Met-rospectives:

A COLLECTION OF THE GREATEST GAMES IN NEW YORK METS HISTORY

EDITED BY BRIAN WRIGHT AND BILL NOWLIN
ASSOCIATE EDITORS: LEN LEVIN AND CARL RIECHERS

Society for American Baseball Research, Inc.
Phoenix, AZ

Met-rospectives: A Collection of the Greatest Games in New York Mets History

Edited by Brian Wright and Bill Nowlin
Associate editors: Len Levin and Carl Riechers

Copyright © 2018 Society for American Baseball Research, Inc.
All rights reserved. Reproduction in whole or in part without permission is prohibited.
ISBN 978-1-943816-87-3
Ebook ISBN 978-1-943816-86-6

Book design: Rachael E. Sullivan
Society for American Baseball Research
Cronkite School at ASU
555 N. Central Ave. #416
Phoenix, AZ 85004
Phone: (602) 496-1460
Web: www.sabr.org
Facebook: Society for American Baseball Research
Twitter: @SABR

Photo credits – Mets book
Front cover photograph: Jerry Coli/Dreamstime

Photographs courtesy of:
Keith Allison: page 116.
Jerry Coli/Dreamstime: pages 10, 19, 27, 32, 35, 40, 42, 46, 48, 52, 63, 66, 87, 91, 96, 100, 109, 111, and 129.
Dwong19/Dreamstime: 44.
National Baseball Hall of Fame & Museum: pages 61, 79, and 83.
Wikipedia Commons: 5, 8, 114, 117, 120, 122, 123, 125, 128, 133, 134.
Brian Wright: 2, 18, 64, and 119.

CONTENTS

INTRODUCTION..................................1
Brian Wright

1. APRIL 23, 1962:
METS EARN FIRST EVER VICTORY BEHIND JAY HOOK'S
COMPLETE-GAME FIVE-HITTER..................................2
Tony Valley

2. JUNE 26, 1963:
TIM HARKNESS HITS GAME-WINNING GRAND SLAM..................4
Alan Raylesberg

3. MAY 31, 1964:
BASEBALL'S LONGEST DOUBLEHEADER..................................7
Alan Cohen

4. JULY 9, 1969:
TOM SEAVER'S NEAR-PERFECT GAME..................................10
Alan Raylesberg

5. SEPTEMBER 15, 1969:
SWOBODA IS CARLTON'S ACHILLES HEEL
ON RECORD-SETTING 19-K DAY..................................13
Richard A. Cuicchi

6. OCTOBER 15, 1969:
SEAVER'S PITCHING, SWOBODA'S
DEFENSE HELP METS BEAT BALTIMORE..................................15
Thomas J. Brown Jr.

7. OCTOBER 16, 1969:
THE METS BECOME THE FIRST EXPANSION
TEAM TO WIN A WORLD SERIES..................................17
Thomas J. Brown Jr.

8. APRIL 22, 1970:
SEAVER STRIKES OUT 19 BATTERS..................................19
Thomas J. Brown Jr.

9. MAY 14, 1972:
WILLIE MAYS HOMERS IN NEW YORK METS DEBUT..................21
Kevin Larkin

10. SEPTEMBER 2, 1972:
"THE KIND OF A NIGHT YOU DREAM ABOUT"..................23
Irv Goldfarb

11. SEPTEMBER 20, 1973:
GETTING ALL THE GOOD BOUNCES..................................25
Brian Wright

12. OCTOBER 10, 1973:
"YA GOTTA BELIEVE" –
METS WIN NATIONAL LEAGUE FLAG..................................27
Steven C. Weiner

13. OCTOBER 14, 1973:
SAY "OH, NO!" TO "SAY HEY" ONE LAST TIME:
WILLIE MAYS HELPS METS PREVAIL IN
12 INNINGS IN WORLD SERIES GAME TWO..................30
Frederick C. Bush

14. OCTOBER 18, 1973:
KOOSMAN, MCGRAW COMBINE ON SHUTOUT
AS METS TAKE LEAD IN SERIES..................................32
Frederick C. Bush

15. JUNE 14, 1980:
THE "STEVE HENDERSON GAME"..................................35
Tom Cuggino

16. APRIL 5, 1983:
TOM SEAVER RETURNS TO THE METS..................................38
Bruce Slutsky

17. SEPTEMBER 7, 1984:
DWIGHT GOODEN ONE-HITS THE CUBS..................................40
Joseph Wancho

18. APRIL 9, 1985:
GARY CARTER HOMERS IN DEBUT FOR METS..................42
Bruce Slutsky

19. JULY 4, 1985:
FIRE(WORKS) AND RAIN: METS AND
BRAVES ENGAGE IN A HOLIDAY EPIC..................................44
Brian Wright

20. SEPTEMBER 12, 1985:
KEITH HERNANDEZ WALK-OFF SINGLE EDGES CARDS..................46
Joseph Wancho

21. OCTOBER 1, 1985:
STRAWBERRY'S 11TH-INNING WALLOP
KEEPS THE METS' HOPES ALIVE..................................48
Richard A. Cuicchi

22. JULY 22, 1986:
METS WIN EXTRA-INNING SLUGFEST
VIA BRAWL AND HOME RUN..................................51
Michael Huber

23. OCTOBER 11, 1986:
LEN DYKSTRA'S HOMER ENDS GAME THREE OF NLCS 54
Rory Costello

24. OCTOBER 14, 1986:
CARTER'S SINGLE WINS GAME FIVE OF 1986 NLCS IN 12TH 56
Rory Costello

25. OCTOBER 15, 1986:
METS SURVIVE 16-INNING BATTLE,
WIN NL PENNANT 59
Rory Costello

26. OCTOBER 25, 1986:
"A LITTLE ROLLER UP ALONG FIRST":
METS WIN WILD GAME SIX ON BUCKNER ERROR 61
Matthew Silverman

27. OCTOBER 27, 1986:
METS RALLY LATE TO BEAT RED SOX IN GAME SEVEN 63
Matthew Silverman

28. AUGUST 11, 1988:
KEVIN MCREYNOLDS' GRAND SLAM IN NINTH BEATS CUBS 66
Brian M. Frank

29. OCTOBER 4, 1988:
METS RALLY FOR THREE IN NINTH,
STEAL GAME ONE OF NLCS 68
Paul Hofmann

30. OCTOBER 8, 1988:
METS BEAT DODGERS, WEATHER IN GAME
THREE TO REGAIN CONTROL OF NLCS 70
Tara Krieger

31. JULY 25, 1990:
METS SURVIVE EXCITING SIX-RUN
NINTH-INNING RALLY BY PHILLIES 73
Michael Huber

32. JULY 28, 1993:
WALK-OFF ENDS ANTHONY YOUNG'S
27-GAME LOSING STREAK 75
Kevin Larkin

33. JUNE 16, 1997:
FIRST REGULAR-SEASON GAME BETWEEN
THE METS AND THE YANKEES 77
Bruce Slutsky

34. SEPTEMBER 13, 1997:
NOT QUITE DEAD AND BURIED 79
Steven C. Weiner

35. SEPTEMBER 16, 1998:
METS KEEP PACE WITH CUBS AS PIAZZA,
HUNDLEY HOMER 81
Mike Wuest

36. JULY 10, 1999:
MATT FRANCO SINGLES OFF MARIANO RIVERA
FOR A WALK-OFF WIN 83
Kevin Larkin

37. OCTOBER 3, 1999:
WIN OR GO HOME: RINSE, REPEAT 85
Seth Moland-Kovash

38. OCTOBER 5, 1999:
BACK FROM THE BRINK, RESOURCEFUL METS WIN 87
Joel Rippel

39. OCTOBER 9, 1999:
JOURNEYMAN TODD PRATT SLAMS METS INTO NLCS 89
Cosme Vivanco

40. OCTOBER 17, 1999:
AFTER FIVE HOURS AND 46 MINUTES...
IT'S BACK TO GEORGIA 91
Brian Wright

41. OCTOBER 19, 1999:
WALK-OFF WALK IN NLCS ENDS METS' SEASON 93
Jack Zerby

42. JUNE 30, 2000:
METS SCORE 10 RUNS IN EIGHTH
INNING VERSUS BRAVES 96
Thomas J. Brown Jr.

43. OCTOBER 5, 2000:
FRANCO SAVES THE DAY, METS EVEN SERIES 98
Paul Hofmann

44. OCTOBER 7, 2000:
BENNY'S BLAST ENDS PLAYOFF DRAMA IN 13TH 100
Rory Costello

45. OCTOBER 8, 2000:
METS ADVANCE TO NATIONAL LEAGUE
CHAMPIONSHIP SERIES 103
Alan Cohen

46. OCTOBER 16, 2000:
THE METS PUNCH THEIR TICKET
TO A SUBWAY SERIES 105
Joe Schuster

47. OCTOBER 24, 2000:
SUBWAY SERIES 2000 - ACT THREE..................................107
Kevin Larkin

48. SEPTEMBER 21, 2001:
NEW YORK CITY'S FIRST BASEBALL GAME AFTER 9/11.................109
Thomas J. Brown Jr.

49. MAY 19, 2006:
DAVID HAS THE WRIGHT STUFF: WALK-OFF HIT
POWERS METS TO COMEBACK WIN.......................................111
Mark S. Sternman

50. AUGUST 22, 2006:
BELTRAN'S WALK-OFF ECLIPSES
DELGADO'S 400TH CAREER HOMER.....................................114
Mike Wuest

51. MAY 17, 2007:
A FATIGUED COMEBACK..116
Gregory H. Wolf

52. JUNE 1, 2012:
SANTANA PITCHES METS' FIRST NO-HITTER THOMAS......................119
Thomas J. Brown Jr.

53. JULY 31, 2015:
FOR FLORES, THERE'S (LIFE AFTER) CRYING IN BASEBALL:
UNWANTED WILMER'S WALK-OFF
BOOSTS METS OVER NATIONALS...122
Mark S. Sternman

54. SEPTEMBER 8, 2015:
NIEUWENHUIS HOME RUN CAPS METS' COMEBACK WIN.................125
Steven C. Weiner

55. OCTOBER 15, 2015:
METS EDGE THE DODGERS TO ADVANCE TO THE NLCS...................128
Bob Webster

56. OCTOBER 21, 2015:
SIXTH STRAIGHT FOR MURPHY KEYS
NEW YORK SWEEP OF CHICAGO..131
David Rickard

57. SEPTEMBER 22, 2016:
METS STAGE THREE COMEBACKS AND DEFEAT
PHILLIES WITH CABRERA EXTRA-INNING WALK-OFF....................133
Michael Huber

CONTRIBUTORS...136

INTRODUCTION

By Brian Wright

In order to make it as a Mets fan, you must be able to conform. This is a franchise known for warming your heart one day and breaking it the next. Nothing comes easy. Even the miraculous championship year of 1969 didn't occur without seven preceding years of futility. And in the dominant 1986 regular season, the road to an expected World Series title didn't happen without gut-wrenching, precipice-of-defeat dramatics in the playoffs.

There has been a fair measure of wondrous and woeful, but this book's 57 game summaries —coinciding with the number of Mets years (1962-2018) – are strictly for the eternal optimist. All, with the exception of one valiant defeat, end in triumph for the orange and blue. The selection process involved various criteria: the time in the season, the dramatic level, and the impact in shaping franchise history. The games are recounted here thanks to the combined efforts of 32 SABR members. Thanks as well to co-editors Len Levin, Bill Nowlin, and Carl Riechers.

They run the gamut of the team's lifespan – beginning with its very first victory in April 1962 at Forbes Field, through Tom Seaver's "Imperfect Game" in July '69, the unforgettable Game Sixes in October '86, the "Grand Slam Single" in the 1999 NLCS, and concluding with extra-inning heroics in September 2016 at Citi Field that helped ensure a wild-card berth.

No matter when your love affair with the Mets began, there will be details you probably forgot and plenty you'll want to relive again. To borrow a saying from former longtime announcer Bob Murphy, enjoy the "happy recaps."

METS EARN FIRST EVER VICTORY BEHIND JAY HOOK'S COMPLETE-GAME FIVE-HITTER

APRIL 23, 1962: NEW YORK METS 9, PITTSBURGH PIRATES 1, AT FORBES FIELD

By Tony Valley

New York City had long been a bastion of National League baseball. The New York Giants (since 1883) and the Brooklyn Dodgers (since 1884) were longtime successful teams whose individual stars and long rivalry riveted generations of baseball fans in and out of New York City.

However, in the mid-1950s, the Dodgers' owner, Walter O'Malley, conceived the idea of moving the Dodgers to Los Angeles. This came about due in part to his clash with New York City Construction Coordinator Robert Moses over the location of a new Dodgers ballpark.[1] He was able to get Horace Stoneham, the Giants owner, who faced similar stadium issues, to agree to move along with him to California's greener (and presumably more profitable) pastures – and so the Giants landed in San Francisco.

These moves, shocking though they were, were perhaps not unexpected. Three other franchises had already moved to new cities in the 1950s, and with the nation's changing demographics and much-improved transportation, expanding the major leagues out of its "rough rectangle" (Bounded by Boston, Chicago, St. Louis, and Washington, D.C.) of the Northeast/Midwest regions of the country began to make sense.

The net effect of these moves, though, was to leave the nation's largest city and its media capital without a National League franchise. Any league expansion would surely include New York City.

New York (along with Houston) was awarded an expansion franchise at the National League meeting in October 1960 to begin play with the 1962 season.[2] William Shea was the team's owner. This New York team took inspiration from the past, naming the club the Metropolitans (or Mets) after a 19th-century New York team, and adopted Dodger blue and Giants orange as the team colors.[3]

Along the same lines, nostalgia for the Dodgers and Giants influenced the Mets' expansion draft selections. The Mets selected four players in all from the two former New York teams, with catcher Hobie Landrith selected as their first player. Other players selected in the draft with ties to the Dodgers and Giants were Roger Craig, Gil Hodges, and Ray Daviault.[4] There was even an element of Yankees nostalgia on the Mets as well, with Casey Stengel (who had also played for the Giants and Dodgers, and had managed the Dodgers) becoming their first manager.

The Mets' infancy was fraught with putrid offense, shoddy defense and bonehead mistakes. But despite a 40-120 record in 1962, the 1962 Mets remain an indelible and lovable part of franchise lore.

The Mets stumbled out of the season starting gate, losing their first nine games. They lost one-run games, and games by 10 runs. They fielded, hit, and/or pitched poorly enough to lose these games, with pitching being the usual culprit. At one point prior to the season, Stengel had said that "The Mets are gonna be amazin'." And so they were – they ended the season last in all meaningful statistical categories. An exasperated Stengel would at one particularly low point in the season mutter, "Can't anyone here play this game?" [5] Finding new ways to lose became commonplace.

Yet, the Mets did have their moments. And their first victory was one of them.

On Monday, April 23, 1962, the Mets played the Pirates at Forbes Field in front of 16,676 spectators. Jay Hook took the mound for the Mets. Among those taking the field that day for the Mets were Gus Bell, Frank Thomas, and Charlie Neal. The Pirates countered with starting pitcher Tom Sturdivant, backed by players such as Dick Groat, Bill Mazeroski, and Roberto Clemente. The Mets were 0-9; the Pirates were 10-0 to begin the 1962 season.

But on this day, the Mets got on top of the Pirates early, scoring two runs in the first and four more in the second. Beginning the game with back-to-back singles, the Mets scored their first-inning runs on sacrifice flies by Bell and Thomas.

After Hook's 1-2-3 bottom of the first, the Mets put together a double, three singles (including a two-RBI single to center field by Hook), three walks, and a sacrifice fly to plate four runs and present Hook with what turned out to be an insurmountable 6-0 lead.

The Mets scored another run in the sixth, on Elio Chacon's run-scoring single to center field, scoring Hook for the second time in the game.

The Pirates scored their only run in the bottom of the sixth on Bob Skinner's run-scoring groundout to first base.

Then the Mets closed out the day's scoring on Bobby Smith's eighth-inning triple to center field, scoring two runs and capping a good offensive day for the Mets. They finished the game with nine runs, 14 hits (including three doubles, a triple, and three sacrifice flies) off four different Pirates pitchers, with Hook, Chacon, and Smith each having two runs batted in.

Hook finished with a complete-game five-hitter, allowing only one earned run.

Reminiscing later about this historic game, Hook had this to say:

"The main thing I remember was that if we would have lost one more, it would have been a record opening the season, and if Pittsburgh won one more, they would have had the record for wins. I had pitched one game before that, and we had been winning in that one, but they took me out and we ended up losing. This time, I pitched a complete game."

After the win, Stengel put Hook to work on the PR front. "After the game, he wanted me to keep talking to the press until there was no one left, so I did, and by the time I was done, everyone was gone from the clubhouse, and there was no hot water left in the showers, so I had to take a bath in the whirlpool in the trainer's room," Hook said.[6] The Mets had won their first game! It was a highlight in a season that did not feature very many. By the end of the decade, though, the Mets were World Series winners. In the end, Stengel was right: the Mets *were* amazin'.

Notes

1 Neil Sullivan, *The Dodgers Move West* (Oxford, England: Oxford University Press, 1999). https://global.oup.com/academic/product/the-dodgers-move-west-9780195059229?q=o%20praise%20the%20gracious%20power&lang=en&cc=us
2 "Astros History: A History of the Astrodome," mlb.com. houston.astros.mlb.com/hou/history/hou_history_feature.jsp?story=5
3 "Mets Timeline," mlb.com. https://www.mlb.com/mets/history/timeline-1960s
4 "Expansion of 1962," baseballreference.com. https://www.baseball-reference.com/bullpen/Expansion_of_1962
5 "Casey Stengel Quotes" Baseball Almanac. http://www.baseball-almanac.com/quotes/quosteng.shtml
6 Dan O'Shea, "Jay Hook," SABR BioProject, http://sabr.org/bioproj/person/11397aad

TIM HARKNESS HITS GAME-WINNING GRAND SLAM

JUNE 26, 1963: NEW YORK METS 8, CHICAGO CUBS 6, AT THE POLO GROUNDS

By Alan Raylesberg

The New York Mets came into existence in 1962 and were one of the worst teams in baseball history, losing 120 games. The 1963 season was much of the same for Casey Stengel's Mets. They lost 111 games and finished last for the second straight year. The Mets of that era were lovable losers, with a host of colorful players who found new ways to lose games and who occasionally provided great winning moments that stood out all the more since victories were few and far between. One of those moments came on the summer afternoon of June 26, 1963 when a little-known first baseman named Tim Harkness etched his name into Mets lore with a dramatic game-winning grand slam in the bottom of the 14th inning.

The Mets started the day at 28-45, in ninth place. The Cubs, at 39-33, were fifth and only three games behind the league-leading Cardinals. There was nothing special about this matchup and only 8,153 paying fans were on hand to witness what unexpectedly turned out to be one of the more memorable games in Mets history.[1]

The Cubs clearly had the better team that day. Their lineup featured three future Hall of Famers: Ernie Banks at first, Ron Santo at third, and Billy Williams in left.[2] A fourth, Lou Brock, started the game on the bench and entered the game in the 10th inning.[3] 1962's Rookie of the Year, Ken Hubbs[4] was at second base.[5] The veteran right-hander Bob Buhl was on the mound.[6]

The Mets lineup paled in comparison. The Mets did have a future Hall of Famer of their own, Edwin "Duke" Snider playing right field. Snider was in his last full season, having been acquired by the Mets in the offseason as part of a pattern of bringing to their team fan favorites of the recently departed Brooklyn Dodgers and New York Giants as their careers wound down.[7] Third baseman Charlie Neal fit that category as well.[8] Ron Hunt, a Rookie of the Year candidate,[9] was at second base and an original Met, Frank Thomas, a legitimate power threat, played left field and hit cleanup.[10] At first base was the 25-year-old Harkness[11] who had been acquired in an offseason trade with the Dodgers in the hope that he could be the Mets regular at the position.[12]7 Pitching for the Mets was "Little" Al Jackson, another original Met picked in the 1962 expansion draft.[13]

The game started out like many other Mets games, with the home squad falling behind 4-0 after five innings. The Mets of that era would often frustrate their fans by creating opportunities to win games only to fall short. This game looked no different as the Mets rallied to tie the game and then managed to blow three opportunities to win the game. Finally, after falling behind by two runs in the top of the 14th inning, a base running blunder cost the Mets again before Harkness came through with his dramatic hit.

The Mets comeback began in the sixth inning when, trailing 4-0, the Mets rallied with two outs. Hunt singled and scored on a double by Snider, Thomas homered, and the Mets were back in the game trailing by a run, 4-3. The Mets tied it in the bottom of the eighth on a single by Thomas, driving in Clarence "Choo-Choo" Coleman who led off the inning with a walk and took second on a balk.[14] With the score tied at four, the drama of the afternoon was only beginning.

Time and again the Mets appeared on the verge of victory. In the bottom of the ninth, the Mets had runners on second and third with two out but Jim Hickman struck out to send the game to extra innings. In the 11th, the Mets threatened again, putting runners on first and second with one out only to see pinch hitter Norm Sherry ground into a double play.[15] The Mets had yet another chance in the bottom of the 12th when Jimmy Piersall walked with two out, only to be promptly picked off first. In the 13th, the Mets threatened once more, this time loading the bases with one out. After Chico Fernandez grounded into a force out at home, Galen Cisco – the

Mets' fifth pitcher of the day – was scheduled to bat with the bases still loaded and now two outs. Of course, the Mets being the Mets, there were no position players left on the bench and Cisco had to bat for himself.[16] He grounded out to end the threat.[17]

Major League Baseball's first mascot, Mr. Met, was introduced in 1964.

Adding to the drama of the game, the Mets went to the 14th inning with their bullpen having pitched eight consecutive innings of hitless ball.[18] With the Mets having squandered four opportunities to win the game, it could not have been surprising to the faithful fans that the Cubs would finally break the tie in the 14th inning with the only hit that they would have over the course of the final nine innings. Of course, this being a Mets game, the tie-breaking hit was a most unusual one, aided by a Mets misplay. With a man on first (from a walk) and two out, Billy Williams hit a liner to left. The Polo Grounds was oddly shaped with a huge expanse in the outfield and Frank Thomas, after getting a bad jump, failed to cut the ball off as it rolled all the way to the wall.[19] Don Landrum raced home from first and Williams circled the bases – an inside-the-park home run - to give the Cubs a 6-4 lead.

In the bottom of the 14th, the Mets were not giving up as the small but enthusiastic crowd cheered on the "Amazin's."[20] Another blunder, however, nearly sealed their fate. Hickman led off with a single and Hunt followed with another single. On Hunt's single, Hickman inexplicably was thrown out at third (by Lou Brock) trying to take the extra base when his run did not matter. The crowd was groaning now but the best was yet to come. With one out, a walk to Piersall put runners at first and second. Paul Toth relieved Jack Warner[21] and got the second out. With two out and two on, Jim Brewer replaced Toth and walked Sammy Taylor to load the bases for Harkness.[22] The count went to three and two. The small crowd was cheering loudly as Harkness connected and sent the ball rocketing into the right-field seats. A two out walk off grand slam in the bottom of the 14th inning! An uncharacteristic ending as the Mets had an amazing comeback win, 8-6.

Writing in the next day's *New York Times*, Gordon White, Jr. described the "feeling [as] one of gloom" as Harkness batted with the 3-2 count. Given that these were the hapless Mets, White wrote that "it looked like another tough defeat" for them. Harkness turned that "gloom" into "complete ecstasy" as his fourth hit of the game was his biggest one. The enthusiastic crowd did not stop cheering until Harkness came out of the dressing room to acknowledge the cheers, something that rarely happened in those days. Casey Stengel put it all in perspective, commenting that "it was one of those good ones. We just had to end it there because I'd run out of men."[23]

1963 was the only season in which Tim Harkness played regularly. He played in 259 games in four seasons, his career ending after 1964. As a career .235 hitter with 14 home runs there is not much to remember him by. Yet, more than 50 years later, legions of Mets fans still remember Harkness for his leading role in one of the greatest games in Mets history.

Sources

In addition to the sources cited in the Notes, the author also consulted Retrosheet.org and Baseball-Reference.com.

The author recalls listening to this game on the radio and remembers the excitement of the moment when Harkness smashed his game-winning grand slam.

Notes

1 According to the *New York Times* account of the game, 18,072 fans were in attendance. In those days, the Mets often had promotions that allowed groups to attend their games for free. Presumably, that Wednesday afternoon was such a game, which would explain the discrepancy between the Times account and the attendance as reported in the official box score. Gordon White, Jr., "4th Harkness Hit Decides 8-6 Game," *New York Times*, June 27, 1963.
2 Banks was not in the starting lineup. Leo Burke started at first base but was ejected in the seventh inning for arguing on a called third strike. Banks then took over at first base as part of a double switch.
3 Brock was in his second full season with the Cubs. In 1964, he would be traded to the Cardinals for Ernie Broglio and others, in what became known as one of the worst trades in baseball history. Brock went on to play 16 seasons with the Cardinals in his Hall of Fame career.
4 1963 was Hubbs' final season as, tragically, he was killed in a plane crash following the season.
5 The rest of the starting lineup consisted of Andre Rodgers at shortstop, Nelson Mathews in center field, Ellis Burton in right field and Dick Bertell behind the plate.
6 Buhl came to the Cubs in 1962 after 10 seasons with the Milwaukee Braves.
7 The "Duke of Flatbush," then 36 years old, was one of the "Boys of Summer" on the great Brooklyn Dodgers teams of the 1950s. After 16 years with the Dodgers, in Brooklyn and Los Angeles, the Mets bought his contract from the Dodgers prior to the season's start. Snider played only one year with the Mets, hitting .243 with 14 home runs. He was a part-time outfielder for the San Francisco Giants in 1964 before retiring.
8 Neal was another former Brooklyn Dodger, who the Mets traded for prior to their inaugural 1962 season. Later in 1963, the Mets traded him to Cincinnati where he

finished what turned out to be his final season.

9 Hunt would go on to finish second for Rookie of the Year, losing out to a young infielder on the Cincinnati Reds by the name of Pete Rose. The 22-year-old Hunt was acquired from Milwaukee in the offseason and became the Mets first young star. The scrappy second baseman went on to play 12 years in the majors, four with the Mets. His "specialty" was being hit by the pitch, as he led the league in that category seven times including 50 in 1971.

10 Thomas slugged 34 home runs in 1962 but only 15 in 1963. He was obtained in a trade with Milwaukee prior to the start of the 1962 season.

11 Harkness was a Canadian, at a time when very few players from Canada were in the major leagues. The Mets traded "Righty" Bob Miller to the Dodgers for him and second baseman Larry Burright. Miller went on to have a 17-year career in the majors. He was known as "Righty" Bob Miller because the 1962 Mets had two Bob Millers, one a righty and one a lefty.

12 The rest of the lineup included Jim Hickman in center, a young hitter who would go on to have a solid 13-year career mostly with the Mets and later the Cubs; Sammy Taylor behind the plate, a career backup who played five seasons for the Cubs before coming to the Mets during the 1962 season; and shortstop Al Moran, a rookie who played only part of one additional season in the major leagues. Hickman, like Neal and Thomas, was an original Met, having been picked in the 1962 expansion draft.

13 Jackson, who was only 5' 10" tall, was an effective left-hander who was a key part of the Mets rotation from 1962 through 1965.

14 Coleman entered the game as a pinch hitter for reliever Larry Bearnarth. "Choo-Choo" was one of the most colorful of all Mets. He ran faster than most catchers and had one of the all-time great nicknames but he could not hit. His career batting average was .197 in 462 major-league at-bats. Coleman, even though a catcher, was a threat to steal and that threat may have caused the balk by Cubs reliever Don Elston that put "Choo Choo" in position to score the tying run.

15 Sherry, whose brother was pitcher Larry Sherry, was a good defensive catcher but a very weak hitter. He was the last position player left on the Mets bench.

16 In 164 career at-bats, Cisco had a career batting average of .128.

17 The Mets used 20 players in the game and only four pitchers were still available when the game ended. White, "4th Harkness Hit Decides 8-6 Game."

18 Writing his game account in the next day's *New York Times*, Gordon White noted that this was "the closest the Mets have come to a no-hitter." Little could he know that it would be nearly 50 years before a Mets pitcher would pitch a no-hitter, a feat achieved by Johan Santana in 2012.

19 White.

20 The Mets got the nickname "Amazings" when "The Old Perfessor," Casey Stengel, while giving a lengthy answer to an interview question, dubbed them the "Amazin' Mets." youtube.com/watch?v=PBjPm_C-53E

21 Warner pitched 4 2/3 solid innings in relief. Toth, who relieved him, was included in the 1964 Brock trade. See n.3.

22 Harkness came into the game batting only .208. He was 3-for-6 on the day going into his final at-bat but was facing a lefty pitcher in Brewer. In 1963, Harkness hit only .156 against lefties.

23 White.

BASEBALL'S LONGEST DOUBLEHEADER

MAY 31, 1964: SAN FRANCISCO GIANTS 5, NEW YORK METS 3 (GAME ONE); SAN FRANCISCO GIANTS 8, NEW YORK METS 6 (GAME TWO, 23 INNINGS), AT SHEA STADIUM

By Alan Cohen

Clouds hung overhead as the first remnants of the crowd entered the new Shea Stadium, situated adjacent to the 1964 New York World's Fair. The time was half past 10 on the morning of Sunday, May 31, 1964. The crowd would eventually number 57,037 paid for the scheduled doubleheader between the Mets and the San Francisco Giants, the largest major-league crowd of the season.

A mist-like rain began to fall. Umbrellas sprung up all over the park, and some spectators elected to purchase hats. The rain stopped just as the first game began at 1:05 PM. Six weeks into the season, the Giants (24-17) were in second place, a game behind the Phillies. The Mets (14-30) looked to be well on their way to their third last-place finish in their three years as a team.

In the second inning of the first game, Joe Christopher, who, as day passed into night, gained a great following in right field, singled off Giants starter Juan Marichal. Ed Kranepool, who had just been called up to the Mets from their Buffalo farm team, singled. The day before, Ed had played a doubleheader in Syracuse, went back to Buffalo, and caught an early morning flight to New York. Jim Hickman cleared the bases with a homer to left.

The Giants took a 4-3 lead in the sixth inning. Orlando Cepeda's double had scored Willie Mays and moved Jim Ray Hart to third base. A sacrifice fly by Jim Davenport scored Hart with the tying run and moved Cepeda to third. Cepeda attempted a steal of home. Reliever Tom Sturdivant's pitch appeared to have the runner beaten by at least ten feet. Catcher Jesse Gonder was slow in applying the tag and the steal was complete.

The Giants completed the scoring in the ninth when Harvey Kuenn drove in Jesus Alou with the Giants' fifth run. Marichal completed the 5-3 Giant win by striking out two batters in the ninth inning, wrapping up his eighth victory of the season. The time of game was 2:29.

The Giants took the second game lead, and the score was 6-3 going into the bottom of the seventh inning. In the Mets' seventh, Roy McMillan and Frank Thomas singled. Christopher then stepped in. Joe hit Bobby Bolin's 3-0 pitch to deepest center field, 410 feet from home plate. Mays leaped against the wall and, with his glove extended, grabbed at the ball as it was leaving the field. He came to the ground with his glove high in the air, signifying for all to see that he had caught the ball. There was one thing wrong, however. There was no ball in the glove. After Christopher circled the bases and touched home plate, the score was knotted at 6-6.

The score remained tied, inning after inning. Shuffling of players between positions became commonplace. In the bottom of the tenth, Mays took over at shortstop. Mays was replaced in center field, temporarily, by Matty Alou.

Gaylord Perry, young and unproven, entered the game to pitch the bottom of the 13th, and there were wholesale changes. Mays returned to center field. He did not have anything hit at him during his three innings in the infield.

In his autobiography, *Me and the Spitter*, Perry devotes an entire chapter to the events of this day. He lists the records set, and concludes by saying that "they saw Gaylord Perry throw a spitter under pressure for the first, but hardly the last, time in his career." Prior to May 31, 1964, Perry "was the eleventh man on an eleven man pitching staff. The twelfth man was in Tacoma." In the 13th inning, Amado "Sammy" Samuel reached Perry for a single. This was followed with a single to right field by McMillan. A great throw by Jesus Alou cut down Samuel trying to advance to third base.

Met-rospectives

In the 14th, Galen Cisco took over for the Mets. The Giants had Jesus Alou on second and Mays on first with none out. The red-hot Cepeda was up. Giants' manager Alvin Dark, with fast runners on base, put on the hit-and-run play. McMillan was racing to cover second when he intercepted Cepeda's liner to center, stepped on second, and fired to Kranepool at first. The Mets had a triple play, and the game went on.

In the Mets' 15th inning, Perry was struggling. Hickman had singled and advanced to second on Charley Smith's sacrifice bunt. Catcher Tom Haller went to the mound and suggested that Perry try out that "new pitch" that he had been working on. If there was ever a time to use it, this was it. Haller said, "It's time to break the maiden, kid. I think you can do it." Before resuming his position behind the plate, Haller told Perry, "Throw it when you can get it on the ball. Don't worry about me. You throw it. I'll catch it. Let's go."

Chris Cannizzaro stepped in and Perry loaded it up. Five spitters later, the count went to three-and-two. What followed was the best argument of the long day. Perry unleashed a fast ball and Cannizzaro checked his swing. Umpire Ed Sudol awarded Cannizzaro first base. Dark argued that Sudol should have conferred with the other umpires before making the decision. Sudol quickly ejected Dark.

Sudol's temper was short because Cannizzaro, earlier in the at-bat, had fouled the 0-2 pitch off Sudol's foot. His temper might have been made even shorter by hunger. Someone had forgotten to bring food to the umpires' quarters between games. Before he left the playing area, Dark put the game under protest. The base on balls proved harmless. While the commotion was going on, Gaylord loaded up another spitter and Cisco hit a ball back to Perry. Perry fired to Davenport, playing shortstop, who threw the still wet ball to Cepeda to complete the inning-ending double play.[1]1

The innings continued to roll past. In the 23rd inning, Davenport stepped in with two out. He hit a ball safely toward the right-field corner. By the time Christopher could retrieve the ball, Davenport was standing at third base with a triple. Cisco intentionally walked Cap Peterson, with Perry, remarkably still in the game, scheduled to hit next. Perry was a worse hitter than even a typical pitcher, but he was pitching great — he had struck out nine batters and allowed seven hits in ten innings. The Giants sent Del Crandall up to pinch hit for Perry. Crandall came through, plating Davenport with a ground rule double to right field. Peterson advanced to third and scored on an infield hit by Jesus Alou. After being shut out for 19 consecutive innings, the Giants had taken an 8-6 lead into the bottom of the 23rd inning, Bob Hendley came in to settle the issue, retiring the three Mets he faced, striking out two.

The strikeouts brought the total by Giants pitchers for the game to 22, eclipsing the mark for strikeouts in an extra-inning game (21), set initially by the Phillies against the Pirates in a 14-inning win on September 22, 1958 and tied by Tom Cheney of Washington in a 16-inning complete game against Baltimore in 1962. When the final out was registered, the game became the longest ever, in terms of time, to be completed in the history of the major leagues – 7 hours and 23 minutes. The doubleheader, also the longest in history, went 9 hours and 52 minutes; the record still stands.

Author's note

I was a high school senior when the Giants first came to Shea Stadium to play the Mets in a four-game series. Each time they came to town, I would go to the local Howard Clothes Store and reserve my ticket. For the May 31, 1964 series finale, it would just be me, as I was unable to find anyone to drag along.

By the 15th inning of the second game, the vendors were gone. I found a discarded program and persevered with my score-keeping. I stepped on a mustard container, splattering its contents on my left leg. When Joe Christopher assumed his position in right field, the few of us remaining waved in his direction, and he waved back.

At the end of baseball's longest day, I put my thoughts together in an article. After I retired, I discovered the paper, dusted it off, and did some updates.

Shea Stadium opened in April 1964 alongside the New York World's Fair.

Sources

Adams, Val. "If it's any help, Mets won TV Rating," *New York Times*, June 2, 1964: 75.

Daley, Arthur. "Sports of the Times: Amazing is Correct," *New York Times*, June 2, 1964: 44.

Durso, Joseph. "Giants Top Mets Twice, as 7 hour 23 Minute 23-Inning Sets Marks," *New York Times*, June 1, 1964.

Kremenko, Barney. "Mets, Giants Go Round and Round to L. P. Record," *The Sporting News*, June 13, 1964: 5.

Kremenko, Barney. "Christopher Heating up Mets with Sizzling Bat," *The Sporting News*, June 13, 1961: 6.

Lipsyte, Robert. "Ball Park Well Built and 'Could have lasted forever'," *New York Times*, May 31, 1964.

Associated Press, "Mets Fans Discussing Marathon," *Hartford Courant*, June 2, 1964: 19A.

Joe Christopher, Jim Davenport, Ed Kranepool, Rusty Staub, and Joan Haller (Tom's wife) were interviewed for this article.

Notes
1 Gaylord Perry (with Bob Sudyk), *Me and the Spitter: An Autobiographical Confession* (New York. E. P. Dutton and Company, 1974), 12-20.

TOM SEAVER'S NEAR-PERFECT GAME

JULY 9, 1969: NEW YORK METS 4, CHICAGO CUBS 0, AT SHEA STADIUM

By Alan Raylesberg

The atmosphere was positively electric at Shea Stadium on the night of July 9, 1969, as the Mets prepared to play the Cubs in the biggest game in Mets history. The upstart Mets, in only their eighth season of existence, were in a position that no one thought possible before the season — contending for first place against a powerful Cubs squad that led the NL's Eastern Division by four games going into the July 9 game.[1] It was a historic night and it would end in a historic game. The Mets' young right-hander, Tom Seaver, came within two outs of a perfect game as the New Yorkers beat Chicago for the second straight day and established themselves as legitimate pennant contenders.

The 1969 Cubs were one of the franchise's all-time great teams. They had not won a World Series since 1908 or a pennant since 1945, and 1969 looked like the year of the Cubs. Led by their fiery and brilliant manager, Leo "The Lip" Durocher," the team from the North Side featured a powerful offense, including three future Hall of Famers: "Mr. Cub" Ernie Banks at first, Ron Santo at third, and Billy Williams in left. Chicago also had a great catcher, Randy Hundley, and a solid middle infield combination with shortstop Don Kessinger and second baseman Glenn Beckert. Veteran Al Spangler shared right field with ex-Met Jim Hickman. The only weak spot in the lineup was center field, where little-known Don Young played most of the games, backed up by several others, including a 22-year-old rookie named Jim Qualls, who had a date with history.

The 1969 Mets had a winning record at midseason for the first time in their history. An expansion team in 1962, the Mets had set numerous records for futility. They lost a record 120 games in 1962 and then lost 90 or more games in each of the next five seasons (through 1967)[2]. Only in 1968 did the Mets finally lose less than 90 games, finishing in ninth place, one game ahead of last place Houston, with a record of 73-89. Former Brooklyn Dodgers star Gil Hodges, a fan favorite, took over as the Mets manager in 1968 and his steady hand had the team in pennant contention by the summer of 1969.

In contrast to the Cubs, the Mets' offense was weak, featuring catcher Jerry Grote, first baseman Ed Kranepool, second baseman Ken Boswell, shortstop Bud Harrelson, third baseman Wayne Garrett, and young outfielders Cleon Jones, Tommie Agee, and Ron Swoboda. The Mets' strength was in their young pitchers, including their Big Three starters: 24-year-old Seaver, 26-year-old Jerry Koosman, and 22-year-old Gary Gentry. The bullpen included a fireballing 22-year-old right hander named Nolan Ryan.

Tom Seaver threw five one-hitters as a Met. When he was able finally able to go wire-to-wire without allowing a hit, he did so as a Cincinnati Red.

The previous day at Shea, the Mets played the Cubs in the opener of a three-game series. Trailing the first-place Cubs by five games at the series start[3], the Mets won the opener in dramatic fashion, scoring three runs in the bottom of the ninth for a 4-3 victory. Thus, the stage was set for July 9, with their fans dreaming of a series sweep to put the Mets within a hair's breadth of first place. On this night, it was the "All-American boy," Tom Seaver, who would take the mound and try to lead the Mets to a place where they had never gone before.

Shea Stadium was packed with more than 59,000 screaming fans. What was about to unfold was not only one of the greatest games in Mets history, but one of the great games in baseball history, given the importance of the game, the record crowd, and the performance of a second-year pitcher who would go on to make the Hall of Fame.

Opposing Seaver was the Cubs' ace lefty Ken Holtzman. Holtzman was only 23 years old and yet in his fifth season with the Cubs. This, however, would not be Holtzman's night. The Mets scored one run in the first and had scored two runs in the second when Durocher pulled Holtzman for reliever Ted Abernathy, who ended the inning. The Mets led 3-0 after two and they had all the runs that they would need.

Seaver joined the Mets in 1967, one year removed from a stellar college career at the University of Southern California. He was a big, strong right-hander with near-perfect mechanics and his arrival gave Mets fans hope that their beloved team would finally become a winning one. Seaver lived up to his billing, going 16-13 in 1967 with a 2.76 ERA and 16-12 in 1968 with a 2.20 ERA. He was off to a spectacular start in 1969, with a 13-3 record going into the big game against the Cubs. The Mets had played the Cubs eight times early in the season, winning only three, at a time when the Mets had their usual below-.500 record. This time was different. As Seaver took the mound on that balmy July evening, the Mets were 46-34 and in a pennant race. For Seaver, it was the biggest game of his young major-league career, on the biggest stage, before the largest crowd in Shea Stadium history.[4]

"Tom Terrific" lived up to his nickname that evening. The Cubs could not touch him. He was pumped, as he struck out five of the first six Cubs batters. The fans were really into it and by the sixth inning it became apparent that on this, the biggest night in Mets history, Tom Seaver was making history. He was pitching a perfect game. No Mets pitcher had done so. No Mets pitcher had thrown a no-hitter and here was Seaver having retired the first 15 batters. The Cubs went down in order again in the sixth and the perfect game was intact. Seaver received a tremendous ovation as he came to bat in the bottom of the frame.

In the Cubs seventh, once again it was three up and three down and you could feel the tension as the excited crowd appreciated the magnitude of what was unfolding before their eyes. The Mets added a run in the seventh, to make it 4-0, but the story of the night now was Seaver. The Mets made some defensive changes in the eighth as Seaver prepared to face the middle of the Cubs lineup. He retired Santo on a fly to center and then struck out the great Banks and then Spangler, to give him 11 strikeouts.

Through eight innings of pitching, it was 24 up and 24 down, 11 on strikeouts. Seaver looked strong as he continued to pump fastballs and the nearly 60,000 faithful could feel his adrenaline as the game moved to the ninth inning.[5]

Randy Hundley led off. Surprisingly, Hundley tried to bunt his way on. As the boos sounded, Seaver fielded the bunt and threw to first for the out.[6] Two outs to go for a perfect game. The fans were on their feet screaming. Up came the weakest hitter in the Cubs lineup – that 22-year-old rookie by the name of Jim Qualls. Qualls was making only his ninth start of the season and came into the game batting only .244. He would have only 120 at-bats in 1969 and after nine at-bats in 1970, for Montreal, he was gone for good from the major leagues. But on this night, on the night that Tom Seaver would make history, the names Jim Qualls and Tom Seaver would forever become linked in baseball lore.

On the first pitch, Seaver came in with a fastball and Qualls (a switch-hitter batting lefty) hit it to the left of second and in front of center fielder Agee – a clean single. Suddenly, the noisy crowd went completely silent. It was an eerie feeling at Shea. All of the air had gone out of the balloon. The disappointment that Seaver felt was shared by the suddenly quiet crowd.[7] Then came the standing ovation for Seaver. The next two batters were retired and the game was over.

The Mets had a huge victory against the Cubs. They were now only three games out of first place.[8] The Franchise, Tom Seaver, had come through. He had pitched the greatest game in Mets history. Despite the disappointment caused by Qualls, Mets fans went home satisfied. They had just witnessed a game that, although not perfect, changed the course of Mets history. Seaver's dominance of the Cubs that night showed, against all odds, that this team was a legitimate pennant contender. As Seaver went on to win 25 games in that magical season, the Mets won the pennant and the World Series. Their performance earned them the moniker "The Miracle Mets." The Miracle began on July 9, 1969.

The author sat in the Upper Deck that evening and nearly 50 years later still vividly recalled the excitement and tension of that night, including how an unbelievably loud crowd went completely silent at the moment Qualls's hit landed in center field.

Sources

Retrosheet (retrosheet.org/boxesetc/1969/B07090NYN1969.htm) and Baseball Reference.com (baseball-reference.com/boxes/NYN/NYN196907090.shtml) were the source of play-by-play information.

Notes

1 There is a discrepancy between Retrosheet and Baseball-Reference.com with respect to the NL standings, and how many games behind the Mets were, on July 8 and 9, 1969. The references herein are based on Retrosheet, which is correct. On June 15, 1969, the Cubs played a doubleheader, losing the first game. The second game was suspended at the end of the seventh inning and completed on September 2, with the Cubs winning. Retrosheet correctly recorded only the June 15 first-game loss in the standings through September 1, recording the Cubs' win in the suspended game only on September 2 when it was completed. Baseball Reference.com counted the September 2 suspended-game victory as a win in the standings on June 15, the day the game was suspended.

2 The Mets finished last from 1963 through 1965, losing 111, 109, and 112 games respectively. In 1966, the Mets were 66-95 and escaped the cellar for the first time, finishing ninth (of 10). In 1967, the Mets were back in last place as they lost 101 games.

3 See n. 1.

4 Shea Stadium's capacity in 1969 was 55,300. On July 9, 1969, there were 59,083 fans in attendance. As reported in the *New York Times*, the paid attendance of 50,709 "was swelled by some junior fans who had been promised tickets in a long-planned promotion. Every seat could have been sold [and] many fans were turned away." George Vecsey, "Single by Rookie Only Chicago Hit," *New York Times*, July 10, 1969.

5 Even though Seaver looked strong, he said afterward that "the feeling was almost gone from my arm." Ibid. In 1969 batters did not work the count and Seaver's gem took only 99 pitches and 2 hours 2 minutes to complete.

6 After the game, Mets first baseman Donn Clendenon said he was not upset with Hundley's effort to bunt his way on to break up a perfect game, commenting, "I don't think Hundley was thinking about the no-hitter. … He was just trying to get on and start a rally." Al Harvin, "Mets Clubhouse Quieted by Single," *New York Times*, July 10, 1969.

7 Seaver said,. "I felt as if somebody had opened up a spout in my foot and the joy all went out of me." Pack Bringley, "Even Tom Seaver Wasn't Perfect," amazinavenue.com/2013/4/1/4164470/tom-seaver-mets-imperfect-game-cub, April 1, 2013. While disappointed after the game, Seaver commented, "I got my breaks. … I just needed one more break." Vecsey, "Single by Rookie Only Chicago Hit." Forty years after the game was played, Seaver still vividly recalled the emotions of that evening, stating that after the game "[The] very first thing [I felt] might have been something like, 'what could have been,'" Michael Bamberger, "Forty Years Ago, Little-Known Qualls Spoiled Seaver's Bid at Perfection," si.com/more-sports/2009/07/08/seaver-tribute, December 11, 2017.

8 See n.1.

SWOBODA IS CARLTON'S ACHILLES HEEL ON RECORD-SETTING 19-K DAY

SEPTEMBER 15, 1969: NEW YORK METS 4, ST. LOUIS CARDINALS 3, AT BUSCH STADIUM

By Richard A. Cuicchi

The National League's 1969 season was one of the most memorable in history because of the legendary collapse of the Chicago Cubs and the improbable rise of the New York Mets to claim the East Division title and go on to win their first-ever World Series. Both teams had reputations for being perennial losers, so it was a crucial season for both in their quest to break out of the stigma of being infamously losing franchises.

The Mets' game on September 15 against the St. Louis Cardinals was characteristic of their late-season surge to glory. The game ended up matching a magnificent 19-strikeout feat by the Cardinals' Steve Carlton, with an improbable two-homer performance by the Mets' Ron Swoboda. In a game they should have probably lost, the Mets came out on the winning end. Swoboda turned out to be Carlton's only Achilles heel in the game.

Just five days before, the Mets had taken the division lead from the Cubs, who had remarkably been in first place since the first day of the season. It was the first time in the Mets' eight-year history that the team held first place. They had won 10 straight games before the Pittsburgh Pirates defeated them the day before the Cardinals game. With the Cubs swooning in the "season from hell," the Mets had climbed to a 3½-game lead.

The Cardinals, defending National League champions, came into the game in third place in the East, nine games behind the Mets. They weren't putting up much of a fight down the stretch, and would finish the season in fourth place.

The Mets were in their second season under manager Gil Hodges. He had inherited a core of young players who had been accumulated beginning in 1965 and now included Tom Seaver, Jerry Koosman, Tug McGraw, Cleon Jones, Ed Kranepool, Ron Swoboda, and Bud Harrelson. All would play key roles in the Mets' drive for the pennant.

The contest on September 15 was played at night in St. Louis before 13,086 spectators. Hodges gave 22-year-old rookie pitcher Gary Gentry (11-11) the starting assignment. Cardinals manager Red Schoendienst countered with 24-year-old lefty Carlton (16-9) against an all-right-handed-hitting Mets lineup. Carlton had lost his last two decisions.

The game's start was delayed for 26 minutes by rain and once it resumed there was another 54-minute delay in the first inning. Carlton had felt feverish all day; and with a sore back, too, he required some pain-killers to suit up.[1] However, he had his strikeout mojo working in the first inning. He struck out the side, although the Mets got two baserunners on an error and a single. The inning was characteristic of Carlton's outing that night: He whiffed multiple Cardinals batters in six of his innings, but also worked around frequent baserunners who reached on nine hits, two walks, and an error.

Carlton struck out the side again in the second inning while yielding a single to Al Weis. In the third, he struck out his seventh opponent, and in the bottom of the inning the Cardinals scored the first run. Lou Brock walked and tried to score from first on Curt Flood's single, but was thrown out at home by center fielder Tommy Agee. Flood advanced to second on the play, and scored on a single by the next batter, Vada Pinson.

In the top of the fourth, Carlton was dealt his first deadly blow by the first two Mets batters. Donn Clendenon walked and Swoboda homered to give the Mets a 2-1 lead. Carlton then proceeded to strike out the side for the third time.

Carlton recorded strikeouts 11 and 12 in the fifth inning, and Cardinals hitters rebounded in the bottom of the frame with four consecutive hits. With two outs, Brock singled and stole second. Flood's single brought in Brock. Pinson's single advanced Flood to second, and Joe Torre's single put the Cardinals ahead again, 3-2.

Carlton appeared to still be in control when he struck out Swoboda for the second time in the sixth. His 14th strikeout (Amos Otis was the victim) came in the seventh inning after the Mets threatened to score with a single and a walk.

Mets reliever Tug McGraw replaced Gentry in the bottom of the seventh and came close to yielding another run to the combination of Brock, Flood, and Pinson, before retiring the side with a strikeout of Torre.

Swoboda struck again in the top of the eighth. After Agee's leadoff single and Carlton's 15th strikeout (Clendenon), Swoboda belted another home run and the Mets regained the lead, 4-3. Carlton also recorded his 16th K that inning.

McGraw retired the side in order in the bottom of the eighth, but so did Carlton in the top of the ninth, when he struck out the side for the fourth time in the game, including Amos Otis's fourth punchout.

McGraw held the Cardinals scoreless in the ninth despite the Mets' fourth error of the game and Brock's single, his fourth time reaching base. The Mets' 4-3 victory was McGraw's eighth of the season.

On a day when Carlton said he had a fever all day before the game,[2] his 19 strikeouts set a new modern-day record.[3] It was the highest total of his Hall of Fame career, which also included three games with 16 strikeouts and one with 15. (He had also taken the loss in one of those 16-strikeout games, against the Phillies in 1967.) It Carlton's sixth game in 1969 with double-digit strikeouts. The loss was his 10th; he finished the season 17-11. When he retired in 1988, he was second on the all-time strikeout list behind Nolan Ryan. (Carlton was subsequently surpassed by Randy Johnson and Roger Clemens.)

Carlton said after the game, "I'm very elated to have done something no other pitcher has ever done. I knew I had something special when I got that standing ovation. That's the first one I ever got. And I got into some elite company – with Sandy Koufax, Bob Feller, and Don Wilson."[4] Those three pitchers held the major-league record of 18 strikeouts in a game at the time. Unaware of how many strikeouts he had until the scoreboard flashed "16" in the eighth inning, Carlton said, "I decided to go all-out for the record. I wanted it badly then."[5]

Nearly 50 years after his game-winning clouts, Swoboda recalled the historic game: "Carlton was a good pitcher having a good day. He had a lot of ways to get you out, possessing a fastball that jumped out at you, an overpowering curve, and an effective slider." Swoboda recalled that his homers, both hit on two-strike counts, came on a fastball in the fourth inning and a hanging slider in the sixth.[6] However, Swoboda wasn't immune to Carlton's strikeouts; the left-hander whiffed the big outfielder twice.

Swoboda remembered, "I had been hot and cold as a batter before this game. In a time before specialized hitting coaches, Mets broadcaster Ralph Kiner took me into the batting cage the day before. He worked with me by setting up the pitching machine with the wheels going in opposite directions, allowing simulated sliders. Kiner kept asking me about my swings against those sliders in the cage, 'How does that feel?' Fortunately, I was able to get to a better place before having to face Carlton."[7]

Swoboda's two-homer game was his first since his rookie season, 1965, when he excited Mets fans by hitting 19 home runs. For much of the 1969 season, he had shared playing time with Art Shamsky and Rod Gaspar, but by mid-August Swoboda had reclaimed his right-field starting job. During the 35-game stretch from August 21 to September 24 (the day the Mets clinched the NL East title), Swoboda had 26 RBIs, including his first career grand slam. He would make one of the most memorable catches in World Series history with his diving backhanded catch of Brooks Robinson's line drive in the ninth inning of Game Four.

In 1969, the first year of division play in major-league baseball, the Mets won the NL East by eight games over the Cubs. They swept the Atlanta Braves in three games in the NL Championship Series, then defeated the Baltimore Orioles in five games in the World Series. That team will forever be known as the "Miracle Mets."

Sources

In addition to the sources listed in the Notes, the author used the following:

Allen, Maury. *The Incredible Mets* (New York: Paperback Library, 1969).

Baseball-Reference.com.

Durso, Joseph. "Swoboda Clouts Pair for All Runs," *New York Times*, September 16, 1969: 51.

New York Mets Media Guide, 1970.

ronswoboda.com.

Notes

1 Neal Russo, "A Record 19 Ks Cure Ailing Carlton," *The Sporting News*, September 27, 1969: 12.
2 Bob Broeg, "Carlton Whiffs 19, but Mets Strike, Too," *St. Louis Post-Dispatch*, September 16, 1969: C1.
3 Carlton's single-game strikeout record was surpassed by Roger Clemens (1986 and 1996), Kerry Wood (1998), and Max Scherzer (2016), all of whom struck out 20.
4 Broeg.
5 Ibid.
6 Author's telephone interview with Ron Swoboda, July 17, 2017.
7 Ibid.

SEAVER'S PITCHING, SWOBODA'S DEFENSE HELP METS BEAT BALTIMORE

OCTOBER 15, 1969: NEW YORK METS 2, BALTIMORE ORIOLES 1, AT SHEA STADIUM
GAME FOUR OF THE 1969 WORLD SERIES

By Thomas J. Brown Jr.

When the Baltimore Orioles and the New York Mets met in Game Four of the 1969 World Series, the sports world was watching closely. The Mets had taken the lead in the Series after winning Game Three, 5-0, behind the pitching of Gary Gentry and Nolan Ryan. When the teams took the field on the afternoon of October 15, Mike Cuellar and Tom Seaver were the starting pitchers in a repeat of the matchup that took place in Game One. Cuellar came out the winner in that pitching duel. Everyone was watching to see if this game would be a repeat.

Seaver started impressively. Although Paul Blair got a single off him in the first inning, he struck out Don Buford and Boog Powell. Frank Robinson flied out to center field and Seaver kept the Orioles from capitalizing on Blair's single. Cuellar also started well. He got Tommie Agee to ground out to third. Bud Harrelson singled to left field, but Cleon Jones hit a groundball to shortstop for a double play to end the inning almost as quickly as it started.

In the second inning Seaver began to show why he was the best pitcher in the National League that season. He got Brooks Robinson to ground out to shortstop. He walked Elrod Hendricks but Davey Johnson hit another groundball to shortstop and Hendricks was forced out at second. The inning ended when Johnson was caught stealing.

In a switch from the first game, it was Cuellar who made the first mistake. He surrendered a leadoff home run to Donn Clendenon in the second inning. Manager Gil Hodges used right-handed hitter Clendenon against lefties in place of Ed Kranepool.[1] After Clendenon's blast, Cuellar got both Ed Charles and Ron Swoboda to ground out to short, then struck out Jerry Grote to end the inning although not without some excitement as Oriole skipper Earl Weaver was ejected for arguing balls and strikes.

As the game progressed, it looked as though that one run might be all that Seaver would need. He kept the Orioles hitters spellbound with his fastball and overwhelming curveball. Orioles got on base in each of the first three innings but Seaver quickly shut them down every time. Baltimore's best chance to take advantage of Seaver took place in the third. After giving up singles to Mark Belanger and Cuellar, Seaver got Buford to hit a groundball to Clendenon. The first baseman threw out Cuellar out at second. This left runners at first and third. Blair, who had 26 home runs and 32 doubles during the season, now came to the plate. Everyone watching expected him to swing away. When Orioles manager Earl Weaver had Blair bunt the ball down the third-base line to score the lead runner, Seaver held Buford at third before throwing out Blair at first. Frank Robinson then hit a foul popup to the first-base side to end the inning.[2]

Cuellar and Seaver continued to battle each other through the sixth inning. The Mets got scattered hits off Cuellar but failed to score any more runs. A pair of singles by Al Weis and Agee in the bottom of the third inning had the Mets with runners at second and third, but Cuellar was able to get out of the inning with groundballs, one to third and second. The Mets got two more hits, one in the fifth and another in the sixth, but failed to score.

Meanwhile, Seaver settled down and took control of the game. From the fourth through the eighth, only one Oriole reached base, Blair on a walk in the sixth.

Coach Billy Hunter, who took over after Weaver was ejected,[3] pulled Cuellar for a pinch-hitter in the top of the eighth inning. Cuellar had kept the Mets from getting any more runs after Clendenon's home run. When he left the game, he had retired 10 of the last 13 Mets batters he faced.[4] Eddie Watt took over in the bottom of the eighth inning and picked up where Cuellar had left off. He got the Mets out in order. Weis flied out to center field, Seaver hit a groundball to second base and Agee struck out. So it was 1-0 going into the ninth inning.[5]

The Orioles finally scored in the top of the ninth inning. Seaver faced the heart of the Orioles lineup. He got Blair to fly out to right field. Then Frank Robinson singled to left and Powell singled to right, sending Robinson to third. Brooks Robinson stepped to the plate and hit a fly ball to short right field, barely over second baseman Weis. Swoboda, the right fielder, could have played it safe. The conservative approach would have been to concede the run and play the ball on a hop. Instead Swoboda practically knocked himself out with an extraordinary catch that would go down as one of the best in World Series history. Swoboda ran at full speed and dived at the last minute to make the catch inches above the ground.[6]

Although Frank Robinson scored, the Mets got an all-important second out. Even more significantly, Swoboda's catch made the Mets and their fans start to believe that they might actually win the Series. Many of those who saw the catch consider it even more momentous than Willie Mays' famous catch in the 1954 World Series.[7] Although the Orioles had finally succeeded in scoring against Seaver, he recovered and got Hendricks to hit another line drive that Swoboda caught in less dramatic fashion.

With the game now tied 1-1, Watt kept the Mets from scoring in the bottom of the ninth even though he gave up singles to Jones and Swoboda. Watt got pinch-hitter Art Shamsky to ground out to second.

The game entered the 10th inning with Seaver still pitching. An error by Wayne Garrett, who had taken over at third for Charles, allowed Johnson to reach first. After Belanger fouled out to the catcher, Hunter sent Clay Dalrymple to the plate as a pinch-hitter for Watt. He singled to center field and Johnson went to second. The next batter, Buford, flied out to deep right field and Johnson took third base. Seaver got out of the inning by striking out Blair. Even though they managed to get a runner in scoring position again, the Orioles could not score. Seaver had kept his focus and continued to dominate the Orioles.

Hunter now sent Dick Hall, who had finished the season with a 1.92 ERA, to the mound in the bottom of the 10th inning. The first batter to face him, Grote, hit a double to left field. Mets manager Gil Hodges sent Rod Gaspar into the game to run for Grote. Hall intentionally walked Weis to set up a possible double play.

With Seaver scheduled to bat, Hodges pulled him for a left-handed pinch-hitter, J.C. Martin. Weaver replaced Hall with lefty Pete Richert. Martin bunted. Richert fielded the ball and threw to first for what looked like an easy out. But his throw hit Martin on the wrist as he ran down the first-base line and bounced into right field. Rod Gaspar, running for Grote, scored from second to win the game. The Orioles immediately protested, claiming that Martin was running too far inside the baseline and had interfered with the throw. The umpires disagreed.[8] The Mets won, 2-1, and took a commanding three-games-to-one lead in the series. Martin's walk-off bunt was only the second one in post-season history. The first was in Game Three of the 1914 World Series when the Boston Braves swept the Philadelphia Athletics.[9]

The Mets were closing in on their first championship. Brian Naylor wrote that this team was "called the Miracle Mets, but in hindsight, they were a solid bunch whose success was due less to divine intervention than to playing good, inspired baseball and, well, perhaps a few lucky breaks."[10] Those lucky breaks were clearly evident on this afternoon.

Sources

In addition to the sources cited in the Notes, Baseball-Reference.com, Baseball-Almanac.com, and Retrosheet.org websites were used.

Notes
1 John Klima, *Pitched Battle: 35 of Baseball's Greatest Duels From the Mound* (Jefferson, North Carolina: McFarland Publishing, 2002).
2 Ibid.
3 *Northwest Arkansas Times*, (Fayetteville, Arkansas), October 16, 1969: 12.
4 Ibid.
5 Ibid.
6 Mark Simon, "Top 10: Mets Best Defensive Plays (Part 2)," ESPN.com, December 17, 2014.
7 Bruce Markusen, *Tales From the Mets Dugout* (Champaign, Illinois: Sports Publishing LLC, 2005): 47.
8 Rick Chandler, "A Postseason Game Being Decided on a Walkoff Bunt? It Also Happened in 1969," SportsGrid.com, October 15, 2014.
9 Paul Casella, "Walk-Off Errors in Postseason Play Rare Events," MLB.com, October 15, 2014. On October 12, 1914, the Braves Herbie Moran bunted with runners at first and second in the bottom of the 12th. The Athletics pitcher, Bullet Joe Bush, fielded the bunt and threw to third base to get the lead runner, Hank Gowdy. His throw was wild and Gowdy scored the walk-off run. Almost exactly a century later, on October 14, 2014, it happened again, in the National League Championship Series between the St. Louis Cardinals and the San Francisco Giants. With Giants runners at first and second in the bottom of the 10th inning, Gregor Blanco bunted and the winning run scored when pitcher Randy Choate threw wild to first.
10 Brian Naylor, "Baseball, Vietnam and Coming of Age at the 1969 World Series," NPR.org, October 15, 2014.

THE METS BECOME THE FIRST EXPANSION TEAM TO WIN A WORLD SERIES

OCTOBER 16, 1969: NEW YORK METS 5, BALTIMORE ORIOLES 3, AT SHEA STADIUM
GAME FIVE OF THE 1969 WORLD SERIES

By Thomas J. Brown Jr.

The New York Mets stopped being the laughingstocks of baseball and became unlikely World Series champions on the afternoon of October 16, 1969. After the Mets joined the National League in 1962, they spent most of the decade known as a bunch of lovable losers. All that ended on a pleasant fall afternoon with temperatures in the mid-60s that made for a perfect day for a baseball game.[1] By the end of the day, New York was celebrating an incredible end to its fairy-tale season.

A crowd of 57,397 showed up for Game Five against the Baltimore Orioles. The Mets led, three victories to one. The unexpected was about to become history. Experts had expected the usual from the Mets in 1969 after their 73-89 record in 1968. Gil Hodges was in his second year as manager, hired to lead the Mets youthful squad, whose core was pitchers, Tom Seaver, Jerry Koosman and Gary Gentry.[2] Besides their young pitchers, the Mets had solid defensive players. Seaver later reflected on the new manager's impact on the team: "[Hodges] brought that presence and that approach to how you play the game. That began to permeate through the club. He never missed a thing."[3]

Hodges chose Koosman to pitch the fifth game. Koosman had earned a 2-1 victory in Game Two, pitching 8⅔ innings and holding the hard-hitting Orioles to just two hits. Now he was given the opportunity to clinch the championship in front of a home crowd. For the Orioles, Dave McNally, the losing pitcher in Koosman's victory, was the starter.

Koosman held the Orioles to one hit in the first two innings, a single by second baseman Davey Johnson in the second, but gave up three runs in the third. Mark Belanger singled to right field, which was followed when McNally hit a home run. Koosman got Don Buford to ground out to shortstop and struck out Paul Blair. But the next batter, Frank Robinson, hit another home run, a blast over the center-field wall, to give the Orioles a three-run lead. Koosman struck out Boog Powell to end the inning.

Meanwhile, McNally dominated the Mets, holding them to three hits through the first five innings and striking out five. It looked as if the Orioles might bring the Series back to Baltimore. But things began to unravel for them in the bottom of the sixth inning.

Leadoff batter Cleon Jones was brushed back from the plate by McNally's first pitch. Home-plate umpire Lou DiMuro called it a ball, but Jones insisted he had been hit. Hodges quickly emerged from the dugout with the ball and showed DiMuro a scuff mark, whereupon DiMuro awarded Jones first base.[4] The next batter, Donn Clendenon, hit a home run and the Mets were just one run behind the Orioles. Years later, the call was still controversial. Frank Robinson is one of those who questioned it. "It's always good planning to have a baseball in the dugout with shoe polish on it, just in case," he said in 2013.[5]

After the two home runs in the third inning, Koosman had allowed just one hit over the next six innings, a single by Powell in the top of the sixth. Another unusual call went against the Orioles in the top of the sixth. It appeared that Koosman hit Frank Robinson but DiMuro ruled against the Orioles again and Robinson ended up striking out.

In the bottom of the seventh inning, Al Weis, the Mets shortstop, who was better known for his defensive skills rather than his bat, hit a home run to deep left field off McNally. It was only the seventh home run of Weis's career and the only time he hit a home run at Shea Stadium.[6] (Weis also surprised everyone by leading the Mets with a .455 batting average during the Series.)

Met-rospectives

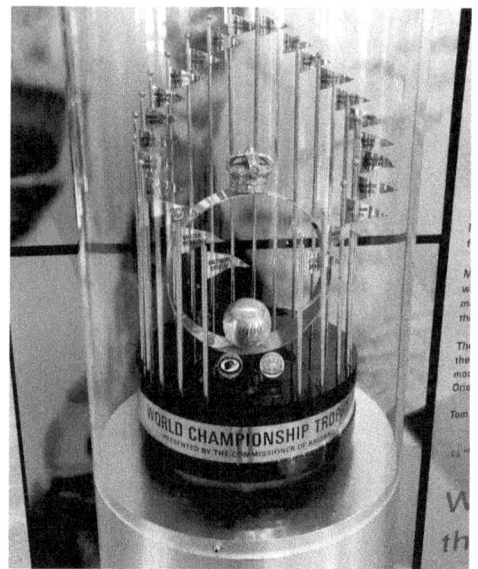

The 1969 World Championship trophy sits in the Mets Hall of Fame & Museum in Citi Field.

Notes

1 thestarryeye.typepad.com/weather/october/page/3/.
2 "1969 The Amazin' Mets," ThisGreatGame.com, accessed November 2, 2016.
3 Ken Belson, "Mets Interrupt Gloom to Recall 1969 Glory," *New York Times*, August 22, 2009.
4 Phil Pepe, "Mets Refuse to Quit, Rally to Beat the Baltimore Orioles 5-3 in Game 5 at Shea Stadium to Win 1969 World Series," *New York Daily News*, October 17, 1969.
5 Clayton Collier, "Frank Robinson Still Swears Miracle Mets Scuffed Ball In Game 5 Of 1969 World Series," Mets Merized Online, June 14, 2013.
6 Ed Leyro, "One Mo-MET In Time: Al Weis," Studious Metsimus.com, accessed November 1, 2009.
7 Phil Pepe, "Mets Refuse to Quit."
8 Tommy Hicks, "Amazing Memory: Mobile's Cleon Jones Recalls Catching Final Out in 1969 World Series," AL.com, November 7, 2009.
9 Jesse Goldberg-Strassler, "Memories of a New York Mets World Series," Ballpark Digest, October 30, 2015. https://ballparkdigest.com/2015/10/30/memories-of-a-new-york-mets-world-series/

After Curt Motton pinch hit for McNally in the top of the eight, Eddie Watt took over on the mound. Jones led off the inning with a double. After Clendenon grounded out to the third baseman, Swoboda doubled to left and Jones scored. Ed Charles flied to left. The next batter, catcher Jerry Grote, hit a groundball down the first-base line. Powell bobbled the ball and then threw it late to Watt, who let the ball get away from him. Both players were charged with errors on the play, which allowed Swoboda to score. Grote was safe at first.[7] Weis ended the inning by striking out.

Koosman walked Frank Robinson to start the ninth inning but the rest of the Orioles batting order was unable to get a rally started. Powell grounded to shortstop Weis and Robinson was forced at second. Brooks Robinson then hit a fly ball to Tommie Agee in center field and Johnson's fly ball to Jones in left field ended the game. Jones later said that he was thinking, "Come on down, baby, come on down. It's all over" as he waited for the ball.[8] Koosman went the distance for the win as the Mets surprised the baseball world by winning the World Series.

After the game, Mets fans poured on to the field to celebrate. *New York Times* columnist Arthur Daley wrote, "They came tumbling from the stands by the thousands, lit red flares, brandished signs and whooped it up in unrestrained glee. They stole all the bases, including home plate, and ripped up the turf for souvenir pieces until it was as pockmarked as a battlefield."[9]

Sources

In addition to the sources cited in the Notes, Baseball-Reference.com, Baseball-Almanac.com, and Retrosheet.org websites were used for box score, player, team, and season pages, pitching and batting game logs, and other pertinent material.

SEAVER STRIKES OUT 19 BATTERS

APRIL 22, 1970: NEW YORK METS 2, SAN DIEGO PADRES 1, AT SHEA STADIUM

By Thomas J. Brown Jr.

The day started well for Tom Seaver on April 22, 1970. He received his Cy Young Award in a pregame ceremony.[1] It was a beautiful spring day in New York. A crowd of 14,197 showed up to see the Mets play the San Diego Padres. The many students who attended the afternoon game at Shea Stadium ended up watching a performance for the ages. While the rest of the country celebrated the first ever Earth Day, those in attendance celebrated Tom Seaver's extraordinary performance that afternoon.[2]

Of Seaver's 311 career victories, 198 came in a Mets uniform. That, plus numerous other exemplary figures, earned him 98.84 percent of the Hall of Fame vote in 1992.

The game began with Seaver taking control from the first pitch. Jose Arcia, the San Diego leadoff batter, flied out to center field. Seaver struck out the next two batters, Van Kelly and Cito Gaston, to close out the top of the first. In the bottom of the first inning, the Mets jumped out to the lead. Bud Harrelson singled, and when Ken Boswell doubled to the left-field corner, the speedy Harrelson scored when Al Ferrera did not field the ball quickly.

The Padres tied the game in the top of the second, Ferrara, when the cleanup batter, led off with a towering home run over the left-field fence. To many in the crowd it was not a vintage Seaver performance so far.[3] After giving up the home run, Seaver got Nate Colbert to hit a foul pop to first baseman Art Shamsky. Then Dave Campbell lined out to left field, and Seaver struck out Jerry Morales for the third out and his third strikeout of the game.

Seaver continued his dominance in the third inning as he collected two more strikeouts. After walking Bob Barton to start the inning, he struck out Mike Corkins and Kelly. Neither even swung at the third strike. Seaver now had five strikeouts and he was just warming up.

The Mets went ahead in the bottom of the third inning. Tommie Agee led off with a single and Harrelson hit a triple to right field that barely missed going out of the park. Agee scored and the Mets had the lead. Seaver had all the runs he would need.

Gaston led off the Padres' fourth and struck out looking. Ferrara walked. Colbert flied out to center field. Campbell singled to left, but Seaver finished the inning by striking out Morales on a fastball. He now had seven whiffs.

Seaver continued to befuddle the Padres in the fifth inning. Barton fanned and Corkins was caught looking. The third out was a grounder to third base.

By the top of the sixth inning, Seaver had yielded just two hits and had nine strikeouts. Since the Mets led by only one run, he would really have to bear down to ensure that they kept the lead.[4] After catcher Jerry Grote caught a foul popup, Seaver got Gaston to fly out to right field, thenstruck out Ferrara to end the inning and get his 10th strike out of the game.

By now the afternoon shadows were starting to creep over home plate. The rest of Shea Stadium was still in the bright sun and the shade around home plate presented problems for the Padres hitters.[5] They were flailing at Seaver's fastball and things would not improve as he showed no signs of slowing down.

Seaver struck out the Padres in order in the top of the seventh inning. Colbert swung at a third strike, and Campbell and Morales were both caught looking. Johnny Podres, the Padres minor-league pitching instructor, was in the dugout. Podres, who had once struck out eight batters in a row for the Los Angeles Dodgers, observed that Seaver"had perfect rhythm, and I don't think he'll ever throw that hard again. It's amazing, as hard as he was throwing he was still hitting the spots. If you didn't swing, it still was a strike."[6]

After Barton struck out looking to lead off the eighth inning, Ramon Webster pinch-hit for pitcher Corkins and struck out. Next, Ivan Murrell pinch-hit for shortstop Arcia, and he was quickly dispatched by Seaver. With just one inning left, Seaver had 16 strikeouts.

When the Padres came to bat in the top of the ninth inning, Seaver and the Mets were still holding on to a one-run lead. As Seaver took the mound, the crowd was excited and there was a buzz throughout the stands. When Kelly led off and struck out swinging for Seaver's eighth strikeout in a row, the crowd made it sound as if Shea Stadium was filled to capacity.[7]Seaver then caught Gaston on a called third strike for the second out.

Ferrara, who had homered for the Padres' only run, now came to the plate. Ferrara said after the game: "The last time up,it was his best shot against my best shot.He challenged me and he won."[8]Seaver struck out Ferrara for his 19th strikeout of the game and his 10th in a row.

Seaver finished masterfully. Over the last five innings, he allowed only three batters to make contact with the ball. He needed only 10 pitches to strike out the side in the ninth inning. "I might as well have played without a glove," said shortstop Harrelson after the game.[9]

Besides the win, Seaverset a record of 10 strikeouts in a row. He also matched Steve Carlton's 19-strikeout game of the previous season. Carlton had lost that game to the Mets when Ron Swoboda hit two home runs.[10]

Seaver's record of 19 strikeouts for a nine-inning game would stand for 16 years until Roger Clemens struck out 20 batters twice during the 1986 season. Seaver's record of striking out 10 in a row still stood as of 2016 as the major-league record.

Sources

In addition to the sources cited in the Notes, the Author also used the Baseball-Reference.com, Baseball-Almanac.com, and Retrosheet.org websites.

Notes
1 Joe Gergen, "Tom Terrific: Seaver strikes out 19," *Newsday* (Long Island, New York), April 22, 1970.
2 "Remembering Mets History (1970) Tom Seaver Ties MLB Record With 19 Strikeouts in a Game," Centerfieldmaz.com, April 21, 2016.
3 Gergen.
4 Stephen Hanks, "Tom Seaver's 19-Strikeout Classic Turns 45," MetsMerizedOnline.com, April 22, 2015.
5 Hanks.
6 Gergen.
7 Hanks.
8 Gergen.
9 Ibid.
10 Hanks.

WILLIE MAYS HOMERS IN NEW YORK METS DEBUT

MAY 14, 1972: NEW YORK METS 5, SAN FRANCISCO GIANTS 4, AT SHEA STADIUM

By Kevin Larkin

In his novel *You Can't Go Home Again*, Thomas Wolfe tells the story of a man returning to his hometown in search of his identity. In May 1972, Willie Mays was sort of a George Webber-like character when he came to the Mets after spending the first 21 years of his career with the Giants – for 15 years in San Francisco and, before that, for six years in New York.

The Mets acquired the future Hall of Famer on May 11 for Charlie Williams and $50,000 and Mays debuted three days later, coincidentally, against the Giants at Shea Stadium. With 646 home runs, 1,859 RBIs, 3,187 hits, and countless defensive gems under his belt, Mays was an unquestioned all-time great.

Now, his role would be far less significant – even though his legend had yet to diminish.

Mets owner Joan Payson was in attendance on this Mother's Day 1972 to watch Mays play. Early in her career Payson had acquired shares in the New York Giants team. Now as part-owner of the New York Mets, she was the third woman to have an ownership stake in a major-league ballclub.[1]

On May 14, Mays played first base and led off against Giants starting pitcher Sam McDowell, who entered the day with a 5-0 record. Pitching for the Mets was Ray Sadecki, without a decision so far in the young season.

Sadecki got the Giants out in the first inning with the only trouble being a double to right field by Tito Fuentes with one out. Fuentes was left stranded and Mays stepped up to the plate for the Mets in the bottom of the first. He walked. So did the next two batters. All three came around to score on a grand slam by Rusty Staub – a four-run New York frame.

Sadecki kept up the good work in the second inning, allowing just a one-out single to Giants third baseman Jim Ray Hart. McDowell settled down, getting the Mets in order including a strikeout of Mays for the third out of the inning.

In the Giants' third, all they could muster for an offense was a one-out single to center field by Fuentes. McDowell then dominated the New York lineup, getting three outs on a fly ball, a strikeout, and a groundout.

It was a 1, 2, 3 inning for Sadecki and the Mets in the top of the fourth. McDowell faltered just a bit for the Giants as he allowed a double to left field by Jim Fregosi. After intentionally walking the Mets catcher, Jerry Grote, McDowell put out this fire by striking out his mound counterpart Sadecki to end the inning.

Sadecki came unraveled in the fifth inning: He walked the leadoff batter, Fran Healy. Bernie Williams pinch-hit for McDowell, and tripled to score Healy with the Giants' first run of the game. Chris Speier, the Giants shortstop, doubled to right field to score Williams and then Fuentes hit a two-run home run to tie the score at 4-4. There were still no outs, but Sadecki struck out Bobby Bonds and got both Dave Kingman and Ken Henderson to fly out.

Don Carrithers replaced McDowell on the mound in the bottom of the fifth, and was to face the number one, two, and three hitters in the Mets lineup: Willie Mays, Bud Harrelson, and Tommie Agee. Mays got his first hit as a Met, a home run to left field that sent the Mets ahead again, 5-4.[2] Agee walked and stole second base. Staub was intentionally walked, but the runners were left stranded when Cleon Jones hit into a 4-6-3 double play to end the inning.

The sixth inning was of little excitement to either team. Hart singled to center field off reliever Jim McAndrew, who had replaced Sadecki. McAndrew got the next three outs to leave Hart stranded at first base. Jim Barr replaced Carrithers and, after giving up a single to Ted Martinez, got Grote to ground into an inning-ending 4-6-3 double play.

Speier led off the seventh inning by grounding out to second base. Fuentes, who had been a pain to every pitcher the Mets used, got his fourth hit of the day, a double to right field. However, he remained at second base as McAndrew got the next two hitters to fly out. With Barr still pitching for the Giants, McAndrew struck out, Mays walked for the second time in the game, but was thrown out trying to steal second base, and Harrelson flied out to right field.

San Francisco was down to its final six outs. McAndrew retired the first two batters in the Giants eighth on a flyout and groundout. Garry Maddox doubled to right field but Dave Rader, batting for Fran Healy, stranded Maddox when he grounded out to the shortstop, Harrelson. In the bottom of the inning, Barr struck out Agee, Staub, and Jones. Now it was the top of the ninth and the Giants were down to their final three outs.

McAndrew was still on the mound for the Mets and the Giants sent up Al Gallagher to hit for Barr. He grounded out to McAndrew on a comebacker. Speier grounded out to shortstop for out number two. Now it was the Giants' last chance. Fuentes, who had tormented the Mets so far, walked to reach base for the fifth time in the game. But Bobby Bonds struck out to end the game.

Mays had pulled out some of that "Say Hey" magic one last time; his home run was the winning margin of victory for the Mets. After the game, Mays said, "That was my first hit as a Met. And my first hit as a Giant was a home run, too."[3]

He played in a total of 135 games for the Mets, he ended his career with 660 home runs (placing him fifth all-time). He also ended up with 3,283 hits and 1,903 runs batted in. Mays announced his retirement after Game Two of the 1973 World Series pitting the Mets against the Oakland Athletics.[4]

Sources

The author consulted Baseball-Reference.com and Retrosheet.org,

Notes

1 Payson followed Helene Hathaway Britton who had a ownership with the St Louis Cardinals (1911-1917) and Grace Comiskey who had partial ownership of the Chicago White Sox between 1940 and 1956.

2 Joseph Durso, "Mets Win on Mays's Homer, 5-4," *New York Times*, May 15, 1972: 47.

3 Ibid. After going 0-for-12 in his first three games as a Giant, Mays homered off future Hall of Famer Warren Spahn of the Boston Braves at the Polo Grounds on May 28, 1951.

4 Phil Pepe, "Willie Mays Retires After Game 2 of the World Series in 1973," *New York Daily News*, October 15, 1973.

"THE KIND OF A NIGHT YOU DREAM ABOUT"

SEPTEMBER 2, 1972: NEW YORK METS 11, HOUSTON ASTROS 8, AT ASTRODOME

By Irv Goldfarb

Every team has comebacks. Miraculous rallies from seemingly insurmountable deficits litter the historical landscape in every major sport. Whether a club ultimately needs that special comeback on their way to a championship, or merely uses it as a springboard for success later in the season, it's often remembered in team lore as a landmark victory.

However, there are also those miracle games that occur during seasons that aren't quite as successful and whose outcomes don't mean as much in the big picture of a full season.

Historically, the New York Mets have experienced their share of the latter. So in a campaign that ended with an 83-73 record and a 13½-game deficit in the National League East standings, their game against the Houston Astros on September 2, 1972, should have been lost deep in the pages of baseball history.

Instead, it will be remembered as one of the biggest comebacks the team ever had.

The 1972 season began with major-league baseball's first strike, over a dispute regarding the players' pension fund. By the time the sides agreed on a $500,000 increase for the plan, 13 days at the start of the regular season had been lost. By September 2, the National League standings told a fairly dismal story for both teams: The Mets were already 14 games back of the eventual division-winning Pittsburgh Pirates, while the Astros still clung to a glimmer of hope for a strong finish: They were on a six-game winning streak and trailed the soon-to-be pennant-winning Reds by seven games. As a matter of fact, they knew they could have gained another game that night, as Cincinnati lost to the Montreal Expos.

Houston had pounded the Mets in the Astrodome, 8-0, the night before, handing franchise pitcher Tom Seaver his 10th loss of the season while beating up on a beleaguered Mets bullpen. And amazingly on this Saturday night, the Astros grabbed another 8-0 lead, sparked this time by Lee May's two-run homer in the first inning, his 28th of the year, a two-run double by Cesar Cedeño in the third inning, and Bob Watson's two-run single in the bottom of the seventh, as the Astros hammered starter Brent Strom and relievers Ray Sadecki and Bob Rauch, the latter a rookie hurler appearing in his only major-league season. Hence, the Mets entered the eighth inning hopelessly behind for the second consecutive game, as veteran right-hander Don Wilson had shut them down over the first seven innings, facing only 24 hitters and allowing just four hits.

But backup catcher Duffy Dyer, a holdover from the Miracle Mets of '69 (as was every starting position player in this game except right fielder John Milner), opened the inning with a single to left. Shortstop Bud Harrelson followed with another base hit and utility outfielder Dave Marshall, pinch-hitting for Rauch, walked to load the bases. Center fielder Tommie Agee hit a sacrifice fly to right for the Mets' first run of the game, which brought up second baseman Ken Boswell, another unheralded contributor to that 1969 team.

Though he had already been responsible for half his club's hits entering the inning (two singles in three at-bats), Boswell had come into the game batting a paltry .177. "I started out the season not hitting badly, but I always came up empty-handed," Boswell remarked after the game. "I kept trying to laugh it off, figuring things would straighten out but they didn't." They straightened out well enough in this at-bat, however, as Boswell launched his eighth homer of the season, a three-run blast that made the score 8-4. "I think it was a hanging slider," he guessed. "I was just trying to get it in the air."[1]

Met-rospectives

Though a home run in the midst of a big comeback is often dubbed a "momentum-killer" and the Mets were still down by four runs, a pitching change from Wilson to journeyman reliever Fred Gladding didn't stop the Mets' sudden offensive onslaught: Milner immediately collected a single, veteran Met first baseman Ed Kranepool followed with another, and left fielder Cleon Jones doubled in a run, with Kranepool stopping at third. Astros manager Leo Durocher then called for reliever Jim Ray to replace Gladding, but it made no difference as third baseman Wayne Garrett singled in Kranepool and Jones to make the score a suddenly tight 8-7.

Dyer made his second plate appearance of the inning and singled again, but Ray got Harrelson to pop out to the shortstop in foul territory and Marshall to fly out to end the Mets biggest inning of the season. They had scored seven runs on eight hits and were now down by only a single run.

To start the eighth, Mets manager Yogi Berra sent out legendary left-hander Jerry Koosman. Koosman, who had faced three batters in relief the night before, had been sent to the bullpen earlier in the season after three early-season losses because he had "lost his rhythm." "I literally forgot how to wind up," he said after his career.[2] Koosman got into some trouble, hitting Tommy Helms with a pitch, then giving up a two-out single to Roger Metzger. At that point, Berra called on Tug McGraw, who struck out Cedeño looking.

Now it was their turn again and the Mets offense didn't miss a beat: Agee walked to start the ninth and Boswell chimed in with another single, his fourth hit of the game. Durocher marched out reliever Tom Griffin, but the Astros' luck didn't change as a sacrifice attempt by Milner was fielded by the usually surehanded third baseman Doug Rader, who made a disastrous throw wide of first. The error scored Agee to tie the game, sending Milner to second and Boswell to third.

Durocher then ordered Kranepool walked intentionally to load the bases, but that strategy backfired as well: Jones singled to right to score Boswell and Milner and give the Mets a two-run lead. Kranepool was thrown out at third as Cleon Jones took second and Garrett singled him in. Dyer followed with a strikeout, but even more action followed – Harrelson singled and even McGraw got into the act as he walked to load the bases. Reliever George Culver got Harrelson on a fielder's choice, however, and the Mets took the field in the ninth with a three-run lead.

With Willie Mays now in center field in one of his last regular-season appearances, McGraw got the side in order in the ninth, closing out the 11-8 victory by getting Watson to ground out to the star of the game, Kenny Boswell.

Boswell, originally from Austin, Texas, said he usually had to have about 30 tickets available for friends and relatives who wanted to see him play when the came to Houston. "but I've never been able to do anything. Guess I was trying to impress them (tonight)," he said later.

For Houston manager Durocher it was just one of those games. "Everything they hit was right between somebody," he lamented after the nightmarish experience. "We got beat with the best we had, so what can you say?"

"It's about time we find a few holes," Berra declared.

For Boswell, who actually ended his career with the Astros five years later, it was the night of his life. "It's nice to know there's a little left," the 26-year-old veteran declared. "It's the kind of a night you dream about."

Sources

In addition to the sources cited in the Notes, the author also consulted Baseball-Reference.com, Retrosheet.org, and the following:

Strauss, Michael. "Mets Score 7 in 8th, 4 in 9th, Win, 11-8, *New York Times*, September 3, 1972: S1

Associated Press. "Mets Down Houston 11-8," *Austin Statesman*, September 3, 1972: D7.

Notes
1 "Boswell Finds a Little Left," *Newsday*, September 3, 1972: 5C. All quotations come from this article unless otherwise indicated.
2 Interview with the author, 2008, in Matthew Silverman and Ken Samelson, eds., *The Miracle Has Landed* (Hanover, Massachusetts: Maple Street Press, 2009), 141.

GETTING ALL THE GOOD BOUNCES

SEPTEMBER 20, 1973: NEW YORK METS 4, PITTSBURGH PIRATES 3, AT SHEA STADIUM

By Brian Wright

They were in a bad place, but at the right time.

The 1973 Opening Day roster weakened under the weight of countless ailments. Right fielder Rusty Staub continued to deal with the hamate bone operation that curtailed his wonderful start to 1972. Catcher Jerry Grote, shortstop Bud Harrelson, first baseman John Milner, and left fielder Cleon Jones each missed significant chunks of the schedule – causing daily lineup cobbling and a lack of stability.

On July 9, the Mets were 34-46. They were sixth in a six-team division and 12½ games out of first. "Who Should Mets Ax?" was the headline of a *New York Post* poll that ran during the summer swoon – with manager Yogi Berra, general manager Bob Scheffing, and team chairman M. Donald Grant as choices. Most put their support behind Berra, given a bad hand with the preponderance of injuries and an unstable bullpen. Nevertheless, Grant was rumored to be considering offering Yogi the pink slip with his team occupying the NL East cellar.

A condition like this prompted the buoyant Berra to generate his greatest pearl of wisdom: "It ain't over 'til it's over." Both the team, and its manager, were knocked down – but not out. As those key pieces were coming back to full service, the rest of the middling divisional conglomerate was generous enough that the Mets weren't left too far astray.

There was no separation of power typical of most pennant races, where the better teams pull away as the bad ones fail to keep up. Instead, mediocrity was spread all around. For the Mets, who received their clean bill of health by late August, this had the makings of an 11th-hour revival.

Even as September beckoned, New York sat in the cellar – yet only 6½ games back. The greater hindrance was the number of teams they had to pass instead of the ground to make up. Embarking on what would be a 21-8 stretch, the Mets closed in and passed other NL East teams still going in quicksand. After September 19, the fight for the title was as congested as the Van Wyck Expressway. Pittsburgh led, but had three teams breathing down its neck – the Expos one game behind and the Cardinals and Mets each 1½ games back.

The Mets, though, were in a more advantageous position vis-a-vis the other pair of teams chasing for first. New York was in the midst of a five-game home-and-home series with the Bucs and going into the game of September 20 was coming off two straight victories to gain ground.

But a seesaw tradeoff of single-run innings appeared to end in Pittsburgh's favor. The Pirates went on top, 3-2, in the top of the ninth on Dave Cash's double off Harry Parker, who had relieved Jerry Koosman. It seemed the Mets' uphill climb toward the NL East summit would take an inopportune setback. In the bottom of the inning, with two outs and Ken Boswell at second, the likelihood of that obstacle increased. However, New York's offense got to reliever Ramon Hernandez for the second time in three nights. Duffy Dyer made it happen – a double to left field that erased the Mets' third deficit, sent the game into extra innings, and unearthed the remnants of good fortune that emanated during the miracle march of four years prior.

In 1969, it came in the form of a black cat scooting behind home plate and in front of the faltering Chicago Cubs dugout. In '73, Lady Luck lent her generous magic hand with a singular play. A play that couldn't possibly be duplicated. A play so distinctive it earned a catchy moniker.

That play occurred in the top of the 13th.

Met-rospectives

With two outs and Richie Zisk on first, Dave Augustine hit one destined for the Mets bullpen –except the ball's trajectory sent it squarely off the top of the left-center-field fence and back toward Cleon Jones. An inch farther and it would have been a home run. An inch shorter, and what followed probably wouldn't be possible.

Jones caught it off the fortuitous bounce, turned, and fired to cutoff man Wayne Garrett while Zisk – the potential go-ahead run – rounded third and headed home. Garrett threw to catcher Ron Hodges, perched behind the plate, who caught it and laid down the tag on a sliding Zisk.

"I knew I had to catch the ball and hold onto it, but I didn't have all that much time," Hodges said. "I had to block the plate. … I squeezed the baseball as hard as I could squeeze it. I didn't want to drop it."[1]

Home-plate umpire John McSherry, after waiting a few moments to make sure, elevated his hand and closed it into a fist. Side retired. The legend of the "Ball on the Wall" play was born.

"Believe it or not, I had it in line all along, I thought it would hit the wall," Jones said, "Luckily, Garrett was at short. If Harrelson had been there, he would have taken the relay much further in the outfield and we would never have gotten Zisk."[2]

Minutes later, the Mets made good on this stroke of wondrous luck.

Walks to Milner and Boswell, followed by Don Hahn's failed bunt try, brought Hodges back to the forefront with one out. Hodges singled against Dave Giusti and just in front of left fielder Willie Stargell to score Milner and pull New York within a half-game.

The following day's report in the *New York Times* said that the Mets had endured a "season that has seem them hurt, slumping, vilified, and resurrected at various stages. But with all their adventures, they will probably remember last night's four-hour thriller as one of the top soap operas of the year."[3]

Roughly 24 hours later, New York won again to reach .500 … and first place – completing its three-week ascent from bottom to top.

That's where they would stay. The Mets prevailed in five of next seven contests – and Cleon Jones was a significant reason why. He hit six home runs over the final two weeks, including one in the first of a presumed October 1 doubleheader at soggy Wrigley Field, played a day after the scheduled end to the regular season, with New York needing one victory to clinch.

The Mets built a 6-2 lead in support of eventual Cy Young Award recipient Tom Seaver, but their ace tired – evidenced by Rick Monday's two-run blast over the ivy – and gave way to 1973's late-year inspiration.

Tug McGraw, countering his dreadful first half with a remarkable second half, saved games – and the season. When he got Glenn Beckert to pop softly to John Milner – who then stepped on first to double off Ken Rudolph, running on contact – for a game-ending double play, Tug ensured that this season would continue.

It was far from conventional, but it was official. At 82-79, the worst record (at the time) for any divisional winner, the New York Mets emerged victors of this NL East slog.

Sources

In addition to the sources cited in the Notes, the author also consulted Baseball-Reference.com, Retrosheet.org, and Ultimatemets.com.

Notes
1 Howard Blatt, *Amazin' Met Memories* (Tampa: Albion Press, 2002), 265.
2 Craig Wolff, "1973 Mets Revive a Month of Glory," *New York Times*, July 31, 1993: 1.
3 "Mets Rally Three Times, Beat Pirates in 13th, 4-3," *New York Times*, September 21, 1973: 1.

"YA GOTTA BELIEVE" – METS WIN NATIONAL LEAGUE FLAG

OCTOBER 10, 1973: NEW YORK METS 7, CINCINNATI REDS 2, AT SHEA STADIUM
GAME FIVE OF THE 1973 NATIONAL LEAGUE CHAMPIONSHIP SERIES

By Steven C. Weiner

Before their 1973 postseason began, the New York Mets had last seen the Cincinnati Reds on August 20 to finish a four-game series at Shea Stadium. But the circumstances bore no resemblance to this day in October. The Mets had lost 8-3 and stood in last place in the National League East – 12 games under .500, seven games behind the NL East first-place St. Louis Cardinals, and about to host the NL West-leading Los Angeles Dodgers in a three-game series. Equally concerning was the work of relief pitcher Tug McGraw, who lost that day by giving up five earned runs in 3⅓ innings – making him 0-6 with a 5.45 ERA.

In his biography of Tug McGraw, Matthew Silverman noted that "McGraw experienced both fame and failure at astonishing levels in 1973."[1] As Silverman describes it, McGraw had picked up the personal mantra "Ya Gotta Believe" earlier that summer through talks with Joe Badamano, a motivational speaker and friend of former manager Gil Hodges.[2] He rarely hesitated to repeat it to fans, teammates, and even to Mets Chairman M. Donald Grant. In fact, when Grant came into the clubhouse one day for a rare pep talk, McGraw was quite vocal and let his phrase be heard. Ed Kranepool, McGraw's roommate and the Mets player representative, spoke to McGraw, sensing trouble when Grant stormed out of the clubhouse. "You better tell Donald Grant you didn't mean anything, that you were endorsing what he was saying," Kranepool said. "We went outside the locker room, Donald was there, and Tug stopped him and he apologized and everything was fine. It cleared the air."[3]

While it might be a stretch to suggest that Grant's midsummer pep talk spurred the turnaround for both McGraw and the Mets, the results after that day in August are quite clear. The Mets finished the season by winning 27 of their last 39. McGraw won five times without a loss and saved 12. The Mets reeled in, then passed their competition in the National League East to finish 1½ games better than the St. Louis Cardinals. With an 82-79 record, their winning percentage (.509) was the lowest ever for a postseason berth and their opponent in the NLCS, the Cincinnati Reds, was a powerhouse, having captured pennants in 1970 and 1972. They won the tough NL West with a mark of 99-63 (.611) – 3½ games clear of the Dodgers. Pete Rose arguably had his best season, batting .338 with

Rusty Staub was the first Met to eclipse 100 RBIs in a single season—doing so in 1975. In a second act, beginning in 1981, he established himself as a first-rate pinch-hitter. Staub missed the deciding game of the '73 NLCS after injuring his shoulder in a collision with the right field wall while making a super catch.

230 hits en route to MVP honors. Five players represented the Reds in the All-Star Game and their lineup included three future Hall of Famers.[4] They had already beaten the Mets in 8 of 12 games in their season series. But that Mets team at playoff time was nothing like the one that steamed through the home stretch.

The Reds' eight hits in the first two NLCS games at Riverfront Stadium were a rather meager production. The split of the first two games meant the Reds faced the prospect of having to win two games on the road to take the National League flag. It didn't sit well with the Reds when shortstop Bud Harrelson (far from a power threat at the plate), innocently said after the second game, "They all look like me hitting."[5] It particularly didn't sit well with Pete Rose. In the top of the fifth inning of Game Three, with Rose on first and the Reds down, 9-2, Joe Morgan hit a sharp grounder to first baseman John Milner, who threw to Harrelson to start a 3-6-3 double play. Rose slid hard into second base. Soon after, "a fight breaks out!"[6] When the dust settled and the Reds took the field, the fans remained in an ugly mood – pelting the field with everything possible. After Rose was nearly hit with a bottle, manager Sparky Anderson took his team off the field. The umpires threatened a Mets forfeit until a group of players – including Tom Seaver, Yogi Berra, Cleon Jones, and Willie Mays – walked out to left field to restore calm and finish out a Mets win. As it turned out, Rose almost singlehandedly got the Reds to the fifth and deciding game by going 3-for-5 in Game Four with what turned out to be a game-winning homer in the 12th inning.[7]

The pitching matchup for the Game Five was a reprise of the opener at Riverfront. In that game, Jack Billingham allowed only three Mets hits. But when he left the mound after the eighth inning, Tom Seaver's RBI double in the second inning had him trailing. Seaver pitched an equally strong game, striking out 13. But a solo home run by Pete Rose in the eighth inning and a walk-off home run by Johnny Bench in the ninth inning were Seaver's undoing in the 2-1 loss.

As it turned out, the first inning of the deciding game foreshadowed the outcome that was to follow. Seaver got off to a shaky start. After a walk, a single, and a wild pitch, an intentional walk to Johnny Bench loaded the bases with two outs. But Seaver got Ken Griffey to fly out to center field to escape without damage, having faced six batters, three of whom would later be enshrined in the Hall of Fame, Joe Morgan, Tony Perez, and Johnny Bench. Jack Billingham was not so fortunate. Singles by Felix Millan and Cleon Jones and a walk to John Milner loaded the bases for Ed Kranepool. His single to left field drove in two runs for the early lead. For Kranepool, making his first start since September 15 and the only Met left from their first season in 1962, it was his first appearance and first hit of the NLCS. It couldn't have been timelier!

The Reds made it back to even with single runs in the third and fifth innings. A double to right field by Joe Morgan, an error by right fielder Cleon Jones and a sacrifice fly by Dan Driessen scored the Reds' first run. In the fifth inning, Pete Rose doubled down the left-field line and Tony Perez lined a two-out single to right-center to get them even, but that didn't last long!

The Mets went ahead for good with four runs in the bottom of the fifth inning with 42-year-old Willie Mays, in his final season, right in the middle of the scoring spree. Doubles by Wayne Garrett and Cleon Jones wrapped around a fielder's choice/bunt by Felix Millan scored the first run. After John Milner walked, Mays pinch-hit for Kranepool. Like Kranepool, Mays was also making his first appearance of the NLCS and, ironically, he also delivered his first hit. His Baltimore chop single drove in Felix Millan. Subsequently, Don Hahn's groundout to shortstop and Bud Harrelson's single gave the Mets a 6-2 lead. Seaver scored New York's final run in the sixth when he doubled and came home on a Cleon Jones single.

The Mets were taking no chances in the top of the ninth inning after Tom Seaver loaded the bases on a single and two walks. Despite having pitched 4⅓ innings in Game Four, Tug McGraw came in to retire Joe Morgan on a pop fly and Dan Driessen on a groundout for the save and the National League championship. Sportswriter Joseph Durso aptly captured the scene at Shea Stadium: "But then, in a swirling scene, thousands of persons in the crowd of 50,323 stormed the field … and clawed huge chunks of fence, sod and fixtures from the arena. Professional sports may have had more clamorous moments. But New York baseball has had none since the Mets won the World Series four years ago, after eight seasons as the comic relief of the leagues."[8]

Next up was the American League champion Oakland A's in the 1973 World Series. As improbable as that might have sounded in August, one needed only to remember what Tug McGraw had been saying over and over again: "Ya Gotta Believe!"

Sources

In addition to the references cited in the Notes, the author also accessed Baseball-Reference.com and Retrosheet.org.

Notes
1 Matthew Silverman, "Tug McGraw," SABR Baseball Biography Project, sabr.org/bioproj/person/0834272a.
2 Ibid.
3 Tara Krieger, "Ed Kranepool," SABR Baseball Biography Project, sabr.org/bioproj/person/f9491612.
4 Johnny Bench, Joe Morgan, Pete Rose, Dave Concepcion, and Jack Billingham represented the Reds in the All-Star Game in Kansas City on July 24, 1973; Tom Seaver and Willie Mays represented the Mets. As of 2018, Bench, Morgan, and Tony Perez have been enshrined in the Hall of Fame at Cooperstown, New York.
5 Eric Aron, "Bud Harrelson," SABR Baseball Biography Project, sabr.org/bioproj/person/cb7f6459.

6 Matthew Silverman, *Swinging '73, Baseball's Wildest Season* (Guilford, Connecticut: Lyons Press, 2013), 146. "Ringside announcer Bob Murphy called Flushing's 'Fight of the Century' on WHN: And a fight breaks out! A fight breaks out! Pete Rose and Bud Harrelson. Both clubs spill out of the dugouts and a wild fight is going on! Jerry Koosman's in the middle of the fight. Everybody is out there. … Rose outweighs Harrelson about 35 pounds. … Another fight breaks out!"
7 Rose batted .381 in the NLCS and the rest of the Reds collectively hit .158.
8 Joseph Durso, "Mets in World Series; Defeat Reds for Flag," *New York Times*, October 11, 1973: 1.

SAY "OH, NO!" TO "SAY HEY" ONE LAST TIME: WILLIE MAYS HELPS METS PREVAIL IN 12 INNINGS IN WORLD SERIES GAME TWO

OCTOBER 14, 1973: NEW YORK METS 10, OAKLAND ATHLETICS 7, AT OAKLAND-ALAMEDA COUNTY COLISEUM
GAME TWO OF THE 1973 WORLD SERIES

By Frederick C. Bush

After losing a tight 2-1 decision in Game One of the 1973 World Series, the New York Mets hoped to salvage a split of the first two games against the Athletics in front of 49,151 spectators on a Sunday afternoon in Oakland. The starters for Game Two, the Mets' Jerry Koosman and the Athletics' Vida Blue, were two of the top lefties in the majors, so another pitching duel appeared to be the order for the day. That turned out not to be the case, however, as both starters were long gone by the time New York finished a 10-7 victory in 12 innings that took a record 4 hours and 13 minutes to complete.[1] Though 17 runs were scored in the game, the focus was on the many errors that affected the game's course and final outcome. The A's committed five errors – one short of the record set by the Chicago White Sox in Game Five of the 1917 World Series against the Mets' predecessors, the New York Giants – and their last two errors cost them the game.

The A's struck immediately against Koosman, taking a 2-0 lead in the bottom of the first. Cleon Jones belted a homer to lead off the second and cut the lead in half, but Oakland quickly recouped that run in the bottom of the frame when Joe Rudi's single drove home Bert Campaneris, who had hit a one-out triple. Wayne Garrett launched the Mets' second solo homer of the day in the top of the third to close the gap to 3-2.

In the bottom of the third Gene Tenace drew a one-out walk, Jesus Alou singled, and Ray Fosse was safe on Koosman's errant throw to first baseman John Milner. Manager Yogi Berra gave his starter a quick hook and brought in reliever Ray Sadecki, who managed to escape the bases-loaded jam without allowing another run and then pitched a scoreless fourth.

After Harry Parker kept the A's off the board in the fifth, the Mets took their first lead in the top of the sixth. Blue issued a one-out walk to Jones and allowed a single to Milner, causing his day on the mound also to come to an end. Reliever Horacio Pina threw gasoline on the fire rather than throwing strikes past Mets batters. He hit Jerry Grote with a pitch and allowed consecutive RBI singles by Don Hahn and Bud Harrelson, after which he was quickly pulled from the mound by Oakland manager Dick Williams. Pina's successor, Darold Knowles, did not fare any better as he "awkwardly tumbled down the mound while fielding a bases-loaded comebacker"[2] from Jim Beauchamp and flipped an errant throw to catcher Fosse that allowed two additional runs to score and gave the Mets a 6-3 advantage. Knowles settled down and kept New York from inflicting further damage over the course of 1⅔ innings of work.

Tug McGraw, the Mets' fourth pitcher of the day, took the mound in the bottom of the sixth. From that point through the eighth inning, he allowed only one run, which scored when Reggie Jackson drove home Campaneris with a double in the seventh.

In the top of the ninth, with the score still 6-4, Rusty Staub hit a leadoff single against Blue Moon Odom and was replaced by pinch-runner Willie Mays. The "Say Hey Kid" was playing out his final season and no longer had the spring of youth in his step, a fact that soon became evident. After Jones fouled out, Milner rapped a single to right field on which Mays should have been able to reach third, but Mays missed second base and then stumbled and fell. After the game, the 42-year-old Mays explained, "Rather than embarrass myself, I stopped. I don't know how it happened that I missed the bag. I guess it was trying to do two things at the same time – watch the ball and touch the bag."[3] Mays' misstep on the basepaths turned out to be inconsequential as Grote fouled out and Hahn grounded out to shortstop for the third out.

Of greater importance was Mays' next mishap with his footing after he took his familiar position in center field in the bottom of the inning. Oakland pinch-hitter Deron Johnson led off with a long fly ball to center field. Mays lost sight of the ball and "then slipped, pitching headlong on the turf and tried to reach out at the last instant with his bare hand to grab it"[4] as the ball got past him for a double. Broadcaster Curt Gowdy lamented on air, "Ten years ago he would have put that ball in his back pocket."[5] Mays later admitted, "I didn't see the ball. I tried to dive for it [at] the last second. We had a two-run lead and I shoulda played it safe."[6]

After McGraw retired Campaneris and Rudi, he walked Sal Bando and then surrendered back-to-back RBI singles by Jackson and Tenace that knotted the game, 6-6. McGraw set down Alou for the final out and – in spite of having pitched two innings in Game One the previous day – remained in the game and set the A's down in order in the 10th and 11th innings.

The Mets had a chance to take the lead in the top of the 10th after Harrelson led off with a single, reached second on McGraw's sacrifice bunt, and went to third when Garrett reached base on an error by Tenace at first base. Felix Millan stepped to the plate and hit a fly ball to short left field, but third-base coach Eddie Yost still sent Harrelson home. Almost 40 years later, Harrelson still recalled the play vividly:

[I] tried to stay up as long as I could to block catcher Ray Fosse's view of the throw. Willie Mays ... was the on-deck hitter and on his knees signaling me to slide, but I saw Fosse reaching down for the ball and I figured my best bet was to go in standing up. ... I was safe, only plate umpire Augie Donatelli didn't agree.[7]

Mays, still on his knees, pleaded Harrelson's case to Donatelli to no avail, as did Berra and the rest of the Mets, and the game remained tied until the top of the 12th.

In the fateful 12th, Mays found redemption for his misplay in the ninth, and the game's goat horns passed to A's second baseman Mike Andrews. Mays came to bat with Harrelson on third, McGraw on first, and two outs. After swinging and missing on Rollie Fingers' first offering, Mays swung at the second pitch and "slapped it straight back, a bounder that hopped high over the pitcher's head and skipped on into center field"[8] and drove in Harrelson with the go-ahead run. Sadecki, by now watching the game in the clubhouse, asserted later, "He had to get a hit. This game was invented for Willie Mays a hundred years ago."[9] It turned out to be the last hit of Mays' storied Hall of Fame career.

After Jones singled to load the bases, Paul Lindblad relieved Fingers. Milner tapped a ball up the middle for what should have been the third out, but the ball bounced through Andrews' legs, allowing McGraw and Mays to score. On the next play, Andrews fielded Grote's grounder cleanly but threw slightly wide of first, where umpire Jerry Neudecker ruled that first baseman Tenace had been drawn off the bag by the throw and that Grote was safe; Andrews was charged with his second error on the play.[10] Television replays showed Neudecker's call to be incorrect – Tenace's foot was still on the bag when he received the throw ahead of Grote's arrival[11] – but it nevertheless allowed Jones to score and increased New York's lead to 10-6. Lindblad retired Hahn, but the A's now found themselves in a deep hole.

A fatigued McGraw allowed a leadoff triple to Jackson and walked Tenace before Berra pulled him in favor of George Stone. Alou promptly knocked home Jackson with a single, but Stone bore down to earn the save – McGraw got the win – after Campaneris grounded to Harrelson for the final out of the game.

Notes

1 Lowell Reidenbaugh, "Tug's Battle Cry Inspires Mets: 'You Gotta Believe,'" *The Sporting News*, October 27, 1973: 10.
2 Jason Turbow, Dynastic, *Bombastic, Fantastic: Reggie, Rollie, Catfish, and Charlie Finley's Swingin' A's* (Boston: Houghton Mifflin Harcourt, 2017), 154.
3 "Say-Hey Days Seem Gone for Ol' Willie," *Chicago Tribune*, October 15, 1973: 80.
4 Ibid.
5 Matthew Silverman, *Swinging '73: Baseball's Wildest Season* (Guilford, Connecticut: Lyons Press, 2013), 175.
6 Red Smith, "The Game They Invented for Willie," *New York Times*, October 15, 1973: 43.
7 Bud Harrelson with Phil Pepe, *Turning Two: My Journey to the Top of the World and Back With the New York Mets* (New York: St. Martin's Press, 2012), 151. Television replays showed that Harrelson was safe; however, in 1973, instant replay was not yet used to confirm or overturn calls on the field, so Donatelli's controversial call stood.
8 Smith, "The Game They Invented for Willie."
9 Ibid.
10 Andrews had been dealing with a long-term shoulder injury, which may explain his poor throw on what should have been a routine play. Oakland owner Charlie O. Finley was so irate with Andrews that immediately after the game he had Andrews examined by team orthopedist Dr. Harry Walker whom Finley ordered to declare Andrews to be disabled. Walker grudgingly complied, and Finley coerced Andrews into signing a memo in which he agreed with the diagnosis. A's players were so upset with Finley that they threatened to strike and not play Game Three in New York. Commissioner Bowie Kuhn stepped in and ordered Finley to reinstate Andrews in time for Game Three, and the potential disaster of a World Series forfeit by the Oakland A's was averted. (A comprehensive account of the entire episode between Finley and Andrews can be found in Turbow, 155-170).
11 Turbow, 156. Once again, with replay not yet in use on the field, Neudecker's call stood, just as Donatelli's call on Harrelson had in the 10th inning.

KOOSMAN, MCGRAW COMBINE ON SHUTOUT AS METS TAKE LEAD IN SERIES

OCTOBER 18, 1973: NEW YORK METS 2, OAKLAND ATHLETICS 0, AT SHEA STADIUM

GAME FIVE OF THE 1973 WORLD SERIES

By Frederick C. Bush

After alternating losses in Games One and Three with wins in Games Two and Four, the New York Mets entered the final game to be played at their home venue with an aim to break that pattern and to take the lead in the World Series. It was a "dark and wintry evening"[1] in New York City on October 18, 1973, when 54,817 fans packed Shea Stadium to watch a rematch between Game Two starters Jerry Koosman and Vida Blue. Neither lefty had received a decision in that contest, but Koosman's outing had been particularly short as he had surrendered three runs in only 2⅓ innings. On this night, Koosman redeemed himself by pitching 6⅓ innings of shutout ball before turning the mound over to the ubiquitous Tug McGraw. Of his sterling performance in sub-50-degree weather, Koosman simply observed, "It helps to come from Minnesota."[2] It also helped the Mets in their quest to become the most unlikely World Series championship team in major-league history.[3]

Koosman breezed through the first two innings, allowing only a harmless two-out walk to Sal Bando in the first, before the Mets provided all of the run support their pitchers would need on this night. Cleon Jones, who had smashed a home run against Blue in Game Two, led off the bottom of the second inning. Jones was still ailing from the flu that had caused him to exit the previous night's game after seven innings, but he found the strength to stroke a double that sailed over left fielder Joe Rudi's head. John Milner came to the plate and promptly slashed a single to right field to drive in Jones for a quick 1-0 Mets' lead. After this rocky start, Blue buckled down to retire the next three batters.

In the top of the third inning, Koosman displayed his tenacity when he made sure that A's speedster Bert Campaneris, who had reached base on a two-out single, would not get into scoring position via a stolen base by picking him off at first. Koosman explained, "I mixed up my moves to first base . . . a head fake, then a foot fake, anything to prevent Campaneris from detecting a pattern."[4] He finally caught Campaneris "still standing 10 feet away" [from first] with his third pickoff attempt.[5] The A's protested that Koosman had balked, but home-plate umpire Russ Goetz disagreed and the pickoff play ended Oakland's half of the inning.

The next scoring opportunity for either team came in the bottom of the fourth inning when Rusty Staub and Jones led off with back-to-back singles for the Mets. Milner attempted a sacrifice bunt, but

While pitching in Tom Seaver's shadow, Jerry Koosman is so easily overlooked. But in terms of postseason performance, the left-hander from Minnesota might be the better.

Blue fielded the ball and threw it to Bando to force out Staub at third base. Jerry Grote fouled out, but then Campaneris mishandled Don Hahn's grounder and the bases were loaded with Mets. Blue escaped the jam unscathed when Bud Harrelson hit a pop fly to first baseman Gene Tenace for the third out.

After Koosman cruised through the top of the fifth, Blue experienced another scare in the bottom of the frame. Wayne Garrett drew a one-out walk, advanced to second when Blue uncorked a wild pitch while facing Felix Millan, and then reached third on Millan's grounder to Tenace. Once again, however, Blue kept the Mets from doing further damage as Staub hit a grounder to Campaneris for the final out of the inning.

The A's finally got a runner into scoring position in the top of the sixth. After Blue struck out to open the inning, Campaneris reached first via a base on balls. Rudi hit a foul fly that Mets backstop Grote caught for the second out before Bando reached base on an error by Garrett at third. Koosman remained as cool as the weather and induced a grounder from Reggie Jackson to Harrelson, who fielded the ball and stepped on second to get the force on Bando.

Jones led off the bottom of the sixth and, just as he had done in the second inning, smashed a ball that looked like it would go over Rudi's head in left field. This time around, Rudi made what was described as "perhaps the best defensive play of the first five games . . . [as he] raced back to his right and made a leaping, one-handed catch of the ball as he crashed into the screen."[6] Blue likely breathed a sigh of relief, but he was soon in trouble again. After Milner grounded out, Grote hit a single and scored on Hahn's triple into the gap in left-center field. The Mets now led 2-0, and Blue's night was at an end as Darold Knowles entered the game in relief for Oakland.

Of all the members in the Mets' anemic lineup, Hahn was the least-likely candidate to power the team to an insurance run. He had batted only .229 with 10 doubles and two homers over 93 games with New York after beginning the season with Tidewater at the Triple-A level. Hahn identified what he believed were the two reasons for his successful at-bat against Blue. The first, he said, was that "The other day, Bud Harrelson pointed out that I was too tense at the plate, so I loosened up and I'm getting back my confidence."[7] He also asserted, "Late in the season, I was pulling pitches, but earlier I was hitting to right field. The A's may not have watched me late in the season because they were playing me as a right-field hitter."[8]

With Hahn on third base, Knowles intentionally walked Harrelson to face Koosman, whom he struck out to quash the Mets' scoring threat.

Koosman returned to the mound in the top of the seventh and got into his first real jam of the game. He walked Tenace, the leadoff batter, and then surrendered a one-out double to Ray Fosse that put A's runners on second and third. Mets manager Yogi Berra called to his bullpen and brought in McGraw for the fourth time in five World Series games.

McGraw flirted with disaster by walking Deron Johnson to load the bases, but he then got pinch-hitter Angel Mangual – batting for Knowles – to pop out to shortstop and struck out Campaneris to preserve the two-run lead. Campaneris was caught off-guard by a Mets' pitcher for the second time on this night. McGraw revealed, "I got that called third strike with a fastball . . . I made it look like a screwball, hoping he'd think it was one, and I guess he did."[9] As he ran off the mound after whiffing Campaneris, McGraw noticed that New York City Mayor John Lindsay was holding up a sign with the Mets' McGraw-inspired battle cry "Ya Gotta Believe" on it. "When I saw him," McGraw said later, "I just yelled, 'Yeah, you gotta believe.'"[10]

McGraw had originated the "Ya Gotta Believe" battle cry as a response to a locker room speech by Mets' owner M. Donald Grant in which Grant asserted, "We believe in you guys, every single one of you." The Mets had not been playing well, and teammates like Harrelson and Garrett believed that McGraw was mocking Grant when he yelled out, "Aaaaahhhh, ya gotta believe." Teammates urged McGraw to apologize to the owner, and he did; however, he still began to shout "Ya Gotta Believe" every time something positive happened for the Mets. Although fellow reliever Buzz Capra initially referred to the phrase as "that 'Gotta Believe' crap," starting pitcher Jon Matlack conceded that McGraw's enthusiasm and motto soon "spread like wildfire."[11]

McGraw pitched the eighth and ninth innings to earn the save and put an exclamation point on both the Mets' win and his own performance by striking out the final two A's batters of the game, Ted Kubiak and pinch-hitter Billy Conigliaro. He also declared that he would be ready to pitch again in Game Six, if needed, saying, "I got all winter to rest."[12]

The Mets now had a one-game edge in the series. However, though they believed in themselves, so did the A's. Bando, who was Oakland's team captain, asserted, "We never do anything easy. We never have. Now we just have to win two games."[13] The A's did indeed win Games Six and Seven, by scores of 3-1 and 5-2, thus claiming their second consecutive World Series championship and putting an end to the idea that the 1973 "Ya Gotta Believe" Mets could pull off the same feat as the "Miracle" Mets had against the Baltimore Orioles in 1969.

Notes

1 Joseph Durso, "Mets Beat A's, 2-0, Lead World Series by 3 Games to 2," *New York Times*, October 19, 1973: 1.
2 Lowell Reidenbaugh, "Hahn's Triple Trips Up A's; Mets Go Ahead in Series," *The Sporting News*, November 3, 1973: 8.
3 The Mets had a season record of 82-79, which is still the worst-ever ledger for a World Series competitor. The 2006 St. Louis Cardinals came within one game of that mark with a record of 83-78. Unlike the 1973 Mets, however, the Cardinals managed to win their World Series against the Detroit Tigers, thus becoming the championship team with the worst regular-season record in major-league history.
4 Reidenbaugh, 8.
5 Durso, 28. There is a minor discrepancy in the news reports as to how many throws to first Koosman made before he successfully picked off Campaneris. Durso reported that Koosman caught the runner on his third throw while Reidenbaugh reported that

the pickoff occurred on a fourth throw; of primary importance, of course, is the fact that the pickoff occurred at all.

6 Reidenbaugh, 16.
7 Reidenbaugh, 8.
8 Ibid.
9 Dave Anderson, "McGraw Wins Guess Game," *New York Times*, October 19, 1973: 29.
10 Ibid.
11 The descriptions of incidents and the quotes included in this paragraph are all from the following source: Matthew Silverman, *Swinging '73: Baseball's Wildest Season* (Guilford, Connecticut: Lyons Press, 2013), 122-23.
12 Anderson, 29.
13 Leonard Koppett, "A's Are in a Precarious Spot, But Confidence Hasn't Sagged, *New York Times*, October 19, 1973: 28.

THE "STEVE HENDERSON GAME"

JUNE 14, 1980: NEW YORK METS 7, SAN FRANCISCO GIANTS 6, AT SHEA STADIUM

By Tom Cuggino

Each baseball season's early summer games take on a mystical quality in cities that endure longer, darker winters. Near June solstice, night patiently awaits dusk's extended loitering, humidity is tolerable, and the schedule is still young enough to keep fans of even the most dismal teams buoyant for revelation. Such was the setting on a calm 70-degree Saturday evening at Shea Stadium as the hometown Mets took the field on Flag Day 1980 against the San Francisco Giants, a franchise that had abruptly abandoned the city for the West Coast a generation prior. Most of the National League followers in town had by then long since adopted the expansion Mets as an irresistibly flawed replacement since the team's inauguration in 1962, priding themselves as anxious patrons of some of the most uncommon euphoria and agony the game had ever seen. The heroes of the franchise's story thus far had frequently been otherwise inconsequential players who fleeted through sparse moments of glory, becoming all the more satirically etched in the forgiving memories of their fans. One more such indelible character would develop that night.

The Mets entered with a record of 26-28, in fourth place trailing the Expos by seven games in the NL East, but were playing inspired baseball of late with seven wins in their previous nine games, including a three-game sweep of the Dodgers at Shea Stadium earlier in the week, the middle game a 10-inning complete game by Craig Swan with Mike Jorgensen's game-winning grand slam, culminated the next night by a comeback from a 5-0 deficit. The Giants were 24-33, bringing up the rear in the NL West, and had no positive momentum since consecutive series sweeps over the Cardinals and Cubs back in mid-May. The Mets offered left-hander and Brooklyn native Pete Falcone to start the game, making his 11th start of the season with a record of 3-4 and an ERA of 5.02. The Giants countered with former Rookie of the Year John "The Count" Montefusco, who grew up in nearby Long Branch, New Jersey.

Before many of the 22,918 fans found their seats, Falcone spotted the Giants four first-inning runs, three of them on second baseman Rennie Stennett's second (and final) home run of the season. The Giants added another in the next frame, sending Falcone to an early shower. He was replaced by right-hander Mark Bomback in long relief, who walked Jack Clark to load the bases but wiggled out of further damage. Bomback issued two more free passes along with

During Lee Mazzilli's first stint with the Mets, from 1976-1981, he was a top player on a bad team. When he returned in 1986, he was a role player on one of the best teams ever.

four singles over the next three innings, but San Francisco managed to convert only one more run from it all.

The score remained 6-0 Giants through the middle of the sixth, and Montefusco was no-hitting the Mets until Doug Flynn led off the bottom of the inning with a single to center. With one out, Lee Mazzilli reached on an error by Stennett and Frank Taveras bunted for a hit to suddenly load the bases for right fielder Claudell Washington, whom the Mets had acquired from the Chicago White Sox a week earlier for minor-league pitcher Jesse Anderson. Washington drove in Flynn with a fly to Larry Herndon in center, but Steve Henderson stranded the two remaining runners with his third strikeout of the night.

The score stayed 6-1 through the middle of the eighth inning and Montefusco kept the Mets to the two hits. New York gathered steam, though, when with one out Mazzilli singled to center and Taveras reached on an infield hit. Giants manager Dave Bristol stuck with his starter to face Washington, who grounded into a fielder's choice at second base. Henderson redeemed his three prior strikeouts with an infield hit as Mazzilli streaked home to make it 6-2. Mike Jorgensen's walk loaded the bases and finally chased Montefusco, who was replaced by reliever Greg Minton. Minton faced a dangerous predicament in catcher John Stearns, a .310 hitter on his way to a third All-Star Game appearance in four years. Minton won the encounter, fanning Stearns in what felt like the final dagger that night for the Mets.

Then came the magical ninth.

After Jeff Reardon set down the Giants in a scoreless top half of the inning, Minton went to work on a seemingly routine effort to finish off the Mets. First came an innocent groundout by Elliott Maddox, but then Flynn bunted his way on base to get the Shea blood flowing again. Jose Cardenal, who had grounded out to shortstop Johnnie LeMaster upon entering the game the previous inning as a pinch-hitter, did the same again here but advanced Flynn to second in the process. This set up Mazzilli to knock Flynn home with a single to center, inching the fans forward in their seats. Taveras then walked, reaching base for the third time and bringing Washington to bat as the potential tying run. Bristol had southpaw Gary Lavelle, his closer the season before, available for a favorable matchup versus the left-handed-hitting Washington, but chose to hang with Minton. This proved costly as Washington dropped a single to center to score Mazzilli for the second straight inning … 6-4. With the New York crowd now fully salivating, Bristol lifted Minton for fellow right-hander Allen Ripley, a strange move in that Ripley had become a budding starter and this would be one of only three appearances for him out of the bullpen all year. As he finished his warmups, Stephen Curtis Henderson sauntered to plate with the scoreboard bursting out in all capital letters: "HENDU CAN DO"!

It was almost three years to the day that Henderson had been acquired in an almost unthinkable trade, part of several the Mets made on a single day in what was dubbed "The Midnight Massacre." He arrived from the Cincinnati Reds along with Doug Flynn, outfield prospect Dan Norman, and starting pitcher Pat Zachry for three-time Cy Young Award winner and future Hall of Famer Tom Seaver, who for a decade had been known simply as "The Franchise."[1] Henderson was the big bet in the deal, and Mets manager Joe Torre endorsed his enthusiasm as similar to that of Willie Mays.[2] He had been a solid line-drive hitter now for several years, finished second in the 1977 Rookie of the Year voting to future Hall of Famer Andre Dawson by just two tallies, and reached base in a Mets rookie record 28 consecutive games during that campaign. He had been something of a defensive enigma, though, and had a penchant for hitting into rally-killing double plays (he had led the league in that dubious category in '78 with 24), something Mets fans were surely mindful of at that juncture of the game. While he hadn't yet homered that season in 188 at-bats, he entered the day among the league batting leaders at .340. Ripley, meanwhile, had surrendered 19 long balls in 150⅓ career innings prior to this showdown. With tension palpable, Henderson laced an opposite-field line drive into the bullpen over the 371-foot marker on the right-center-field wall, unleashing the ballpark's signature enormous plastic Big Apple from its upside-down top hat, and sending the hometown fans into an unmitigated October-esque frenzy. The Mets, having been no-hit for five innings and down 6-1 in the eighth, had rebounded for a preposterous 7-6 victory. An appropriate exclamation point to Flag Day, to be sure. The scoreboard's final retort: "HENDU DID DO"!

That wasn't the only lifetime highlight in Henderson's day. Just hours before the game that day, he became engaged, asking his future wife, Pam, to marry him. "She had just come into town and I gave her a ring at the airport – LaGuardia," Henderson later fondly recalled during a pregame interview at Citi Field as the hitting coach of the Philadelphia Phillies. "Then I homered. That was the first homer I hit that year. I picked the right time."[3]

The euphoria was short-lived. After the dramatic victory, the Mets lost their next seven games and eventually finished 67-95, and Henderson was traded a year later to the Cubs for another headliner, Dave Kingman.[4] However, a week and a half prior to that sublime evening, they had drafted one of the generation's greatest raw talents in Darryl Strawberry, who would become the initial face of the franchise's winningest decade. That subsequent renown seemed a mountain away in 1980, but for a flash in that summer's pan, an impossible recovery had kindled an aura of hope for the blue and orange.

Sources

In addition to the sources cited in the Notes, the author also consulted Baseball-Reference.com and four New York Mets blogs:

Ultimate Mets.com, Independent Mets Database, ultimatemets.com/profile.php?PlayerCode=0260&tabno=7.

MetsMerizedOnline.com, Independent Mets Database, metsmerizedonline.com/2010/06/a-mets-magic-moment-turns-30.html/.

Mets360.com, Mets Blog, mets360.com/?p=31252.

AmazinAvenue.com, Mets Blog, amazinavenue.com/2013/6/3/4391810/this-date-in-mets-history-june-3-darryl-strawberry-gregg-jefferies-drafted.

Notes

1 Associated Press, "Mets Trade Tom Seaver, Dave Kingman," *Wilmington* (Delaware) *Star-News*, June 16, 1977: 23, news.google.com/newspapers?nid=1454&dat=19770616&id=dbosAAAAIBAJ&sjid=JRMEAAAAIBAJ&pg=5196,3178841.

2 Peter Gammons, "This Stevie Is Also a Wonder," *Sports Illustrated*, August 15, 1977: 42, si.com/vault/1977/08/15/643744/this-stevie-is-also-a-wonder.

3 Anthony McCarron, "Where Are They Now? Former Met Steve Henderson, Once Traded for Tom Seaver," *New York Daily News*, April 22, 2015, nydailynews.com/sports/baseball/mets/steve-henderson-traded-seaver-article-1.2195267.

4 Joseph Durso, "Kingman Back With Mets; Henderson Traded to Cubs," *New York Times*, March 1, 1981, nytimes.com/1981/03/01/sports/kingman-back-with-mets-henderson-traded-to-cubs.html.

TOM SEAVER RETURNS TO THE METS

APRIL 5, 1983: NEW YORK METS 2, PHILADELPHIA PHILLIES 0, AT SHEA STADIUM

By Bruce Slutsky

Tom Seaver became a New York Met in a very usual way. In 1966 a rule prevented any team from signing a college player while his season was still in progress. Since the Atlanta Braves had signed Seaver illegally, Commissioner William Eckert voided the contract and allowed any team to match the Braves' offer of $51,500. The Indians, Phillies, and the Mets were interested in signing Seaver, so the commissioner held a lottery to determine who would get him. The Mets won the lottery and Seaver joined their Triple-A team at Jacksonville.[1]

Seaver was "The Franchise" for the New York Mets. He turned the team from perennial losers when he arrived in 1967 and won the Rookie of the Year Award to World Series champions in 1969, when he won the first of his three Cy Young Awards. Team broadcaster Ralph Kiner described Seaver as "the driving force behind the players, always pushing the team to be better than they were, never letting them settle."[2]

In early 1977, Seaver grew increasingly dissatisfied with Mets Board Chairman M. Donald Grant for not trying to improve the team. The Mets had signed Seaver to a three-year contract extension in 1976 for $675,000, making him baseball's highest-paid pitcher. A new collective-bargaining agreement reached in July of that year led to the first wave of free-agency signings after the season. The Mets stood pat, and Seaver was upset that there wasn't much motivation to upgrade a club that was coming off a third-place finish. After quarreling with Grant and general manager Joe McDonald over the team's performance and a new contract, he was dealt to the Cincinnati Reds for pitcher Pat Zachry, second baseman Doug Flynn, and outfielders Steve Henderson and Dan Norman on June 15, 1977 – forever known as the "Midnight Massacre." The Mets entered the darkest era in their history.[3]

Seaver pitched for the Reds for six seasons, compiling a record of 75-46, and tossed a no-hitter against the St. Louis Cardinals in 1978. On December 12, 1982, Seaver came home again. The Reds traded him back to the Mets for Charlie Puleo, Lloyd McClendon, and Jason Felice. Seaver was 38 years old and had recently suffered from a sore right shoulder and sore hip.[4]

Despite Seaver's age, the still-rebuilding Mets made him the Opening Day starter on Tuesday, April 5, 1983. Seaver left his home in Greenwich, Connecticut. at 10:30 A.M. and arrived at Shea Stadium 45 minutes later. When fans entered the ballpark, they began to post banners welcoming him back. As usual, Seaver went to the bullpen to warm up. When the final member of the Mets' starting lineup was announced, cheers resonated throughout the park. After Seaver completed his warm-ups, he gave the ball to a handicapped boy in the stands and walked to the dugout to an even louder ovation. New York Governor Mario Cuomo and New York City Mayor Ed Koch participated in the pregame ceremonies, but those dignitaries paled in comparison to the one who would take the mound minutes later.[5]

Seaver's return involved a classic matchup against an old rival, the Philadelphia Phillies' Steve Carlton. The two had dueled nearly 10 years prior – April 6, 1973 – and several more times before and since. Collectively, Seaver and Carlton had won 549 games, pitched 106 shutouts, struck out 6,571 batters, and won seven Cy Young Awards. Not surprisingly, both were later elected to the National Baseball Hall of Fame almost unanimously on the first ballot. The crowd, announced at 46,687, was the largest Opening Day crowd at Shea Stadium since 1968 as everyone wanted to welcome "Tom Terrific" back to New York.

The fans received more remnants of past glories. Seaver began this beautiful sun-drenched afternoon by striking out Pete Rose, and embarked on a sterling day. In fact, both pitchers were nearly flawless over the first six innings. Seaver allowed three hits while Carlton allowed only two. Neither gave up a run. Since Seaver was nursing a strained thigh, he had to depart after six innings – to be relieved by Doug Sisk. The Mets offense was unable to get Seaver a win, but they were able to win the game. They broke through in the bottom of the seventh, when Mike Howard got an RBI single through a drawn-in infield. Brian Giles hit a sacrifice fly to Rose in right field for the second run, which was enough for New York to improve its record against Carlton to 32-27.

Seaver's reunion with the Mets lasted for only one season. In 34 starts he won 9 games and lost 14 for the 68-94 Mets. (He did lead the pitching staff with 135 strikeouts in 231 innings.) Back then, there was a compensation pool to reimburse teams that lost free agents. Every club could protect 26 players. Since the Chicago White Sox lost Dennis Lamp to the Toronto Blue Jays, they were allowed to pick one player not protected by any team. The Mets thought that at age 39 no team would want Seaver and left him unprotected. To the Mets' and Seaver's dismay, the White Sox took him. Mets owners Nelson Doubleday and Fred Wilpon were devastated by this development, as it was their intention to bring Seaver back to complete his career with the Mets.[6]

Seaver pitched with Chicago until June 29, 1986, when he was traded to the Boston Red Sox for Steve Lyons. The highlight of his tenure with the White Sox was his 300th win on August 4, 1985, at Yankee Stadium. After posting a 7-13 record in an injury-plagued 1986 season, Seaver was left off the Red Sox' postseason roster and retired at the end of the season. When several pitchers for the Mets were injured early in 1987, he attempted a comeback, but quickly realized that he couldn't return. But despite his other stops in his storied big-league career, he'll forever be remembered as a New York Met.

Sources

In addition to the sources cited in the Notes, the author also consulted Baseball-Reference.com.

The author was on jury duty that April 5. He was released early from his civic obligation and took the subway to Shea only to find out the game was a sellout.

Notes

1 "Tom Seaver," Society for American Baseball Research, January 25, 2016. Accessed January 18, 2018. sabr.org/bioproj/person/486af3ad.
2 "Tom Seaver," Baseball Hall of Fame. Accessed January 18, 2018. baseballhall.org/hof/seaver-tom.
3 Bill Madden, "The Midnight Massacre," New York Daily News, June 17, 2007. Accessed January 18, 2018. nydailynews.com/sports/baseball/mets/midnight-massacre-article-1.224970.
4 Joseph Durso, "Mets and Reds in Agreement on Seaver Trade," New York Times, December 10, 1982. Accessed January 18, 2018. nytimes.com/1982/12/11/sports/mets-and-reds-in-agreement-on-seaver-trade.html.
5 Steve Wulf, "It Was a Terrific Homecoming," SI.com, October 13, 2015. Accessed January 18, 2018. si.com/vault/1983/04/18/619590/it-was-a-terrific-homecoming.
6 Joseph Durso, "Mets Are Stunned," New York Times, January 20, 1984. Accessed January 18, 2018. nytimes.com/1984/01/21/sports/white-sox-take-seaver-mets-are-stunned.html.

DWIGHT GOODEN ONE-HITS THE CUBS

SEPTEMBER 7, 1984: NEW YORK METS 10, CHICAGO CUBS 0, AT SHEA STADIUM

By Joseph Wancho

The Chicago Cubs were as hot as a summer's day as they began a three-game series with the New York Mets at Shea Stadium. They sported a 15-4 record since August 18 and increased their National League East lead over the Mets from 1½ games to 7 games.

Two reasons for this uprising on the North Side were two deals that brought instant success. Chicago acquired Dennis Eckersley from Boston on May 25, 1984. Eck pitched his way to a 10-8 record with a 3.03 ERA in 24 starts. But the real haul came three weeks later. On June 13, in a seven-player deal with Cleveland, Rick Sutcliffe came over to the Cubs and went 16-1 with a 2.69 ERA in 20 starts. The 1982 American League ERA champion had fallen on hard times (4-5, 5.15 ERA). Nobody could have predicted how well this deal would work out for Chicago. Sutcliffe was so dominating during his 3½-month stint in the new league that he was selected as the NL Cy Young Award winner in 1984.

The Mets still measured up well. It had been 1973 since their last postseason appearance, and they had been relegated to the basement of the NL East five times since 1977. But the pendulum was swinging their way as the front office put together a solid nucleus of a ballclub. Second baseman Wally Backman, third baseman Hubie Brooks, and center fielder Mookie Wilson had all made their major-league debuts while wearing Mets uniforms in 1980. First baseman Keith Hernandez and left fielder George Foster were acquired in trades to lend leadership and evoke some fear in the opposition. Darryl Strawberry, who manned right field, was named the NL Rookie of the Year in 1983 by both *The Sporting News* and the Baseball Writers Association of America.

Their starting pitching was young, with Walt Terrell and Ron Darling in only their second seasons. But the jewel of the staff was the youngest one of all: Dwight Gooden. The Tampa, Florida, native dominated Class-A opponents in 1983. Pitching for Lynchburg in the Carolina League, the 18-year-old Gooden posted a 19-4 record with a 2.50 ERA. He struck out 300 batters in 191 innings pitched. He earned a brief call-up to Triple-A Tidewater, beating Denver in an International League playoff game.

It was a big jump from Class A to the big leagues. But Mets skipper Davey Johnson, who managed at Tidewater in 1983, felt it was merited. "I was expecting to start the season at Tidewater and would

Dwight Gooden, a teenage revelation in 1984, enhanced his Rookie of the Year performance with a wondrous 1985 that included a 24-4 record and a 1.53 ERA.

not have been disappointed if I did," Gooden said. "I didn't think I was ready yet, but they do."¹

Gooden's apprehension was squelched with a 14-8 record and a 2.98 ERA heading into the September 7 game against Chicago. He racked up 224 strikeouts, earning him the nickname Doctor K. The Cubs' Dick Ruthven (5-9 with a 4.67 ERA) opposed him, marking the fourth such time these two faced each other in '84 (with Doc holding a 2-1 edge so far).

A crowd of 46,301 packed their way into Shea for the Friday night affair. Bob Dernier led off the game with a walk, and stole second base – only to be stranded. The Mets wouldn't have as much difficulty cashing in. Backman led off the bottom of the frame with a triple to center field that soared over Dernier. He waltzed home on a fly to right field from Wilson.

The Mets held that 1-0 advantage until the third inning. New York scored five times with the big blow coming on Foster's 20th home run of the season. After a walk to Brooks, Cubs manager Jim Frey yanked Ruthven in favor of Warren Brusstar.

Meanwhile, Gooden began to exert total control of the Cubs – having not allowed a hit through four innings. Although Gooden was having his way with the Cubs batters, he also contributed on offense as well. With one down, he singled and moved to second base when Backman walked. Gooden scored on Wilson's base hit.

Keith Moreland led off the top of the fifth inning, and got aboard when he singled to third base. Third baseman Ray Knight tried to make a play on the ball hit down the line, but it was a tough chance.

"I was playing back and off the line," Knight said. "Nobody had been pulling Doc, and Moreland goes the other way and he doesn't run well. I came in at such a sharp angle, I had to catch the ball and throw it all at once. But I never got the ball out of my hand. My momentum was carrying me toward their dugout and there was no way I could throw the ball."²

Unshaken, Gooden retired the next three batters. And he had every reason not to be rattled: His offense had built a 7-0 advantage. That grew even larger when New York scored three more in the sixth to complete the 10-0 blowout. Strawberry provided two of those runs on his 21st homer of the season.

Gooden surrendered three more walks in the final three frames, but no more hits. It was the only one-hitter of his career. Doc had two hits of his own, but of more historical significance were his 11 strikeouts.

When he whiffed Ron Cey in the second inning, he surpassed Grover Cleveland Alexander's NL record of 227 strikeouts in a rookie season, set in 1911. Five days after his mastery of the Cubs, Doc fanned 16 more in a 2-0 triumph over Pittsburgh to surpass Herb Score's major-league mark for most K's in a rookie campaign. Gooden would finish with 276 – which as of 2018 remained the top mark for freshman pitchers.

"Tonight was one of my better games," said Gooden. "I felt great going into the game and I felt strong at the end."³

Frey also noticed how the 19-year-old appeared to get better as night wore on. "He threw a couple of fastballs to Henry Cotto in the ninth inning that were as hard as he threw in the first inning," the Cubs manager said. "He's just an outstanding pitcher, what else can you say? You're going to hear that for 15 more years."⁴

As for coming up short of a no-no, Gooden placed the emphasis on the greater priority. "I'm not disappointed. The hit doesn't matter. I just wanted to win the game."⁵

Gooden ended the season with a 17-9 record and a 2.60 ERA. To nobody's surprise, he was selected the NL Rookie Pitcher of the Year by both *The Sporting News* and the BBWAA.

Gooden had the hardware, but the Cubs won their season-long battle with the Mets – taking the NL East by 6½ games. New York improved further, but ended up bridesmaids again in 1985 with the St. Louis Cardinals emerging as the victor. But those two near misses bolstered the motivation to complete the deal in 1986.

Sources

In addition to the sources cited in the Notes, the author also consulted Retrosheet.org.

Notes

1 Jack Lang, "Rookies Earn Way Into Mets' Rotation," *The Sporting News*, April 9, 1984: 23.
2 Murray Chass, "Gooden Pitches 1-Hitter and Strikes Out 11 Cubs," *New York Times*, September 8, 1984: 27.
3 Murray Chass, "Mets Top Cubs, 10-0," *New York Times*, September 8, 1984: 28.
4 Ibid.
5 Chass, "Gooden Pitches 1-Hitter."

GARY CARTER HOMERS IN DEBUT FOR METS

APRIL 9, 1985: NEW YORK METS 6, ST. LOUIS CARDINALS 5 (10 INNINGS), AT SHEA STADIUM

By Bruce Slutsky

Gary Carter earned the nickname "Kid" when he first came to spring training with the Montreal Expos at age 19 in 1973.[1] He, along with Larry Parrish, Ellis Valentine, André Dawson, and pitcher Steve Rogers, would turn out to be the core players of this franchise in the late 1970s and early 1980s. But Carter, with his affable personality and hard-nosed play, was the recognizable star. *Sports Illustrated* put him on its front cover in early 1983, proclaiming him the "Best in Baseball."[2] From 1974 to 1984, Carter hit 220 home runs for the Expos and was picked for seven All-Star Games. But Carter's stay in Montreal resulted in only one playoff appearance. That came in the split season of 1981, when the Expos reached the National League Championship Series before falling to the Los Angeles Dodgers in heartbreaking fashion.

In 1984 the Mets seemed to have found their way after a decade in the wilderness since their last appearance in the postseason, in 1973. A 90-72 record put them in second place, 6½ games behind the '84 Chicago Cubs. The Mets felt they needed to make roster moves before they could be true pennant contenders. In one of the biggest trades since they dealt Tom Seaver to the Reds in 1977, the club obtained Carter from the Expos in exchange for shortstop Hubie Brooks, catcher Mike Fitzgerald, and minor leaguers Herm Winningham and Floyd Youmans. Since Carter had 10 years of major-league service time and at least five years with the same team, he could have vetoed the trade. But he didn't, aware of the fine nucleus of playoff potential the Mets possessed. Certainly, playing in New York City would improve his visibility.[3]

Dwight Gooden, the teenage pitching prodigy who was voted the 1984 NL Rookie of the Year and was the runner-up in the Cy Young Award voting, got the 1985 Opening Day assignment. In addition to Carter making his New York debut, other notable starters included Wally Backman, Mookie Wilson, Keith Hernandez, and Darryl Strawberry. Joaquin Andujar, who won 20 games in 1984, was the St. Louis Cardinals' starting pitcher. The group behind him included Lonnie Smith, Tommy Herr, and future Hall of Famer Ozzie Smith. With Vice President George H.W. Bush tossing out the ceremonial first pitch, the game had a playoff atmosphere. It was also a portent of the fierce NL East battle that would heat up come late September and early October.

After compiling several Hall of Fame-worthy seasons in Montreal, Gary Carter came to New York in December 1984 and enhanced the Mets' reputation as a championship contender.

But there was little heat in the air. At game time, the temperature was 45 degrees. That didn't stop a crowd of 46,781 from coming to Shea Stadium. By the bottom of the fifth, the Mets were ahead, 5-2, on of RBIs from Hernandez, Howard Johnson, Rafael Santana, and George Foster (home run). Andujar departed the game after five innings — tagged for eight hits. Gooden, meanwhile, was removed in the top of the seventh after giving up singles to Andy Van Slyke and Ozzie Smith.

By the ninth inning, the Mets were clinging to a 5-4 advantage. But an ineffectual Doug Sisk walked Jack Clark with the bases loaded. With the score now even at 5-5 in the bottom of the ninth, Neil Allen, a former Mets closer, came in to pitch for St. Louis. He had departed from New York on June 15, 1983, a date legendary in Mets history and infamous in Cardinals lore. Allen and Rick Ownbey were sent by the Mets to St. Louis for Hernandez. Former Mets catcher John Stearns called the trade "the biggest heist since the Thomas Crown Affair."[4] The main reason for the exchange was the deteriorating relationship between Whitey Herzog and Hernandez. Herzog was quoted as saying, "Keith Hernandez was dogging it. … He's the best defensive first baseman I've ever seen. But on offense, he was loafing. He loafed down the line on groundballs and he wasn't aggressive on the bases."[5]

The Mets loaded the bases against Allen in the bottom of the ninth on a hit, a walk, and an error, but Allen got Mookie Wilson on a fly ball to retire the side. Tom Gorman gave up a double to Ozzie Smith in the top of the 10th but the Cardinals couldn't push a run across.

Hernandez led off the bottom of the 10th inning against Allen and struck out. That merely set the stage for Carter to have a storybook finish in his orange and blue debut. A hanging curveball by Allen turned into a rope as it came off Carter's bat. Left fielder Lonnie Smith reached up at the wall, but the ball snuck over his glove and the fence in front of the visiting bullpen. The Mets were 6-5 walk-off winners. The Mets had a 6-5 win and reason to think that, with the best-hitting catcher in baseball, there would be many more special victories ahead. The only blemish in the game for Gary Carter was a passed ball in the third inning that led to a run for the Cardinals.

Carter, the Mets' cleanup batter, was selected for the All-Star Game in his first four seasons with the team, and was one of the stars of the Mets' victory over the Boston Red Sox in the 1986 World Series. Hobbled by knee injuries,[6] he was released by the Mets in 1989 and signed as a free agent with the San Francisco Giants. After the 1990 season for the Giants, he signed with the Los Angeles Dodgers in 1991 and then in 1992 returned to the Expos, for whom he completed his playing career. After retirement he served as a color commentator for the Florida Marlins and the Expos. Carter also worked as a minor-league catching instructor for the Mets. He was elected to the Baseball Hall of Fame in 2003.

In 2011 Carter was diagnosed with glioblastoma, an aggressive form of brain cancer. He died on February 16, 2012.[7]

Sources

In addition to the sources mentioned in the Notes, the author consulted baseball-reference.com and retrosheet.org.

Notes

1 "Gary Carter," Baseball Hall of Fame. Accessed January 19, 2018. http://baseball-hall.org/hof/carter-gary
2 Rory Costello, "Gary Carter," Society for American Baseball Research. Accessed January 19, 2018. http://sabr.org/bioproj/person/1a995e9e
3 Joseph Durso. "Mets Get Expo's Carter for Broks and 3 Others," *New York Times*, December 10, 1984. Accessed January 19, 2018. http://www.nytimes.com/1984/12/11/sports/mets-get-expo-s-carter-for-brooks-and-3-others.html
4 "Why Cardinals dealt Keith Hernandez in 1983," RetroSimba. December 31, 2017. Accessed January 19, 2018. https://retrosimba.com/2013/06/12/why-cardinals-dealt-keith-hernandez-30-years-ago/
5 Whitey Herzog and Kevin Horrigan. *White Rat: A Life in Baseball* (New York: Harper & Row, 1987), 148.
6 Costello.
7 "Gary Carter," Baseball Hall of Fame.

FIRE(WORKS) AND RAIN: METS AND BRAVES ENGAGE IN A HOLIDAY EPIC

JULY 4, 1985: NEW YORK METS 16, ATLANTA BRAVES 13 (19 INNINGS), AT ATLANTA-FULTON COUNTY STADIUM

By Brian Wright

The Mets have an unusual affinity for finding themselves in notable marathons.

Take that late May 1964 game at Shea Stadium, for instance -- a nightcap of a doubleheader that went on for 23 innings and nearly 7½ hours and ended in a San Francisco Giants victory behind Gaylord Perry's 10 frames of relief.

Fast-forward almost four years later. The Astrodome saw New York and Houston play to the longest scoreless tie in major-league history. It wasn't until the bottom of the 24th, and a bad hop that eluded Mets shortstop Al Weis, before the Astros brought this seemingly endless struggle to a close.

The Mets and Cardinals set their own offensively-challenged record in 1974. Forty-five men left on base became a single-game high, in addition to 175 official at-bats. A botched pickoff attempt in the top of the 25th led to Bake McBride scoring the winning run. When New York was set down in the bottom half, the Shea clock read 3:13 A.M. In terms of innings played, it is the longest uninterrupted game ever.

All of these strange events, though, are modest compared to what unfolded inside Atlanta-Fulton County Stadium beginning on the evening of the 1985 Independence Day holiday – a game scheduled to begin at 7:30 P.M. on July 4 which ended up finishing at 3:55 A.M. on July 5. There were 29 combined runs, 46 hits, 43 players used, 14 pitchers, three blown saves, two rain delays, two ejections, a formal protest, and a dumbfounding homer by a relief pitcher.

But the game that seemingly wouldn't end almost never got going. Precipitation pushed the start back by an hour and a half. When the skies temporarily cleared, both New York manager Davey Johnson and Atlanta skipper Eddie Haas sent their respective aces to the hill.

Neither would be there for long. Dwight Gooden, in the midst of a unanimous Cy Young season at age 20, lasted only 2⅓ innings before a second rain delay put an end to his outing. Braves starter Rick Mahler departed in the fourth after surrendering six hits and three earned runs.

New York, which came into the game 4½ games behind St. Louis in the NL East, yet in fourth place, eventually took a 7-4 lead into the bottom of the eighth following a Keith Hernandez homer, leaving him just a single short of a cycle. But Jesse Orosco, nursing a sore shoulder, couldn't shut the door on the Braves, initiating a theme that would afflict pitchers on both sides. Atlanta scored four times in its half of the eighth, including a three-run double by Dale Murphy. The Mets responded in the ninth with a Lenny Dykstra RBI single off Bruce Sutter. Extra innings allowed Hernandez to complete his cycle in the 12th, but it took until the top of the 13th

Ron Darling was acquired from the Texas Rangers organization in 1982 in a deal that involved Lee Mazzilli.

for New York to break the 8-8 tie, when as Howard Johnson smashed a two-run homer. The Braves were one strike from defeat before Terry Harper answered the "HoJo" long ball. With a runner on, his drive to left field dinged the foul pole. Ten apiece.

Scoring was absent through the 14th, 15th, and 16th. The 17th lacked for runs, but not intrigue. Darryl Strawberry got the heave-ho from home-plate umpire Terry Tata for disputing balls and strikes. Davey Johnson chimed in with choice words and earned his ticket to the clubhouse, too. Finally, the Mets broke through in the top of the 18th by way of Dykstra's sacrifice fly. Tom Gorman was asked to hold the one-run advantage. He retired Gerald Perry and Harper on groundouts. Up came the pitcher's spot. But Haas, to no surprise, had used up his pinch-hitting options.

Reliever Rick Camp remained the only hope – and a faint one at that. Camp's batting record was terrible, even by hitting pitchers' standards. He toted a meager .060 average to the plate, with 83 strikeouts in 167 career at-bats.

It would stand to reason that in this "Twilight Zone" atmosphere, *anything* was possible. But Camp hitting a home run? That was far too much to ask … or was it?

After Gorman got two easy strikes, Camp connected. The reactions of the Mets players told the story. Third baseman Ray Knight, as the ball took flight to left-center field, threw his arms out and palms up in disbelief. Left fielder Danny Heep, as he watched the ball go beyond the fence, placed his hands on his head. Howard Johnson, at shortstop, dropped to his knees. Dykstra, in center field, squatted in exhaustion. Second baseman Wally Backman barked – probably with words not safe for work – as Camp passed him.

But nobody felt worse than the man who served up the unlikeliest of home runs.

"There's not one thing you can say you feel at that moment," said Gorman, the eventual winner after six innings of relief. "It's not like pitchers don't hit home runs; they do. But in that situation, with two strikes and no balls and you give the guy a pitch he can hit out, it's embarrassing."[1]

"That's luck, pure luck," Camp rightfully admitted. "If we have to rely on me to hit a home run to win a game, we're in bad shape."[2]

Camp assumed his normal role in the top of the 19th with the score tied at 11. What he had taken from the Mets, he gave away (and then some). Knight atoned for the 11 men he left on base by doubling in Gary Carter (who caught all 305 pitches from Mets hurlers) to put New York on top, 12-11. The Mets were far from through, however. Heep singled in two runs and came around when Backman produced an RBI hit of his own. Ron Darling came in to protect the seemingly comfortable 16-11 lead, only to watch the Braves make one more

tireless charge. Harper's two-out single drove in two and brought the tying run to the plate – Rick Camp.

But dramatics, like those still in attendance, had been exhausted. Camp struck out on four pitches. At five minutes to 4 A.M., Darling put a period on perhaps the wackiest baseball chapter ever written. This night-turned-morning would still end with a bang. Several, in fact. The Braves went ahead with the postgame fireworks show. Residents near the ballpark reportedly made panicked calls to police, with some fearing this was the onset of a nuclear war with the Soviet Union.[3]

In summation, Hernandez, speaking for everyone, said: "I saw things I had never seen before."[4]

Sources

In addition to the sources cited in the Notes, the author also consulted Baseball-Reference.com, Retrosheet.org, and Ultimatemets.com

Notes
1 Michael Martinez. "29 Runs, 46 Hits, 19 Innings, 7 Hours, 1 Game," *New York Times*, July 5, 1985: 1.
2 Ibid.
3 Greg Stephenson. "30 Years Ago Saturday, Atlanta Braves Battled New York Mets in One of MLB's Craziest Games Ever," AL.com. al.com/sports/index.ssf/2015/07/30_years_ago_saturday_atlanta.html. Accessed March 28, 2018.
4 Howard Blatt, *Amazin' Met Memories* (Tampa: Albion Press, 2002), 280.

KEITH HERNANDEZ WALK-OFF SINGLE EDGES CARDS

SEPTEMBER 12, 1985: NEW YORK METS 7, ST. LOUIS CARDINALS 6, AT SHEA STADIUM

By Joseph Wancho

It was like old times in New York City. Both of Gotham's professional baseball teams were in late-season division races. A quirk in the schedule had both the Mets and Yankees as home teams on September 12. And both clubs were hosting their closest adversary in their respective divisional races.

The Mets had a matinee tilt with the St. Louis Cardinals – each sporting identical 83-54 records and sat atop the National League's East Division. The Yankees were hosting the Toronto Blue Jays in an evening affair. The Bombers trailed the Jays by 2½ games in the American League East. With both teams in the postseason mix, was it possible for an All-New York World Series? The fans for both clubs certainly hoped that would be the outcome.

The different starting times caused a traffic tie-up on the Triborough Bridge as Mets fans leaving Queens passed Yankee supporters headed to the Bronx. The Number 4 and 7 subway trains were packed tighter than patrons quaffing beer in an Irish bar on St. Patrick's Day. Yes, pennant fever had swept into New York City.

The Mets and Cardinals were wrapping up a three-game set at Shea Stadium; they had split the first two games, both victories by a scant one run, the Mets by 5-4 in the first game and the Cardinals 1-0 in 10 innings in the second. Newly acquired Cesar Cedeno had led off the extra frame with a solo home run to give the Cards the winning run.

The pitching matchup for the rubber game was Joaquin Andujar (20-9, 3.00 ERA) for St. Louis and Ed Lynch (10-7, 3.09 ERA) for New York. It was the second straight 20-win season for Andujar. He was one-third of a trio of quality starters for the Cardinals, along with Danny Cox and John Tudor. Lynch's 10 victories matched his career high, achieved in 1983. He was the third starter on the Mets rotation behind Dwight Gooden and Ron Darling. In this game, neither starting pitcher would get a decision.

A crowd of 46,295 filled Shea (no doubt boosted by Senior Citizen Day) on a beautiful, sunny afternoon that held a slight hint of a nip in the air. The Mets proved to be unwelcoming hosts, as they roughed up Andujar by scoring four runs in the bottom of the first inning. Mookie Wilson led off the proceedings with a walk and Wally Backman followed with a single to center field that sent Wilson scurrying to third base. Former Cardinal Keith Hernandez

The June 15, 1983 trade with the St. Louis Cardinals that brought Keith Hernandez to New York in exchange for Neil Allen and Rick Ownbey is arguably the greatest trade the Mets ever made.

hit into a 6-4-3 double play. Wilson scored, but the chance for a big inning looked wasted.

But the Mets kept the line moving as Gary Carter reached first with a looping single to center field. Then three consecutive doubles to right field by Darryl Strawberry, Danny Heep, and Howard Johnson plated three more runs and the Mets led, 4-0.

It did not get any easier for Andujar in the second frame. With one out, Wilson reached via a bunt single and Backman doubled him home for the Mets' fifth run. That was the end of the day for Andujar, who was replaced by left-hander Ricky Horton. After Hernandez's groundout to the pitcher that froze Backman at second base, Carter was walked intentionally, and a walk to Strawberry loaded the bases. Horton, who was not providing much relief, hit Heep to force in Backman with the Mets' sixth run. All six runs were charged to Andujar, as the book was closed on him for the day.

Meanwhile, Lynch retired the first six Cardinals batters he faced. But he too ran into trouble as St. Louis scored three runs in the third to cut the Mets lead in half. With one out, Tom Nieto singled to left field. Curt Ford, batting for Horton, followed with a single to right field and Nieto checked into second base. Vince Coleman struck out, but Willie McGee followed with another single; Nieto scored the Cardinals' first run. Tom Herr doubled to left, scoring Ford and McGee to trim the Mets advantage.

St. Louis inched closer in the top of the fourth inning. With runners on first and second, Nieto doubled to left field and both runners scored. The Mets now led by a single run, 6-5.

By the sixth inning the game was in the hands of the bullpens, and for the next three innings, neither team could score. Doug Sisk, Roger McDowell and Jesse Orosco all saw duty out of the pen for the Mets. First out of the pen for the Cardinals was Pat Perry, making his major-league debut. After four solid innings, he was replaced by Ken Dayley in the seventh.in the seventh.

In the top of the ninth, the Cardinals tied the score when Willie McGee socked his ninth home run of the season, depositing a 2-and-2 fastball from Orosco over the wall in left-center.

Wilson led off the bottom of the ninth and sent a chopper to short. Ozzie Smith charged in and fielded the grounder, but his throw to first was in the dirt and first baseman Brian Harper could not come up with it. It was a tough chance with the speedy Wilson streaking down the first-base line, and no error was charged to Smith. "It's one of those plays, that if it's made, it's a super play," said Smith. "People take it for granted because I've made it a lot of times. We didn't make it."[1]

Backman bunted back to Dayley, who made the putout unassisted. But Wilson moved into scoring position at second base. Hernandez stepped to the plate and singled between short and third. Vince Coleman charged the ball from his left-field position and fired it home, but Wilson beat the throw standing up to deliver the winning run.

New York took over first place in the East. "We had to win this one," said manager Davey Johnson. "We had to show the Cardinals that we're going to win."[2] The Mets played St. Louis 18 times in 1985, posting an 8-10 record against their nemesis. Eleven of those games were decided by one run, while six went into extra innings. "If we had lost, after being six runs up," said Hernandez, "that would have hurt us. And if they had won after being six runs down, they would have kept rolling for who knows how long."[3] Hernandez added, "That was a big hit in my career, no question."[4]

And what was the outcome for the Yankees? They were victorious as well, scoring six runs in the bottom of the eighth inning to turn a 4-1 deficit into a 7-5 victory. Ron Hassey's three-run blast was the big blow.

But both the Mets and the Yankees were left on the outside looking in as far as a postseason berth. The Cardinals won the NL East by three games and Toronto finished two games up on the Yankees in the AL East.

Those baseball fans of New York, who had dreamed of a possible Subway Series, would need to be patient. Their wishes would come to fruition in 2000

Notes
1 Rick Hummel, "Mets Batter Fading Andujar," *St. Louis Post-Dispatch*, September 13, 1985: D2.
2 Craig Wolff, "New York: Mets Win and Retake First," *New York Times*, September 13, 1985: A1.
3 Wolff.
4 Hummel.

STRAWBERRY'S 11TH-INNING WALLOP KEEPS THE METS' HOPES ALIVE

OCTOBER 1, 1985: NEW YORK METS 1, ST. LOUIS CARDINALS 0, AT BUSCH STADIUM

By Richard A. Cuicchi

The New York Mets entered the 1985 season looking to build on their success (second-place finish in the NL East) under manager Davey Johnson the year before. Indeed, the Mets became embroiled in a battle for the division title for most of the season, and ultimately it came down to a two-team race between the New Yorkers and the St. Louis Cardinals. The extra-inning game between these two rivals on October 1 contributed to the end-of-season excitement, with Darryl Strawberry hitting one of the most dramatic home runs of his career to capture the much-needed win for the Mets.

The Mets had relinquished their division lead to St. Louis on September 14 and were desperate to stay in contention down the stretch. They managed to do just that, as they entered a three-game series with the Cardinals that began on October 1. A Mets sweep would put them in a tie for first place, with three games remaining after that.

The game was played at night in St. Louis's Busch Stadium before a crowd of 46,026. Cardinals manager Whitey Herzog and Mets manager Johnson played a poker game involving their starters, both skippers wanting to avoid a contest between their number-one pitchers during the series. With pitcher Ron Darling next up in the Mets rotation, Johnson decided to stick with him over Dwight Gooden, his ace, to start the first game. Herzog countered with his ace, John Tudor. Johnson said before the game, "Whitey knew all along I was going to start Darling. I've got to win three games here, not one. I don't have the luxury of changing around my rotation at this point." Saying, "I'm not conceding the next game to Gooden," Herzog figured that the Cardinals just needed to win two games in the series to be in position to win the division.[1]

Tudor, the second-best pitcher in the National League behind Gooden, had won 19 of his last 20 decisions, and sported a 2.04 ERA. He was seeking a record-tying 11th shutout for a left-hander.[2] In his last outing against the Mets, on September 11, he posted a 10-inning, three-hit shutout win. Darling's record wasn't too shabby either; he had 16 wins (including his last six in a row since August 14) and a 2.94 ERA going into the game.

Tudor and Darling locked into a pitcher's duel for nine innings. For some fans, the game to this point might have been considered boring. But the best drama would follow.

The right-handed Darling was especially efficient as he allowed more than one baserunner in only two innings. With the aid of a

The No. 1 overall draft pick in 1980, Darryl Strawberry had his share of highs and lows. But he remains the Mets' all-time leader in home runs.

caught-stealing play (second inning) and a double play (seventh inning), Darling escaped run-scoring threats by the Cardinals. Altogether he gave up only four hits and three walks in his nine-inning stint. As for Tudor, he held the Mets to six hits in his 10 innings on the mound.

The seventh inning was the only time a batter for either team reached third base during the two starters' outings. The Mets had their first real chance to score in that inning. With one out, Tudor allowed a single to Ray Knight and a double to Rafael Santana, whose one-hop liner struck Tudor's foot and bounced past first base into foul territory down the right-field line. Darling, hitting next, didn't execute on a suicide-squeeze play, and Cardinals catcher Darrell Porter caught pinch-runner Howard Johnson in a rundown. Darling fouled out to end the threat.[3]

The Cardinals had their best chance for a run in the bottom of the inning on Terry Pendleton's double and a walk to Mike Jorgensen. But Ozzie Smith grounded into a double play to end the inning.

Tudor pitched the top of the 10th inning for the Cardinals before exiting the game for a pinch-hitter.

Left-hander Jesse Orosco came on in the 10th in relief of Darling, who had been lifted for pinch-hitter Tom Paciorek in the top of the inning. After retiring leadoff batter Pendleton on a pop foul to the catcher, Orosco walked Cesar Cedeno, who stole second base. Orosco struck out Ozzie Smith, then issued an intentional walk to Tito Landrum, pinch-hitting for Tudor, in order to get to Vince Coleman, who had been hitless against Orosco in his last 15 at-bats. Cardinals manager Herzog sent Jack Clark, who was still recovering from a torn rib muscle, to the plate to pinch-hit for Coleman. Orosco retired Clark on a fly ball to right field to end the inning.[4]

Left-hander Ken Dayley relieved Tudor in the top of the 11th inning. The month of September hadn't been particularly kind to Dayley, who suffered two blown saves and a blown lead while losing two decisions among his 10 outings.

Dayley's fortunes appeared to be changing when he struck out Keith Hernandez and Gary Carter to start the inning. But then Darryl Strawberry hit a towering drive that hit the digital clock in right field, estimated at 440 feet from home plate.[5] While the fans may have been bored for 10 innings, those who stuck around until the 11th witnessed one of the most dramatic home runs in Strawberry's career. After the game Strawberry said, "It's a mistake pitch. A hanging curve. You want to be up there in that situation, you want to help, you're happy that a guy like Tudor is gone, you suddenly see it there."[6]

Orosco returned to the hill for the bottom of the 11th. Apart from Mookie Wilson's error on a fly ball, Orosco had no trouble retiring the Cardinals to clinch the 1-0 victory for the Mets.

The New Yorkers were able to stay alive, reducing the Cardinals' lead to two games. Davey Johnson's pitching plans appeared to be working when Dwight Gooden shut down the Cardinals the next day, 5-2, to pull the Mets to within one game of the Cardinals. However, the Mets' hopes for gaining a first-place tie were dashed in the third game of the series when they lost, 4-3.

The Cardinals clinched the East Division title when they took two games from the Chicago Cubs in the last series of the season. The Mets didn't help themselves, losing two of their remaining three games to the Montreal Expos.

The Cardinals went on to win the National League pennant, but lost to the Kansas City Royals in the World Series.

Strawberry did his part during the last nine games of season to keep the Mets in contention by getting 11 hits, including four home runs. The slugger finished the season with 29 home runs, 79 RBIs, and a team-leading .947 OPS. He missed considerable playing time when he required surgery on May 11 for a tear of an inner ulnar collateral ligament on an elbow of his throwing arm and wasn't able to return until June 28. During that stretch, the Mets had a 20-23 record. After he returned from the disabled list, the Mets posted a remarkable 60-33 record.[7] Perhaps had he not missed all that time, the Mets would have been in a different position going into the last few weeks of the season.

The Mets finished the 1985 season with the second-best record (98 wins) in their history, so their final outcome was devastating to their rabid fans. It was the second year in a row that they finished in second place in the division. Davey Johnson, in his second season at the helm of the team, said about the season, "I'm disappointed, very disappointed. I feel like the bridesmaid, never the bride."[8] However, they would make up for their disappointing finish by winning the East Division in 1986 and advancing to the World Series against the Boston Red Sox.

Sources

In addition to the sources cited in the Notes, the author also consulted the following:

Anderson, Dave. "Sports of the Times; Playing Pennant Poker," *New York Times*, October 2, 1985.

Baseball-Reference.com.

Moran, Malcolm. "Tudor Superb, but His Effort Wasted," *New York Times*, October 2, 1985.

Notes

1 Joseph Durso, "Strawberry Blast in 11th Closes Gap to Two Games," *New York Times*, October 2, 1985.

2 Prior to this game, Tudor was tied with Carl Hubbell with 10 shutouts, while Sandy Koufax held the record with 11. Rick Hummel, " 'Career Years' Spur Redbirds," *The Sporting News*, October 21, 1985: 18.

3 Rick Hummel, "Cards Magic Number Holds at Four," *St. Louis Post-Dispatch*, October 2, 1985: 4.

4 Hummel, "Cards Magic Number."

5 1986 *New York Mets Media Guide*, 126.

6 Durso.

7 1986 *New York Mets Media Guide*.

8 Jack Lang, "Johnson Tired of 'Bridesmaid' Role," *The Sporting News*, October 21, 1985: 18.

METS WIN EXTRA-INNING SLUGFEST VIA BRAWL AND HOME RUN

JULY 22, 1986: NEW YORK METS 6, CINCINNATI REDS 3, AT RIVERFRONT STADIUM

by Michael Huber

Rodney Dangerfield is credited with saying, "I went to a fight the other night, and a hockey game broke out."[1] If we replace *hockey* with *baseball*, we could get an idea of what happened in Cincinnati on July 22, 1986. In what he termed "the strangest game I've ever been in,"[2] New York Mets manager Davey Johnson piloted his team to a 6-3 victory over the Cincinnati Reds before 23,707 fans, in a game that included a bench-clearing brawl, several ejections, and two Mets pitchers playing musical chairs. Johnson juggled his players on a carousel trying to cover positions and pitch to Reds batters. The slugfest actually had a few long fly balls, including a Howard Johnson home run with two aboard in the top of the 14th for the win.

Bob Ojeda took to the mound for the visiting Mets, with Scott Terry as the Reds' starting pitcher. Each team had two hits but no runs through the first two innings. In the bottom of the third, Terry helped his own cause and singled to left. He moved to second on a sacrifice. With two outs, Dave Parker crushed his 21st home run of the season, giving Cincinnati a 2-0 lead. Rafael Santana led off New York's half of the fifth inning with a walk. Ojeda tried to sacrifice him to second, but first baseman Tony Perez fielded the bunt and gunned down Santana at second, putting the Mets pitcher on at first. Lenny Dykstra tripled to the gap in right-center and Ojeda scored. Wally Backman hit a grounder to second and Cincinnati's Ron Oester threw home, nailing Dykstra at the plate and preserving the 2-1 lead. In the bottom half of the fifth, Kal Daniels pinch-hit for Terry and singled up the middle, but he was picked off at first by Ojeda. That proved to be a crucial lapse by Daniels because one out later, Buddy Bell connected for his sixth home run of the season, restoring the Reds' two-run cushion.

In the sixth inning New York's Darryl Strawberry led off and argued a called third strike with umpire Gerry Davis, who sent the Mets outfielder to the showers. Kevin Mitchell replaced him in right field. Tim Teufel hit for Backman in the seventh, using yet another position player for New York. From the sixth through the ninth, New York used three relievers (Rick Anderson, Randy Myers, and Doug Sisk).

In the top of the ninth, still trailing by two runs, Davey Johnson brought in Howard Johnson as a pinch-hitter for Santana. Johnson struck out, but the ball bounced off the glove of catcher Bo Diaz, and Johnson ran for first base, kicking the ball in the process. Reds

No Mets manager has more victories than Davey Johnson, who averaged nearly 96 wins in his six full seasons.

pitcher Ron Robinson scooped up the ball and fired to first, but Johnson appeared to be running out of the baseline and the ball hit him in the back. Safe at first. Reds coach Billy DeMars raced out to argue and after some heated exchanges he was ejected by home-plate umpire Davis. Mookie Wilson, who had entered the game as a defensive replacement in the eighth inning, then grounded into a 4-3 double play. New York was down to its final out trailing 3-1. Dykstra worked Robinson for a walk. Teufel doubled to deep center, and Dykstra pulled up at third, playing it safe because his run would not decide anything. Reds skipper Pete Rose then walked to the mound and called for a double switch: He brought in closer John Franco from the bullpen and signaled for Sal Butera to catch for Diaz (the pitcher's position would be up third in the bottom of the ninth). Franco faced Keith Hernandez, who lifted a fly ball to the warning track in right field. Dave Parker waited under the ball, only to have it pop out of his glove for a two-run error (both runs unearned). The game was suddenly tied, and both teams had to consider extra innings. Five more extra innings.

The Mets had two walks and a single in the top of the 10th, but Franco scattered three strikeouts, the last with the bases loaded, to get out of the jam. In the bottom of the inning, Rose pinch-hit himself for Franco, setting up "the main event."[3] He singled off the Mets' fifth pitcher of the game, Jesse Orosco, and then pulled himself from the game for pinch-runner Eric Davis. Davis stole second, his 46th swipe of the season. On the next pitch, he took off for third and easily beat the throw from catcher Gary Carter for steal number 47. As Davis popped up from his slide, a pushing match began between him and third baseman Ray Knight. Said Knight: "When he elbowed me, I said to him, 'What's your problem?' He said, 'You pushed me.' We had hit each other solidly, but I knew he had the base. I'm at peace with myself about it. I don't like to fight with anybody, but I felt threatened."[4] Words and punches were exchanged and both benches cleared. The brawl delay lasted for 16 minutes.[5] Dave Parker told reporters after the game that the fight "was triggered by Knight. He pushed Davis off the base. That's the second time in this series that it's happened, and both times it was at third base with him. He was aggressive, and Eric just reacted."[6] Davey Johnson said, "I want to say we show a lot of fight, but that's not what I mean. We're hard competitors, but we're not malicious. We don't like people to cuss us, and that's what Davis did. That's what caused tempers to flare."[7]

After the game, instead of "laughing over the lunacy of the game,"[8] Mets players resented the fact that George Foster had not left the bench to participate in the brawl. Manager Johnson decided to not use Foster as part of his left-field platoon, and within weeks Foster was no longer with the team. When the dust settled and all the gloves and caps were picked up, four players had been ejected (Knight and Mitchell of the Mets and Davis and Mario Soto of the Reds). Cincinnati pitcher Tom Browning came on to run for Davis at third (remember, Davis was safe). Davey Johnson put catcher Gary Carter in at third replacing Knight,[9] and Ed Hearn went in to catch. Johnson also moved Orosco to right field to replace Mitchell, and summoned Roger McDowell to pitch. At this point, there was no one else to play for the Mets. The Mets manager noted, "I'm out of pitchers, and I'm out of extra players."[10] The only players left in the dugout were starting pitchers Dwight Gooden, Ron Darling, and Sid Fernandez. McDowell retired Wade Rowdon on a groundout to second to end the inning and extend the game into the 11th.

In the 11th, Cincinnati's Tony Perez singled and moved to second on a sacrifice. With two outs, Orosco and McDowell switched positions – Orosco returned to the mound and McDowell replaced him in right field. The strategy succeeded when Orosco struck out the Reds' Max Venable. In the 12th, after the Reds' Buddy Bell reached on an infield hit with nobody out, McDowell and Mookie Wilson changed positions; Wilson moving to center field and McDowell to right. After the switch, Orosco gave up another hit, but got out of the inning on a bunt that turned into a double play, and a fly ball.

In the bottom of the 13th McDowell returned to the mound and Orosco went to right field. With one out, Cincinnati's Perez hit a line drive to right field. Center fielder Dykstra couldn't reach the ball, so Orosco had to make the play. "I squeezed it so hard, the stuffing could have come out," he said after the game.[11]

In the top of the 14th inning, Hearn led off with a double to right center. Right fielder Orosco walked and reliever Ted Power struck out pitcher McDowell, bringing up Howard Johnson, who sent a pitch from Power over the right-field wall for a three-run home run. McDowell then retired the Reds on three groundouts to preserve the win.

Both Orosco and McDowell had entered the game in the bottom of the 10th inning as pitchers. McDowell then played right field, moved to left field, and returned to the mound for the last two innings. Orosco also pitched in the 10th, went to right field, pitched again, and returned to right field. In the 12th and 14th innings the Mets had pitchers Orosco and McDowell batting back-to-back. In the 12th, Orosco was the guy on the mound and McDowell was in right field, and in the 14th, Orosco was in right and McDowell was on the hill. Orosco had pitched two innings and McDowell three after the regulation nine innings.

In the losing cause, the Reds had left 11 men on base; the Mets had stranded 16 runners. The Mets' victory increased their lead in the National League East to 14 games, their largest margin of the season to that date.

Sources

In addition to the sources mentioned in the notes, the author consulted baseball-reference.com and retrosheet.org.

Notes

1 brainyquote.com/quotes/quotes/r/rodneydang100124.html.
2 "Mets Win on Clout in 14; Four Ejected After Brawl," *New York Times*, July 23, 1986.
3 Shane Tourtellotte, "Baseball's craziest game?" hardballtimes.com/baseballs-craziest-game/.
4 *New York Times*.
5 You can watch the action on a YouTube video (youtube.com/watch?v=jQLZaVIX-FJM).
6 *New York Times*.
7 Ibid.
8 Tourtellotte.
9 Carter had brief experience, having played third base in one inning in a 1975 game for the Montreal Expos.
10 *New York Times*.
11 Tourtellotte.

LEN DYKSTRA'S HOMER ENDS GAME THREE OF NLCS

OCTOBER 11, 1986: NEW YORK METS 6, HOUSTON ASTROS 5, AT SHEA STADIUM

GAME THREE OF THE 1986 NATIONAL LEAGUE CHAMPIONSHIP SERIES

By Rory Costello

"This is a great feeling," said Len Dykstra after the game. "The last time I hit a home run in the bottom of the ninth to win a game, I was playing my Strat-O-Matic baseball game, rolling dice against my brother Kevin."[1]

During the 1986 regular season, Dykstra was the most frequent leadoff hitter for the Mets. Wally Backman was the team's most frequent number-two batter. They were often known as the "little pests" – a label they wore with pride. They were tobacco-chewing dirty-uniform guys who set the table well for the big bats in the lineup. Yet that Saturday afternoon, with lefty Bob Knepper starting, both were on the bench as the game began. And it was Backman who sparked the ninth-inning rally with a drag bunt to lead off. One out later, Dykstra – who had just eight regular-season homers – took Houston closer Dave Smith deep to end the game.

Smith (who died at age 53 in 2008) was a good closer, if not a great one. He had a career-high 33 saves in 1986, and although blown saves weren't tabulated back then, a retroactive calculation shows just six for him in the regular season that year. He relied on a sinker and forkball, and he was not prone to giving up the long ball: five in 56 innings in 1986, and just 34 in 809⅓ regular-season innings lifetime.

He had not been effective against the Mets in '86, though – especially in back-to-back games on July 19 and 20 in Houston. The Astros eventually won both of those, but Smith blew the save in the first game by giving up a ninth-inning homer to Darryl Strawberry. The next afternoon he was largely responsible for losing a three-run lead in the ninth, though technically the blown save was Frank DiPino's.

Like all closers, though, Smith tried not to dwell on the past. After Game Three of the NLCS, he was forthcoming with the media. "You approach a hitter like (Dykstra) differently," he said. "He's not a slugger. You try to make him hit it on the ground. I was trying to throw him a forkball, low and away. It stayed out over the plate and it was up a bit." Even though a stiff wind was blowing from right field at Shea Stadium, Smith knew it was gone as soon as Dykstra hit it.[2]

"Dykstra does like to swing for the fences," said Davey Johnson. "I tell him all the time: 'If you hit line drives, you'd hit .330 every year.' But I forgive him today."[3] Johnson was more critical in the spring of 1988, when "Nails" reported to camp after packing on more than 20 pounds of muscle.[4] Ever after that, the cloud of performance-enhancing drugs would hang over Dykstra.

Hal Lanier's postgame comments were curt. Setup man Charlie Kerfeld, the goofy chowhound from Knob Noster, Missouri, had breezed through a 1-2-3 eighth inning. "I didn't see any reason not to bring in my number-one man," Lanier said. "If you get beat with your number-two guy, you leave yourself open to a lot of second guesses. What would you guys write if Dykstra hit that off Kerfeld and Smith was still in the bullpen?" He also dismissed the idea of bringing in Smith to start the eighth.[5]

Early on, it didn't seem that a save situation would arise. Mets starter Ron Darling allowed two runs in the first inning and another pair in the second, on a two-run homer by Bill Doran. Davey Johnson said, "Darling was a little tentative and not very aggressive, like he was during the season. But we battled back, and that's the big thing."[6] Indeed, that was the hallmark of the Mets' entire season.

Knepper shut out New York through five innings, but the Mets tied it in the sixth. The big blow was a three-run homer by Strawberry. The Astros promptly went ahead again, though, scoring an unearned run. Third baseman Ray Knight stood to be the goat because of his throwing error.

In the bottom of the seventh, even though Knepper was still pitching, Johnson decided to send Dykstra up as a pinch-hitter for Rick Aguilera. "I was taking a gamble putting Dykstra in the game," the manager later said.[7] "I called upstairs and found out that Knepper had thrown about 100 pitches. I thought Hal Lanier would probably hook Knepper after that inning and then I'd have Lenny in the game against their right-handed relief pitchers. And when I saw Hal shake Knepper's hand in the dugout after the seventh, I knew I was all right."[8]

Johnson was also looking ahead when he replaced Tim Teufel at second base with Backman in the top of the ninth. As Mookie Wilson later wrote, "Wally … could always be counted on to get on base in a big spot. I wanted Wally to bunt, walk, slash, dive into first, whatever it would take to get on base."[9] After laying down his drag bunt, Backman wriggled around the tag of first baseman Glenn Davis. "I felt Wally went two to three feet out of the baseline," said Lanier, "and Glenn couldn't touch him." Dave Smith said, "I was surprised that they didn't call him out of the baseline because I saw him run on the grass."[10]

First-base umpire Dutch Rennert told Lanier, however, that Backman was already by Davis. "I was conscious of the three feet at all times," Rennert said, referring to the limed line three feet to the right of the first-base foul line. "And the home-plate umpire, Frank Pulli, could also call him out, but there was no doubt in my mind."[11]

Backman agreed with Rennert. "The first baseman was out of my vision behind me," he said. "The key for me on that bunt is to make the first baseman field it. And after I got past him, I was just trying to slide head-first into the bag and grab it with my left hand. He added, "I didn't think they'd have had me even if I went in straight up. I slid right on top of the line and kicked up all the chalk. I didn't think there was much of an argument there."[12]

Danny Heep, pinch-hitting for Rafael Santana, was ordered to bunt. After Heep fouled one off, an inside pitch got by catcher Alan Ashby for a passed ball. "That's when I thought the momentum changed," Davey Johnson said later. "I don't like to bunt and now I didn't have to."[13]

Heep worked the count full but then flied out to short center field. That brought up Dykstra, batting ninth because he'd entered in a double switch.

When Dykstra came to the plate, he remembered another Astros game at Shea from that Fourth of July, when he had doubled home the winning run against Smith with the score tied 1-1. "He threw me a fastball that time. This time, I didn't think he would. He threw me a fastball on the first pitch, and I fouled it off. Then I knew I wouldn't get a fastball, and sure enough the next pitch was a forkball."[14]

"He's got pop in his bat," said Smith. "And anybody in a big-league lineup can hit the ball out of the park if he guesses right on a pitch."[15]

Had Smith been able to nail down the save, Lanier had previously stated that he would turn to his number-four starter, rookie Jim Deshaies, in Game Four. His alternate decision was already made too. Seeking the equalizer – and looking ahead to a possible Game Seven as well – the call went to Mike Scott.[16]

Notes
1 John Nelson, "Dykstra's Homer Gives Mets Comeback Victory," Associated Press, October 12, 1986; Dave Anderson, "Dykstra 'Nails' Astros," *New York Times*, October 12, 1986.
2 John Nelson; Hal Bock, "Wrong Time for Smith," Associated Press, October 12, 1986.
3 Joseph Durso, "Homer Gives Mets 6-5 Win," *New York Times*, October 12, 1986.
4 Joseph Durso, "Dykstra Displays New Look," *New York Times*, February 25, 1988.
5 "Wrong Time for Smith."
6 John Nelson.
7 Durso, "Homer Gives Mets 6-5 Win."
8 Dave Anderson.
9 Mookie Wilson with Erik Sherman, *Mookie Deluxe: Life, Baseball, and the '86 Mets* (New York: Berkeley Publishing Group, 2014). The irony is that Wilson was referring to Game Six of the World Series, when Backman failed to get on base to start the fateful bottom of the 10th inning.
10 Ira Berkow, "Smith Speaks of 'Terrible Pitch' to Dykstra in 9th," *New York Times*, October 12, 1986.
11 Dave Anderson.
12 John Nelson.
13 Dave Anderson.
14 John Nelson.
15 Ira Berkow.
16 Durso, "Homer Gives Mets 6-5 Win;" "Lanier Names Pitchers," wire service reports, October 11, 1986.

CARTER'S SINGLE WINS GAME FIVE OF 1986 NLCS IN 12TH

OCTOBER 14, 1986: NEW YORK 2, HOUSTON 1 (12 INNINGS), AT SHEA STADIUM
GAME FIVE OF THE 1986 NATIONAL LEAGUE CHAMPIONSHIP SERIES

By Rory Costello

Before the 1986 NLCS started, many observers pointed to the greatest mutual strength of the teams: pitching. Games One through Four surpassed those expectations. "I didn't think it would be that great a pitching series," said Mets batting coach Bill Robinson.[1]

In Game Five, it got even better. Nolan Ryan pitched nine innings for the Astros, allowing just one run on two hits while striking out 12. Houston scored just once off Dwight Gooden in 10 innings. Finally, in the 12th, Mets cleanup hitter Gary Carter singled up the middle to bring in the game's only other run.

Carter entered Game Five with just one hit in 17 at-bats, and he was 0-for-4 before coming through with his game-winner. Before the game, teammate Ray Knight said, "Gary's pressing, there's no question. He wants to do well. He drives himself very hard, and he's his own worst critic. Anytime you take the game to heart the way Gary [does], it's hard. Every time he makes an out, it wears on him. I told him, 'You'll get hot. He's capable of exploding at any time."[2] After the game, Keith Hernandez said, "Strong men rise to the occasion."[3]

The game was scheduled for Monday, October 13, but rain postponed it. Therefore, Hal Lanier again passed over rookie left-hander Jim Deshaies and gave the start to Ryan, who returned on a normal four days' rest after losing Game Two. Exactly 17 years before, Ryan – then a Met – had made the only World Series appearance of his long career, and it was also at Shea Stadium. "Was it the same date?" asked Mets third-base coach Bud Harrelson, the team's shortstop in 1969. "No wonder I felt a strange twitch today."[4]

Ryan was remarkably durable, but he had spent two stretches on the disabled list in 1986 with elbow problems. The Astros were counting his pitches, something that was anathema to him. "I was available," he had said on Monday. "I'm not surprised [by Lanier's original plan to use Deshaies] but I'm a little disappointed. After being put on the disabled list, I guess there are no surprises." He admitted that a rain delay could give him problems, though, and agreed that it would have been nice to pitch Game Six – potentially a clincher – at home in Texas.[5]

It was still rainy in New York City on Tuesday afternoon – Game Five finally started after a 22-minute delay. The sun broke through in the middle innings, though, and the field was fairly dry by the end of the game.[6]

A pivotal moment came in the second inning, when a dubious call deprived Houston of a run. Kevin Bass led off with a single and went to third on a looping base hit to shallow center by the next batter, José Cruz. Alan Ashby struck out. Then Craig Reynolds grounded to second base. Wally Backman got the force at second, but the relay throw from Rafael Santana appeared to arrive late. Nonetheless, first-base umpire Fred Brocklander called Reynolds out, so Bass did not score.

The crafty Hernandez may have swayed Brocklander. "I cheated a little bit because I felt it was going to be a close play," the first baseman said. "I yelled 'Out' when I caught the ball because I saw the umpire a little bit in question and I just wanted to put the out in his head."[7]

Reynolds exploded. He charged Brocklander and appeared to bump the ump in the chest. Someone remarked to Reynolds, "Some of your teammates say they've never seen you that mad." The shortstop responded, "I haven't been." He also said, "If I bumped (him) it was accidental, and I'm glad Fred didn't throw me out of the game."[8]

Lanier ran out right behind Reynolds to argue. He later said, "When my first-base coach Matt Galante argues, I have to figure (Brocklander) missed the call. I thought Reynolds beat the ball by half a step."[9] He added, "It's not going to do me any good to rant and rave or tear the clubhouse apart. We had some other opportunities to win, and we didn't."[10]

Brocklander stood by his call even after viewing replays. He said, "It was just a question that his foot was this far off the bag. It was a bang-bang play. … There was just a little daylight." He also claimed that "depth perception" was why the TV cameras made it appear that Reynolds was safe.[11] If today's expanded replay review rule had been in effect then, Lanier would have been able to issue a challenge.

Houston got on the scoreboard in the top of the fifth. Ashby doubled to lead off and Reynolds singled him to third. Ryan tried to move Reynolds up with a bunt, but Gooden got a force out. Bill Doran then grounded sharply to second; it looked like a perfect double-play ball, but it got stuck in Backman's glove long enough for the speedy Doran to beat Santana's relay to first. This time there was no question about Brocklander's call.

Doran stole second, and Billy Hatcher walked, but Denny Walling flied out to end the inning. Houston's best scoring chance after that came in the eighth, and it featured the same three batters. Doran bunted his way on to lead off and Hatcher sacrificed him to second. "Hernandez let Hatcher's bunt roll and roll and roll, hoping it would go foul, and picked it up just in time to tag Hatcher. Walling then lined hard toward left. Off the bat it sounded like a single, and Doran was running full speed."[12] Instead, Mookie Wilson came in, picked off the liner, and turned it into an easy double play.

Meanwhile, Ryan had retired the first 13 batters he faced, striking out eight. But then, on a full count, Darryl Strawberry homered off a low fastball. Many of Strawberry's homers were majestic moon shots. This one was a tracer that he ripped down the right-field line, just over the wall.

Ryan and Gooden were both renowned for their fastballs, but that day, they relied on other parts of their repertoire. "I didn't have a very good curveball," said Ryan, "but I went to the changeup in the middle of the game."[13] Gooden, who struck out just four, said, "I went into the game wanting to establish my off-speed pitches early in the count. I was able to do that, and that prevented the Astros from sitting on the fastball."[14]

Houston threatened again in the 10th. With two out, Terry Puhl, pinch-hitting for Ryan, singled. Ryan, who had thrown 134 pitches, called it "the right decision," adding, "I was tiring. I would have given them one more inning, but it made sense to hit for me."[15] Puhl stole second and Doran then walked. Gooden escaped by getting Hatcher to fly out.

"I let everything I had go in the ninth inning because I had never pitched 10 innings before," said "Doctor K". "I figured that was my last inning. Then, when I came back to the dugout after the ninth, nobody said anything. It was like getting ready for the game all over again." He also said, "I was surprised when they told me to go back in there. I was worried that I wouldn't have anything left. But I felt fine. I think I could have gone longer."[16]

Charlie Kerfeld replaced Ryan and retired the side in order in both the 10th and 11th. That brought his string of consecutive outs in the series to 10. Jesse Orosco also set down all six men he faced in the 11th and 12th.

The Mets finally reached Kerfeld in the bottom of the 12th. Backman led off with a hard one-hopper that bounced high off the glove of third baseman Walling for a single. He took second base on Kerfeld's wild pickoff throw. The Astros then walked Hernandez intentionally to bring up Carter – "I had the matchup I wanted," said Lanier.[17] Kerfeld fell behind 2-and-0, but got back to a full count. Carter fouled off two pitches. He then lashed a grounder behind Kerfeld and into center field.

"I'd be less than honest to say I wasn't frustrated at that point," said Carter. "But I didn't bring one negative thought to the plate with me. I believed something good was going to happen – and it did."[18] The Mets mobbed and embraced The Kid, whose reaction was typically ebullient. The image of Carter with two fists in the air, leading the crowd's postgame cheers, wound up on the cover of his 1987 book, *A Dream Season*.

At least one headline said that the Mets were in the driver's seat as the series shifted back to Houston. Veteran New York sportswriter Dick Young put it differently: "The Mets were supposed to be in what Red Barber called 'the catbird seat.' … And yet, I didn't feel that way, and I don't think the Mets did either."[19] If New York didn't win Game Six, the specter of Mike Scott loomed.

Notes

1 "Mets Accuse Houston's Mike Scott of Scuffing Baseball," *St. Petersburg Evening Independent*, October 14, 1986: C1.
2 Ibid.
3 Hal Bock, Associated Press, "New York Uses Hits Wisely to Escape Grip of Ryan," October 15, 1986.
4 George Vecsey, "Ryan Returns to New York," *New York Times*, October 16, 1986.
5 "Ryan Returns to New York."
6 Associated Press, "Mets Outduel Astros, 2-1, in 12 Innings," October 15, 1986.
7 Associated Press, "Ump Says Runner Out at 1st Base," October 15, 1986.
8 Mark Whicker, "On Replay After Replay, Reynolds Is Safe," *Philadelphia Inquirer*, October 15, 1986.
9 "Ump says runner out at 1st base."
10 Gene Guidi, "Mets back in driver's seat," Knight-Ridder Newspapers, October 15, 1986.
11 Harry Atkins, "Ump Stands by Critical Out Call on DP," Associated Press, October 15, 1986.

Met-rospectives

12 John Nelson, "Carter's Hit Gives NY Series Lead," Associated Press, October 15, 1986.
13 "Mets take Series lead as Carter gets winning hit," Associated Press, October 15, 1986.
14 Robbie Andreu, "Bang-Bang Play Shot Down Astros' Early Scoring Threat," *Palm Beach Sun-Sentinel*, October 15, 1986.
15 "Ryan returns to New York."
16 "Carter's Hit Gives NY Series Lead"; "Bang-Bang Play Shot Down Astros' Early Scoring Threat".
17 Bruce Keidan, "A mad twist," *Pittsburgh Post-Gazette*, October 15, 1986, 13.
18 "Mets back in driver's seat."
19 Dick Young, "Scottphobia," *New York Post*, October 16, 1986.

METS SURVIVE 16-INNING BATTLE, WIN NL PENNANT

OCTOBER 15, 1986: NEW YORK 7, HOUSTON 6 (16 INNINGS), AT THE ASTRODOME

GAME SIX OF THE 1986 NATIONAL LEAGUE CHAMPIONSHIP SERIES

By Rory Costello

Time and again during their run to the world championship in 1986, the Mets clawed back in desperate situations. Later this October, they were all but eliminated in Game Six of the World Series, when the Red Sox were one strike away from winning it all for the first time since 1918. Yet in Game Six of the NLCS that year – an excruciating 16-inning battle – the Mets also climbed out of a deep hole. The incredibly suspenseful game had sportswriters from around the nation at their best. Mike Downey of the *Los Angeles Times* wrote, "(The Astros) made the Mets sweat and suffer, made them charge from behind and gasp to stay in front. … They were enervated, drained, battle-fatigued."[1] In his chronicle of the '86 Mets, *The Bad Guys Won*, author Jeff Pearlman also vividly portrayed the mental and physical exhaustion that the players felt. *Newark Star-Ledger* columnist Jerry Izenberg devoted an entire book to this single contest entitled *The Greatest Game Ever Played*.

Unlike Game Six of the '86 World Series, New York's season would not have ended with a loss to Houston. The Mets had won three of the first five games, including a 12-inning 2-1 victory the day before at Shea Stadium. Had the Astros won Game Six, though, they would have sent Mike Scott to the mound the next day. Scott had thrown a five-hit shutout in Game One, making a single second-inning run stand up. He went all the way again to win Game Four, 3-1. He was on a lethal roll with his split-finger fastball.

The Mets continued to believe that something else was helping Scott's splitter to "drop off the table." Davey Johnson showed a group of reporters eight balls that were scuffed in exactly the same spot – a mark about the size of a 50-cent piece. Johnson said, "It [sandpaper] is in his palm. He doesn't rotate the ball, he just makes a grinding motion. It's blatant to me." However, NL President Chub Feeney called Scott "innocent until proven guilty" – though he added, "We will be watching closely the next time he pitches."[2]

Had the series gone to Game Seven, Scott would have faced Ron Darling. Darling had pitched well during the regular season (15-6, 2.81) but had given up four runs in five innings in Game Three, which the Mets came back to win on Len Dykstra's two-run homer in the bottom of the ninth. In 2006 Darling said, "I felt I couldn't give up any runs because Mike Scott wasn't going to."[3]

The adverb "desperately" has often been used to depict how much the Mets wanted to win Game Six. In their own words, this supremely confident team – viewed as arrogant in many quarters – didn't evince desperation. It is fair to say, however, that the lingering threat of Scott was a strong psychological undercurrent as the series shifted back to the Astrodome. Plus, the Mets' poor long-term record there led Hal Bock of Associated Press to dub it "their personal house of horrors" after Game Five.[4]

Another aside on that venue is in order, too. The Astrodome – once known as the Eighth Wonder of the World – hosted its last big-league game in 1999. It then fell into disuse and disrepair. In 1986, however, the Dome was also home to the Houston Oilers of the NFL. The Oilers had hosted the Chicago Bears just three days before Game Six – yard lines were still visible on the Astroturf.

The starters in Game Six were both lefties: Bob Knepper for Houston and Bob Ojeda for the Mets. The reliable Ojeda had gone the route as the Mets won Game Two, 5-1. But the Astros got to him for three runs in the first inning, and it might have been more except that Kevin Bass was tagged at home on a missed suicide squeeze attempt. Ojeda settled down after that and did not allow another run before coming out for Rick Aguilera in the sixth inning. Aguilera pitched three shutout innings, giving up just one hit.

Meanwhile, Knepper – 17-12, 3.14 in the regular season, with a no-decision in Game Three – was cruising. He'd given up just two hits and a walk as he took a shutout into the ninth inning. Yet the Mets broke through for the tying runs; pinch-hitter Dykstra ignited the rally. As he had in Game Three, Johnson again made the unorthodox choice to send the lefty swinger up to lead off against Knepper. Bass in right field and José Cruz in left were playing deep, but center fielder Billy Hatcher remained shallow. He could not get back to make the play on Dykstra's fly ball, which became a triple.

Mookie Wilson singled off the tip of Bill Doran's glove to score Dykstra. One out later, Keith Hernandez doubled, Wilson scored, and Houston closer Dave Smith entered. Smith, who'd given up Dykstra's homer in Game Three, was ineffective again. He walked the first two men he faced. With the count 1-and-2 to Ray Knight, home plate umpire Fred Brocklander – whose controversial call at first base took a vital run away from Houston in Game Five – had the Astros screaming again when he called a ball. Two pitches later, Knight brought in the tying run with a sacrifice fly.

Roger McDowell entered in the bottom of the ninth for the Mets and went on to pitch five superb innings. He faced the minimum 15 batters; the only baserunner he allowed, Bass, was caught stealing second base. It was McDowell's longest relief stint ever in the majors; his only longer outing came in one of his two big-league starts as a rookie in 1985. Smith pitched a scoreless 10th for Houston, and Larry Andersen blanked the Mets from the 11th through the 13th.

In the 14th the Mets got a run against veteran reliever Aurelio López. The portly Mexican was no longer "Señor Smoke" at this stage of his career, allowing a single and a walk to lead off before Wally Backman's one-out RBI single. However, López contained the damage with runners on second and third. Jesse Orosco came on to try to get the save for the Mets, but with one out Hatcher pulled a drive high and deep. Would it stay fair? It hit the screen on the left-field foul pole, and the game was tied again.

After a scoreless 15th, New York put up three runs in the top of the 16th. López gave up one on a double and a single, then gave way to Jeff Calhoun, who fueled the rally with two wild pitches. One question about this game is why Hal Lanier chose not to use lefty Jim Deshaies – twice passed over for starting assignments and thus well rested – at any point. Lanier said that Deshaies had not faced that kind of pressure before. But bullpen coach Gene Tenace apparently told Lanier that Deshaies didn't have good stuff while warming up.[5]

Yet the tension was far from over – the Astros chipped away for two. They had the tying run on second base and the winning run on first with two out and Bass at the plate. Hernandez warned the weary Orosco (accounts vary as to the choice of words) not to throw a single fastball. The count ran full, and Mets announcer Bob Murphy said, "Pulsating baseball. ... Nobody has sat down for the last four or five innings. ... Incredible." Finally – on the sixth straight breaking ball – Bass fanned.[6] The Mets had won the NL pennant, and Orosco leaped in exultation. It had been the longest game in terms of innings in postseason history.[7]

Even if Houston had extended the series, at least some of the combative Mets still liked their chances against Scott. After Game Four, Ray Knight said, "You have to get that [the talk of scuffing] out of your mind and start thinking, 'What approach is best suited to hit this pitch?' and then you have to make adjustments at the plate."[8] The scrappy Backman said, "We're ticked and we're not going to take this lying down. I don't care if he scuffs 400 balls. I don't care if they're scuffed before the game. I don't think any pitcher can beat us three times in a row."[9]

On the flip side, however, Backman admitted, "If we had lost and had to face Scott tomorrow, I wouldn't have slept at all." Gary Carter said, "Mike Scott was our incentive to win."[10] Davey Johnson added, "Amen. I feel like I'm on parole, like I've just been given a pardon."[11] Perhaps a better choice of words would have been "reprieve" – the 1986 Mets just went from one grueling drama to the next.

Notes

1 Mike Downey, "All That Houston Has Ahead of It Now Is a Winter of Wondering," *Los Angeles Times*, October 16, 1986.
2 Bob Harig, "Mets accuse Houston's Mike Scott of scuffing baseball," *St. Petersburg Evening Independent*, October 14, 1986, C1. "Feeney clears Scott – for now," Associated Press, October 15, 1986.
3 Richard Sandomir, "Mets' Announcers Slide into New Roles," *New York Times*, October 14, 2006.
4 Hal Bock, "New York uses hits wisely to escape grip of [Nolan] Ryan," Associated Press, October 15, 1986.In the 22 seasons from 1965, when the Astrodome opened, through 1986, the Mets had a regular-season record there of 54-90 (.375). Over that period, their overall winning percentage was .472 and their winning percentage in road games was .450. They had a winning record at the Astrodome in just three seasons, though two of them were in 1984 and 1985.
5 Gordon Edes, "Mets Admit They're Glad to Get Off Scott-Free," *Los Angeles Times*, October 16, 1986.
6 Mike Downey described Bass as "overanxious" and Bass later confirmed this in a December 2010 meeting with SABR's Larry Dierker (Houston) chapter. See Bill McCurdy, "1986 NLCS Game 6: A Sacher Masoch Revisitation" (bill37mccurdy. wordpress.com/2010/12/15/1986-nlcs-game-6-a-sacher-masoch-revisitation/).
7 On October 9, 2005, the Astros and Atlanta Braves played 18 innings in Game Four of the National League Division Series.
8 Harig, "Mets accuse Houston's Mike Scott of scuffing baseball."
9 Terry Taylor, "Mets complain Mike Scott is 'scuffing' their attack," Associated Press, October 14, 1986.
10 Wire service reports, October 17, 1986.
11 Associated Press, October 16, 1986.

"A LITTLE ROLLER UP ALONG FIRST: METS WIN WILD GAME SIX ON BUCKNER ERROR"

OCTOBER 25, 1986: NEW YORK METS 6, BOSTON RED SOX 5 (10 INNINGS), AT SHEA STADIUM

GAME SIX OF THE 1986 WORLD SERIES

By Matthew Silverman

Right from the first inning it was obvious this was not going to be a typical game. Even by World Series Game Six standards, this one was out of this world. And that is where Mike Sergio came from, drifting down onto the Shea Stadium infield in a parachute with a modest "Go Mets" sign hanging off it. A veteran skydiver and a middling actor, he made the jump because he was incensed by a balloon-festooned banner at Fenway Park that he had seen on TV. He would serve jail time the following summer for his breach of airspace and flouting of an untold number of laws. But he was quickly hustled off the field in Game Six and the first pitch by Bob Ojeda was thrown less than a minute after he landed. The game was what mattered. And what a game.

After being so rudely interrupted from above, the Red Sox scored in the first on a double by Dwight Evans and added another in the second on Marty Barrett's RBI single. That seemed as though it could go a long way with Roger Clemens on full rest pitching full bore and no-hitting the Mets through four innings, but the Mets were making Clemens work. He threw 72 pitches (49 strikes) to get that far and the crowd was working him, too. Chants of "Ro-ger! Ro-ger" were payback for the derisive catcalls by the Fenway faithful of "Dar-ryl! Dar-ryl!" Darryl Strawberry started the home fifth with his second walk of the night and – just as he'd done in the second inning – he stole second. On the next pitch Ray Knight singled through the middle and Strawberry crossed the plate to cut Boston's lead in half. Mookie Wilson singled to right field and Knight took third with no one out when Evans bobbled the ball. That proved key since Danny Heep, batting for Rafael Santana, bounced into a double play that tied the game. It marked the first time, other than 0-0, that a 1986 World Series game was tied.

Given a reprieve, Bobby Ojeda batted for himself (he grounded out) and threw another inning. Going six innings was quite a feat for Ojeda since Boston had runners on base in all but one inning yet left eight on base against Ojeda. The Red Sox took advantage of shoddy defense by the Mets in the seventh against Roger McDowell, with Knight's errant throw pulling Keith Hernandez off first to put runners on the corners. Boston, without a steal attempt in the Series, tried the hit-and-run several times and usually sent runners on 3-and-2, as the Red Sox did with Jim Rice in the seventh. His

Among the most popular Mets ever, Mookie Wilson earned adoration with his hustle, joviality, and a special at-bat in the 1986 World Series.

jump enabled him to beat a throw to second on what looked like a double-play ball. The Mets got Dwight Evans at first, but because Rice was safe at second, Marty Barrett crossed home plate for a 3-2 Boston lead. When Rich Gedman followed with a single it looked as if Boston would double its lead, but for the second time in the Series, Mookie Wilson, who had a notoriously weak arm and had undergone shoulder surgery the previous winter, threw to Gary Carter on the fly and the catcher rode Rice away from the plate for the third out. Rice's speed, or lack thereof, had kept him from scoring on Evans's rattling ball in the gap in the first inning, and it haunted Boston again, but not nearly as much as much as a decision by John McNamara that would stay with Red Sox fans for years to come.

A blister on Roger Clemens' pitching hand kept him from being effective with his breaking pitches and he logged 134 pitches through seven innings, but it was a time when the number of pitches was often ignored and Clemens had thrown 10 complete games during the season while logging 155⅔ more innings than the previous year (not even counting his five postseason starts covering an additional 34 innings). But with a runner on first and no one out in the eighth inning against McDowell, McNamara had Spike Owen bunt, and then he batted for Clemens with Mike Greenwell – highlight on "green" for the 23-year-old outfielder who had yet to even play enough to qualify as a rookie. He fanned on three pitches.

With Clemens done, ex-Met Calvin Schiraldi came in in the Mets eighth to try to finish off the first Red Sox title in 68 years. He gave up a hit to the first batter he faced, Lee Mazzilli, batting for Jesse Orosco, who had thrown one pitch to finish the Red Sox eighth. Lenny Dykstra followed with a bunt and Schiraldi bounced the throw to second. The Mets wound up tying the game on Gary Carter's sacrifice fly. The tension trebled.

The bottom of the ninth seemed like a carbon copy of the eighth, with the Red Sox messing up the force play on a bunt. This time it was Rich Gedman who made a bad throw. The difference was that Davey Johnson, never a fan of the sacrifice, bunted twice in a row in the eighth and the Mets scored; in the ninth, pinch-hitter Howard Johnson looked bad trying to bunt the first pitch, swung away on the next, and fanned on the third pitch. The Mets did not score and the game moved to the 10th.

The second-guessers took a front-row seat when Dave Henderson homered just above the "a" in the *Newsday* sign. Many scribes started moving toward the visiting clubhouse, where champagne – loaned to the Red Sox by the Mets – was now being iced. The championship indeed looked for all the world to be on ice when Boston scored a second run off Rick Aguilera on Marty Barrett's single.

With two outs in the bottom of the 10th, with the baseball world wondering how the Mets hadn't bunted a second time in the ninth, with writers – depending on where they hailed from – either spouting lyrically about the end of an epic New England baseball drought or New York's failure to get down a bunt, and with frustrated Keith Hernandez sitting in his manager's office drinking a beer, the game changed. Gary Carter singled. Pinch-hitter Kevin Mitchell singled. Ray Knight, down 0-and-2, singled to center to score Carter and send Mitchell to third. John McNamara came out, took the ball, and handed it to Bob Stanley.

Stanley, who led Boston with 16 saves – Schiraldi, not called up from the minors until late July, was third on the club with nine – faced Mookie Wilson, whom he'd faced three times, retired twice, and struck out once in the Series. With the count 2-and-2, Wilson jackknifed out of the way of a slider that, in the words of the man who called it, Rich Gedman, "ran inside a little bit and I didn't get it."[1] The ball went to the backstop, Kevin Mitchell scored, and the game was tied. With Shea Stadium shaking, the Mets dugout ecstatic, Keith Hernandez superstitiously refusing to leave the manager's office during the rally, and Mookie Wilson still at the plate, the game hurtled toward its implausible climax.

On the 10th pitch from Stanley, Wilson hit a "little roller up along first," as Vin Scully said of almost every such groundball in the Series, but this was no routine grounder. The ball skipped through Bill Buckner's legs and Ray Knight scored. "Behind the bag! It gets through Buckner! Here comes Knight and the Mets win it!"[2]

No words were spoken on NBC for three minutes as announcer and network let the reactions on camera and the screaming by the fans say it all. Sometimes words just can't adequately capture a moment. When Marv Albert put microphones in front of Wilson and Knight, they didn't have much luck, either. There wasn't much left to say, or give. "I'm just exhausted right now," Knight admitted. "I'm happy, but I've never been more tired than I am right now."[3] Boston was sick and tired, especially given that Dave Stapleton had replaced the ailing Buckner at first base for defense every time Boston held the lead in the final inning during the postseason. With one unforgettable exception.

This article originally appeared in The 1986 New York Mets: There Was More Than Game Six *(SABR, 2016), edited by Leslie Heaphy and Bill Nowlin.*

Notes
1 Author interview with Rich Gedman, August 14, 2014.
2 *New York Mets 1986 World Series Collector's Edition*, Game Six. MLB Official DVD, A&E Home Video, 2006.
3 Ibid.

METS RALLY LATE TO BEAT RED SOX IN GAME SEVEN

OCTOBER 27, 1986: NEW YORK METS 8, BOSTON RED SOX 5, AT SHEA STADIUM
GAME SEVEN OF THE 1986 WORLD SERIES

By Matthew Silverman

In the years that followed, it was simple to say that victory in Game Seven was preordained after their miraculous escape from Game Six, but triumph in the deciding game was far from assured. As in the 1975 World Series, the Red Sox — after their own legendary '75 Game Six win on Carlton Fisk's home run — took a 3-0 lead in Game Seven. Both 1975 and 1986 ended with Game Sevens Boston wished it could it forget but could not; those with longer memories recalled Game Sevens from 1946 and 1967.

First, all parties had to wait an extra day in 1986. After the Mets' dramatic Saturday-night victory, Sunday was a washout and the teams convened again on Monday night. The two baseball teams did not only have to contest each other, but the game also went up against Giants-Redskins from the Meadowlands on *Monday Night Football*. The competition was a total rout in terms of ratings, with baseball on NBC garnering a 38.9 rating and 34 million viewers, while the football game had just an 8.8 rating, ABC's lowest since *MNF* debuted in 1970. In addition, the reactions from the crowd at Giants Stadium were such that they confused the football players on the field who were not following the goings-on at Shea Stadium.[1] What a game they missed.

Dwight Evans and Rich Gedman hit back-to-back home runs for the Red Sox in the second inning, with Gedman's ball bouncing off irate Darryl Strawberry's glove on its way over the fence. Then Wade Boggs singled home Dave Henderson and it was 3-0. Two innings later, with a man on second and two outs, Mets starter Ron Darling was replaced by Sid Fernandez, an All-Star who had been bounced from the rotation when the Mets fell behind two games to none. Now he played as important a role as any Met in 1986. Standing between the Mets and oblivion, "El Sid" walked his first batter, batting champion Wade Boggs, to bring up Marty Barrett, who had already tied a World Series record with 13 hits. Fernandez got him to fly to right to end the inning and start a stretch of seven straight batters retired to take the Mets through the top of the sixth.

Like Ron Darling, Boston's Bruce Hurst was making his third start of the World Series. The rainout bumped Oil Can Boyd from the rotation, and Hurst, pitching on three days' rest, was brilliant. He

Sid Fernandez's deceptive downward motion helped average 8.5 strikeouts per nine innings from 1985 through 1992.

retired 16 of the first 17 batters with Rafael Santana grounding out to start the home sixth. And just like that, everything changed.

Lee Mazzilli, batting for Fernandez, singled to left. Another switch-hitter, Mookie Wilson, followed with a single. The tying run came to the plate for the first time in the game, yet Hurst could have gotten out of the jam by getting Tim Teufel to hit into a double play. He pitched carefully to Teufel, who had hit him better than any other Met in the Series, going 4-for-9 and breaking up Hurst's string of 15⅓ innings of shutout ball in the Series with a home run in Game Five. In Game Seven, Teufel walked on five pitches to load the bases.

That brought up a left-handed batter against the southpaw, but lefty vs. lefty was secondary as Keith Hernandez stepped to the plate. He was as qualified for the job as any player in Mets history. To that point he had the franchise's highest career average by 22 points (Hernandez at .309 topped Steve Henderson's .287 for best average in at least 1,000 at-bats by a Met through 1986) and he had led the juggernaut '86 Mets in batting average, runs, hits, and doubles.[2] And Hernandez as a St. Louis Cardinal had come through in almost this exact same spot in the 1982 World Series against the Milwaukee Brewers, following a walk by a lefty (Bob McClure) to a right-handed batter (Gene Tenace). Back then Hernandez cracked a game-tying two-run single off McClure and the Cards went on to beat the Brewers.

"I was like, 'You've got to be kidding me,'" Hernandez said of the similarities between his sixth-inning World Series at-bats in Game Seven in '82 and '86. "It was the same situation basically, which I thought was kind of ironic."[3]

And he came through again. Hernandez's two-run single got the Mets on the board. And while Hernandez didn't tie the game as he had in the 1982 World Series, Gary Carter followed by knocking in the tying run.

Hurst got through the inning, but when Tony Armas pinch-hit for him the following inning, it became a battle of bullpens – and that played to the Mets' strength. Roger McDowell, who had won 14 games and saved 22 during the season, fanned Armas while setting down the Red Sox in order in the seventh. In the bottom of the inning Calvin Schiraldi returned to the scene of New England's nightmare two nights earlier. Ray Knight, who scored the winning run on Bill Buckner's fateful error in Game Six, scored the tiebreaking run again, this time under his own power. He drilled Schiraldi's fastball over the wall in left-center as the Mets took a 4-3 lead. Schiraldi allowed a hit to Lenny Dykstra, a wild pitch, and an RBI single to Rafael Santana. After McDowell's sacrifice, John McNamara replaced Schiraldi with Joe Sambito, who walked two batters (one intentionally) and permitted an insurance run when Hernandez drove home another run home against a lefty. Bob Stanley ended the rally by retiring Gary Carter.

Boston came ever so close to tying the score in the eighth inning. In his 82nd appearance and 142nd inning of relief (postseason included), McDowell was done. The first three Red Sox got hits off him, with Dwight Evans' two-run double making it a 6-5 game. Jesse Orosco, who had saved 21 games during the year, plus three wins and a save in October, came in with the tying run on second and no one out. Rich Gedman hit a bullet that was snagged by Wally Backman, brought in for defense. Orosco fanned Dave Henderson, and Don Baylor, in his only at-bat of the Series in the NL park, grounded out to end the threat.

The Mets opened up the lead when Darryl Strawberry homered and Jesse Orosco – in the old "butcher boy play" – pulled back a bunt attempt and singled through the vacated hole to drive in the final tally and allow the Mets to take an 8-5 lead into the ninth. With two down, nobody on, and New York preparing to explode, Marty Barrett swung through the fastball. Orosco's glove went airborne, and the Mets were world champions.

What had been a rather ho-hum World Series for five games turned into an all-time classic thanks to the comebacks in the final two games. Parachutists dropping in, balls going through infielders' legs, balls bouncing off gloves into the stands for home runs, teams skipping workouts, botched bunt plays, muffed rundowns, designated hitters, pitching changes that were made, pitching changes that weren't, and curses unleashed by long-dead sluggers – it wasn't a work of art, but the images produced in the 1986 World Series were indelible marks on the baseball landscape. The pain stayed with Red Sox fans for 18 years, until they finally won their next World Series, and the memory

Alongside the 1969 trophy rests the reward for the Mets' 122 victories, including the eight hard-earned wins in the postseason.

of '86 glory would have to last as Mets fans endured decades without a title and their own brand of demons.

This article originally appeared in The 1986 New York Mets: There Was More Than Game Six *(SABR, 2016), edited by Leslie Heaphy and Bill Nowlin.*

Notes
1 Michael Goodwin, "NBC Scored in Game 7, Too," *New York Times*, October 29, 1986.
2 1987 Mets Information Guide: 216.
3 Author interview with Keith Hernandez, December 22, 2014.

KEVIN MCREYNOLDS' GRAND SLAM IN NINTH BEATS CUBS

AUGUST 11, 1988: NEW YORK METS 9, CHICAGO CUBS 6, AT WRIGLEY FIELD

By Brian M. Frank

Kevin McReynolds and Rich "Goose" Gossage were teammates for three years with the San Diego Padres and were major contributors to a Padres team that played in the 1984 World Series. After McReynolds was traded to the New York Mets during the 1986-87 offseason, Gossage had some unkind words for his former teammate. The outspoken closer suggested McReynolds was lazy, and reportedly said, "I wonder about his work habits."[1] McReynolds would have the opportunity to face Gossage nine times in his career after leaving San Diego. Their most notable meeting came on an afternoon in 1988 at Wrigley Field with the game hanging in the balance.

Despite being in first place in the National League East, the Mets entered their final game of a three-game series with the Cubs on a bit of a slide. The Cubs won the first game of the series, the first nine-inning night game at Wrigley Field, 6-4.[2] After dropping the second game, the Mets saw their division lead shrink to five games over Pittsburgh and 5½ over Montreal. Trying to avoid a sweep in the series finale, New York sent Dwight Gooden to the mound to face Cubs right-hander Al Nipper.

The game got off to a good start for the Mets, when Gary Carter blasted his 300th major-league home run in the second inning. Carter had spent 225 at-bats chasing the milestone home run after hitting number 299 on May 16. After the game he said, "I feel as though a weight has been lifted off me."[3] Carter became the 59th player to hit 300 home runs, and just the fourth catcher to do so.

The Mets lead was short-lived, as the Cubs jumped on Gooden in the bottom of the second for a pair of runs. The low point of the inning came when Darryl Strawberry misplayed a fly ball by Andre Dawson, pulling up shy of the brick wall and turning what could have been an out into a triple. Strawberry, who was slumping at the plate, explained the play after the game, saying, "It was lack of concentration in the field, when I'm going bad at the plate."[4]

The Mets retook the lead in the third, scoring a pair of runs, highlighted by a run-scoring single by Kevin McReynolds. But Strawberry's rough day continued. He was thrown out when he rounded too far off second base after McReynolds' single. He then misplayed another ball in the outfield that turned a Mitch Webster double into a triple in the bottom of the inning. The play, along with a two-run single

Reticent and unassuming, Kevin McReynolds followed up a 29-homer, 95-RBI campaign in 1987 with 27 round-trippers and 99 driven in as the Mets claimed the 1988 NL East crown.

by Vance Law, an RBI single by Ryne Sandberg, and an RBI double by Angel Salazar, put the Cubs in front, 6-3. After just three innings, the Cubs already had three triples and everyone in their lineup except the pitcher had a hit. Gooden managed to tough it out through the fifth before giving way to the bullpen. The fireballer described his atypical outing: "It was hot, it was frustrating. I had no rhythm, pitching so much from the stretch. And I made some bad pitches."[5]

Terry Leach relieved Gooden and held the fort admirably, allowing just three hits in three shutout innings. New York inched closer in the seventh, when leadoff hitter Lenny Dykstra hit a ball over the ivy to cut the Cubs lead to 6-4.

Trailing by two runs entering the ninth inning, the Mets got their first two men on against southpaw Frank DiPino, with singles by shortstop Kevin Elster and pinch-hitter Mookie Wilson. Cubs manager Don Zimmer brought in a fresh lefty, Pat Perry, to face Lenny Dykstra. Dykstra hit a single to left, scoring Elster and cutting the Cubs' lead to one. With runners at first and second and nobody out, Tim Teufel was unsuccessful in a sacrifice attempt, popping out to first baseman Mark Grace. But both runners advanced when, with Keith Hernandez at the plate, Wilson and Dykstra pulled off a double steal to put the tying and winning runs in scoring position. Hernandez was then hit by a pitch, loading the bases.

Strawberry came to the plate with a chance to redeem himself after his rough day in the field and on the bases. But the Mets cleanup man struck out chasing a 2-and-2 slider. With the Mets down to their last out, and right-handed batter Kevin McReynolds due up, Zimmer brought in right-hander Rich Gossage. Once the game's preeminent closer, the 37-year-old Gossage was no longer as dominant as he once was. As Zimmer quipped, "Goose doesn't throw the ball like he did six years ago, but who the hell does?"[6]

As Gossage entered the game, Mets manager Davey Johnson recalled his derogatory comments about McReynolds when the outfielder left San Diego. Johnson remarked after the game, "I really liked that matchup, I remember what Goose once said about Kevin."[7] McReynolds himself tried to downplay the comments, saying, "Goose came over and told me it was written out of context."[8]

McReynolds stepped to the plate with two outs, the bases loaded, and the Mets trailing by one. He was the only man standing between the Mets and a four-game losing streak. The always intimidating Gossage stared in from the mound, with the Wrigley Field faithful on their feet, imploring the closer to end the game and complete the series sweep. Gossage threw a slider for strike one and then another slider for ball one. McReynolds jumped all over the next pitch, sending it an estimated 415 feet "three rows up into the vacant center-field bleachers" for a grand slam to give the Mets the lead, 9-6.[9]

After Gary Carter grounded out to end the ninth for the Mets, the Cubs did not go quietly in their half of the ninth. Lefty Randy Myers recorded the first two outs of the inning, but also allowed a pair of singles to Mitch Webster and Mark Grace. Right-hander Roger McDowell entered the game to face Andre Dawson, who represented the game's tying run. McDowell induced Dawson to hit a comebacker to the mound for the final out of the afternoon.

After the game, Davey Johnson, frustrated by his team's sloppy play during the series, disclosed that he had been ready to call a team meeting if Gossage had retired McReynolds. "We played terrible," the manager said. "… I was thinking if I should have a meeting, because I thought some things needed to be said. We played like Little Leaguers. We didn't execute, we didn't run the bases, we were down three runs and swinging at 2-and-0 pitches over our heads. … I can't be upset after that effort to come back, but we were all embarrassed out there. If you watched the three games here, you would have thought (the Cubs) were in first place and we were in fourth. But we managed to salvage a win instead of a disaster."[10]

The hero of the day, Kevin McReynolds, was a bit more diplomatic in his assessment, saying, "Will this wake us up from our daze? … I have no idea."[11]

Despite the Mets' lackluster play, they managed a late rally to allow the game to come down to a matchup of two former teammates. As Gossage said of the dramatic at-bat, "I get paid to get McReynolds out and that's the bottom line. … I didn't get him out."

Notes
1 Bob Klapisch, "Mac's Slam Salvages Sloppy Mets," *New York Daily News,* August 12, 1988: 69.
2 The Cubs played a 3½-inning rain-shortened contest against the Phillies on August 8, 1988, but the Mets game was the first official nine-inning night game at Wrigley Field.
3 Joseph Durso, "McReynolds Slam Saves the Day," *New York Times,* August 12, 1988: B13.
4 Ibid.
5 Durso: B15.
6 Joe Goddard, "Cubs Are Slammed," *Chicago Sun Times,* August 12, 1988: 84.
7 Klapisch.
8 Goddard: 104. It's highly questionable whether Gossage's comments were out of context. In his 2000 autobiography, he didn't mince any words about McReynolds, calling him the "poster boy for indifference and nonchalance," "as contented as a pig in slop," and "the quintessential couch potato." Richard Gossage with Russ Pate, *The Goose Is Loose* (New York: Ballantine Books, 2000), 216.
9 Alan Solomon "Mets Cook the Cubs Goose," *Chicago Tribune,* August 12, 1988: Section 4, 1.
10 John Harper, "McReynolds' Slam Cooks Cubs' Goose," *New York Post*, August 12, 1988: 81.
11 Klapisch.

METS RALLY FOR THREE IN NINTH, STEAL GAME ONE OF NLCS

OCTOBER 4, 1988: NEW YORK METS 3, LOS ANGELES DODGERS 2, AT DODGER STADIUM

GAME ONE OF THE 1986 NATIONAL LEAGUE CHAMPIONSHIP SERIES

By Paul Hofmann

The 1988 National League Championship Series was a matchup of a pair of teams that had comfortably won their division. The NL East Division champion New York Mets finished with a record of 100-60, 15 games ahead of the second-place Pittsburgh Pirates. The NL West Division champion Los Angeles Dodgers finished with a record of 94-67, seven games ahead of the Cincinnati Reds. The Mets were heavy favorites to win the series. They were only two years removed from the team's 1986 world championship and had owned the Dodgers during the regular season, winning 10 of their 11 games. What appeared to be a potential mismatch turned out to be an epic seven-game series.

Game One pitted two of the National League's best right-handed starters against each other. The Dodgers started the hottest pitcher on the planet, Orel Hershiser, who finished the season with a 59-inning scoreless streak that began in the sixth inning of an August 30 game against the Montreal Expos. The 30-year-old right-hander finished the season with a 23-8 record and a sterling 2.26 ERA. The Mets countered with Dwight Gooden, who finished the season with a mark of 18-9 and a 3.19 ERA, including a 3-0 record and 1.53 ERA against the Dodgers.

A sold-out crowd of 55,582 was crammed into Dodger Stadium when Hershiser delivered the first pitch at 5:25 P.M. under a clear twilight sky. The game-time temperature was 63 degrees, slightly below average because of the misty marine layer that had enveloped the City of Angels earlier in the day.[1]

The first inning was like Hershiser's previous 59 as he retired the side without yielding a run. Leadoff batter Mookie Wilson was retired on a line drive to right field, then Gregg Jefferies laced a clean single to right. The top of the first ended when Keith Hernandez lined out to second baseman Steve Sax, who easily doubled Jefferies off first.

The Dodgers scored in the bottom of the inning. Sax took Gooden's first offering, a high fastball, the other way for a base hit to right. After a game of cat-and-mouse that saw Gooden throw over to first base four times, the ever-aggressive Sax easily stole second. Franklin Stubbs struck out on a 3-and-2 fastball that tailed out of the strike zone. Kirk Gibson, soon to be named the NL MVP, moved Sax to third when he fought off a fastball in on the hands and sent a little looper to second that Wally Backman fielded on one hop. Mike Marshall then dropped a single in front of right fielder Darryl Strawberry to score Sax and put the Dodgers up 1-0.

Neither team was able to mount much of a threat in the ensuing innings. The Mets put runners on first and third with two outs in both the third and sixth innings but Hershiser escaped unscathed both times with inning-ending groundouts. Similarly, the Dodgers failed to move a baserunner past second against Gooden and the score remained 1-0 until the bottom of the seventh.

Mike Scioscia doubled to right to lead off the bottom of the seventh. The Dodgers catcher advanced to third when third baseman Jeff Hamilton hit a weak grounder to first, and scored on Alfredo Griffin's single to right that increased the Dodgers' lead to 2-0. With Hershiser on the mound, the game seemed to shape up exactly the way Dodgers manager Tommy Lasorda would have liked.

Hershiser extended his scoreless innings streak to 67 with a 13-pitch bottom of the eighth.[2] The Dodgers ace stuck out Backman looking to start the inning before Lenny Dykstra, pinch-hitting for Gooden, walked. Wilson, swinging at the first pitch, hit a sharp two-hop grounder to Griffin at short who stepped on second and threw to first for a tidy 6-3 inning-ending double play.

Manager Davey Johnson turned to Randy Myers to keep the Mets close. Myers enjoyed a rock-solid season for the Mets. The left-handed reliever, who finished 16th in the NL MVP voting, pitched in 55 games for the Mets and finished 7-3 with 26 saves and a 1.72 ERA. Myers retired the Dodgers in order on only six pitches.

Hershiser went to the mound to start the ninth with a two-run lead, three outs away from putting the Dodgers ahead in the series. Jefferies led off with a single and moved up to second when Hernandez grounded out to first. Strawberry lined a double to right-center to score Jefferies and make it 2-1. That brought Lasorda to the mound to make a pitching change. Hershiser recalled the conversation on the mound in which he pleaded to stay in the game. "Tommy, don't take me out. I'm fine. I'm fine." Lasorda replied, "Bulldog, you're tired," to which the pitcher replied, "Tommy, I'm fine, I just look tired because it's the first run I've given up in 67 innings." Lasorda had the last word, "Bulldog, get off the mound."[3] Hershiser exited to a thunderous standing ovation.

Jay Howell was summoned to get the last two outs and preserve the Dodgers' one-run lead. The hard-throwing Howell, who had a reputation for being effectively wild, had been acquired by the Dodgers the previous December as part of an eight-player, three-team trade. The hope was that he would shore up the back end of the team's bullpen. Howell went 5-3 with 21 saves and a 2.08 ERA during the regular season.

Kevin McReynolds, the first hitter Howell faced, walked, bringing up fastball-hitting Howard Johnson. Howell refused to give in to Johnson and threw him five consecutive curveballs. The fifth one struck out a flailing Johnson. With the Mets down to their last out, catcher Gary Carter was all that stood between the Dodgers and a one-game series lead.

With the outfield playing deep to guard against an extra-base hit, Howell started Carter off with a pair of curveballs and went ahead in the count, 0-and-2. With the sellout crowd rising to its feet in anticipation of the final strike, Carter connected with a curveball, low and away, and sent a blooping liner to center that caromed off diving center fielder John Shelby. With the runners going on contact, Strawberry scored easily to tie the game while McReynolds raced around third and ran over Scioscia in a violent collision ahead of the throw to give the Mets a 3-2 lead. Backman grounded out to Sax to end the inning but the damage was done.

Carter's hit and the sequence of events that followed were dissected and relived after the game and for years in the future:

Howell shared his reaction with the *Los Angeles Times's* Sam McManis after the game. "My first reaction was that I was surprised he swung," Howell said of Carter's chasing an 0-and-2 curve that was tailing out of the strike zone. "Then I was surprised he hit it."[4]

During the nationally televised postgame interview that followed the game, Carter said he was looking for the curveball. "I wasn't looking for anything else but," Carter said. "I looked bad on the second pitch that he threw to me and all I was trying to do was make contact. … I was just trying to stay on the ball. Fortunately, I was able to make contact."[5] Carter went on to credit Shelby with making an outstanding play on the ball and it just "snuck in there."[6] The Dodgers center fielder said, "I had a good feeling I could get the ball. That is why I dove."[7] Had Shelby not dived for the ball, McReynolds would have been held at third base and the game would have remained tied.

Years later Scioscia recalled the collision at the plate, which resembled a fullback barreling into a waiting linebacker. The solidly built Dodgers catcher said, "McReynolds scored the go-ahead run and knocked me into, I guess, San Bernardino County from Los Angeles County."[8]

Myers returned to the mound for his second inning of work with a slightly different task than he had when he entered the game in the eighth. Instead of keeping the Mets in the game, Myers was left to close the game out for the Mets. For the second consecutive inning he retired the Dodgers in order and the Mets had stolen Game One to start the series.

Notes
1 "Weather History for KLAX – October 4, 1988," wunderground.com/history/airport/KLAX/1988/10/4/DailyHistory.html?req_city=&req_state=&req_statename=&reqdb.zip=&reqdb.magic=&reqdb.wmo=.
2 Officially, Hershiser's scoreless innings streak remained at 59. Postseason statistics are not aggregated into regular-season statistics.
3 "Oral History of Epic Mets-Dodgers 1988 NLCS," mlb.com/news/oral-history-of-epic-mets-dodgers-1988-nlcs/c-152995440.
4 Sam McManis, "Dodgers Come Up Empty on Last Grasp: Carter Lifts Mets to Win, 3-2, in Game 1," *Los Angeles Times*, October 5, 1988. articles.latimes.com/1988-10-05/sports/sp-2818_1_dodger-stadium.
5 "1988 NLCS Game 1 New York Mets at Los Angeles Dodgers PART 2," youtube.com/watch?v=iMtV5hOS9O4.
6 Ibid.
7 Sam McManis.
8 "Oral History of Epic Mets-Dodgers 1988 NLCS."

METS BEAT DODGERS, WEATHER IN GAME THREE TO REGAIN CONTROL OF NLCS

OCTOBER 8, 1988: NEW YORK METS 8, LOS ANGELES DODGERS 4, AT SHEA STADIUM
GAME THREE OF THE 1988 NATIONAL LEAGUE CHAMPIONSHIP SERIES

By Tara Krieger

Wet, wild, and weird – with a dash of pine tar. So went the third game of the 1988 National League Championship Series at Shea Stadium on a damp, frigid Saturday afternoon in October.

There were players stumbling and skidding all over the field – recorded in the official box score as "soaked."[1] In the end, the Mets floated to an 8-4 victory on the heels of a five-run eighth-inning rally after Dodgers reliever Jay Howell was tossed with the sticky substance on the heel of his glove.

Mercury had slipped into retrograde the previous week. Across the river, the Columbia University football team, playing Princeton, was on the verge of ending its five-year deluge of 44 straight losses. October 8, 1988, was that kind of day.

The Mets and the Dodgers had last seen baseball over 60 hours and 3,000 miles ago, when Los Angeles shocked New York in Game Two to knot the series at a game apiece. It was 30 degrees warmer and desert dry then.

Granted, the Dodgers might have been buoyed by some choice words in a ghostwritten column by the Mets' Game Two starter, young pitching phenom David Cone. After the Mets had staged a ninth-inning comeback against Dodgers ace Orel Hershiser and closer Howell in Game One, Cone had called Hershiser merely "lucky" for holding New York scoreless for eight innings and compared Howell's curveball to a high school pitcher's.[2] The fired-up Dodgers had sent Cone to the showers after two innings.

Was Game Two an anomaly? The Mets couldn't wait to board a red-eye and find out on their home turf behind 17-game winner Ron Darling. But the day after the designated travel day, Friday, October 7, rain and what NL President A. Bartlett Giamatti called "manifestly chilly" conditions[3] washed away the evening's contest, leading to the noon Saturday deferment.

The rainout worked in the Dodgers' favor. With the extra day off, they could rest scheduled Game Three starter John Tudor and his sore hip[4] and instead start Hershiser, who was poised to win the NL Cy Young Award and would now be available were there a Game Seven.[5] Also in the Dodgers' favor: They had the NL's best road record during the season, at 49-31.

On the other hand, the Mets had undoubtedly the best home record, at 56-24, and had beaten the Dodgers in 10 of 11 meetings before October. Darling hurled a complete-game shutout against Los Angeles on September 2. Opposing Hershiser, who had ended the regular season with 59 straight scoreless innings, could spell a speedy pitchers' duel.

Not so much. Although the rain had slowed to a drizzle by game time, the puddled tarp remained on the field as the teams warmed up. Dark clouds forced the lights on, in spite of it being midday. Fans – 44,672 of them – wore layers and huddled under multicolored umbrellas in the 43-degree weather.

The 8½-inning game slogged in at 3 hours and 44 minutes and featured 13 walks and four errors.

"Worst day I ever played baseball. Should've never played. Brutal conditions," said Darling, who lasted six innings.[6]

"Jay Howell is suspended for the pine tar incident, because it was so cold we were trying to figure out any way to hold the ball," recalled Hershiser, who went seven.[7]

Howell had a 3-and-2 count against Kevin McReynolds to start the eighth inning when Mets first-base coach Bill Robinson saw him pulling at his glove. Robinson motioned to manager Davey Johnson, who rose from the dugout to alert umpire crew chief Harry Wendelstedt. In a gathering at the mound, home-plate umpire Joe West yanked Howell's glove off his hand, tested the string and the pocket, and threw him out of the game.

The glove was tossed to Giamatti in the stands for further inspection. Howell, who exited to a rousing chorus of "Cheat! Cheat! Cheat!," said he had been greasing his pitches with pine tar to get a "better grip on the ball" in the cold weather.[8]

"It's not cheating," Howell said. "It doesn't change the flight of the ball. I'm certainly not the first pitcher to use pine tar."[9]

But he was the first to be ejected from a postseason game for its use.[10] The Mets then batted around off three Dodgers relievers, permanently tilting the game in their favor after an inauspicious start.

Poor control and fielding put Darling in a two-run hole in the top of the second. He walked the leadoff batters, Mike Marshall and John Shelby, on full counts. Mets first baseman Keith Hernandez, who would win his 11th Gold Glove that November, was anticipating that the next hitter, Mike Scioscia, would swing away. When Scioscia bunted up the line, Hernandez had to scramble for the ball and backhanded it beyond Wally Backman covering first. Hernandez's error – he'd made just two all season – scored Marshall and put Shelby on third. Shelby scored on an infield groundout.

More Mets misjudgment in the third cost another run. With speedy Steve Sax on third and one out, the middle infielders were playing too far back. When the slumping Kirk Gibson grounded to second, Backman could only throw to first while Sax trotted home. 3-0, Dodgers.

Hershiser nearly had the second out in the bottom of the third, but the muddy mound turned strike three into a wild pitch and Mookie Wilson reached safely. Gregg Jefferies's single followed by Darryl Strawberry's double to the right-field corner put the Mets on the board.

The soggy circus continued even on what should have been routine plays, such as when Gibson stumbled on the wet grass chasing Wilson's left-field fly in the bottom of the fifth and had to make a one-handed dive to put it away.

In the bottom of the sixth, with Hernandez on first, Gibson juggled a bad hop on Strawberry's single. Taking advantage of Gibson's hesitation, Hernandez, who initially held up after rounding second, broke for third. But his foot gave way on the grimy basepaths. On all fours with his helmet rolling adrift, Hernandez awkwardly tried to wriggle his way toward the bag, falling twice. He was out by half a hand's length.

The Dodgers returned the favor in the Mets' next at-bat, a high hop from McReynolds to the infield. Third baseman Jeff Hamilton bounced the ball across the diamond, and first baseman Mickey Hatcher juggled it too much to have had control when McReynolds crossed the bag. Safe, E-5.

After Howard Johnson forced out McReynolds and sent Strawberry to third, right-handed-hitting Gary Carter uncharacteristically sprayed a single into shallow right to score Strawberry. Backman drove in Johnson on a grounder off the glove of a diving Hatcher. His string of "yeahs" upon reaching base were as remotely audible as Dodgers manager Tommy Lasorda's string of obscenities from the bench. Tie game.

"This is one of the zaniest, craziest innings I've ever seen in my life," remarked announcer Tim McCarver.[11]

In the top of the eighth, Mets reliever Roger McDowell slid like a banana peel trying to field Scioscia's tapper back to the mound. What should have been the third out wound up in foul territory. An infield single by Hamilton and a walk to Mike Davis loaded the bases. The Mets summoned lefty Randy Myers from the bullpen to face lefty-hitting Danny Heep, pinch-hitting for Hershiser. But Lasorda replaced Heep with right-handed-hitting Mike Sharperson – and Myers (ultimately also the winning pitcher) forced in the go-ahead run on a bases-loaded walk.

Had the bottom of the eighth played out differently, perhaps Howell, who had 21 saves, would've shut the Mets down the final two innings. Instead, he lasted five pitches before the pine tar incident.

"Did it change my strategy?" recalled Lasorda. "You throw my best relief pitcher out of the game, and you change my strategy."[12]

Howell's ejection was a catalyst in the Mets' offensive onslaught, as his replacement, Alejandro Peña, allowed a two-out RBI double to Backman to tie the game (and blow the save). After walking pinch-hitter Lenny Dykstra, Peña was relieved by Jesse Orosco, whom the Dodgers acquired in a trade from the Mets that offseason. Orosco then hung a curve to Wilson for an RBI single, hit Jefferies to load the bases, and threw ball four to Hernandez to walk in a run and off the field. Strawberry's bloop single to shallow left off Ricky Horton scored two more, and the Straw celebrated his third hit with his fists in the air. *Heyyyyyyy!*

Up by four, the Mets called on Cone to prove that the Dodgers hadn't spooked him. Cone delivered a 1-2-3 ninth, and New York was two wins away from the World Series.

"I can see why we're called the Amazing Mets," said Backman, who was 2-for-4 with two RBIs. "We don't die. We just keep fighting until we win."[13]

But the Mets would not win another at home, as the Dodgers snatched away the next two en route to taking the series in seven.

Notes

1 Statistics, unless otherwise noted, are taken from Baseball-Reference.com. baseball-reference.com/boxes/NYN/NYN198810080.shtml.
2 Bob Klapisch ghostwrote the column with David Cone's byline. It ran in the *New York Daily News* on October 5, 1988, entitled, "It Was Justice – Not Luck."
3 NLCS ABC broadcast, October 7, 1988.
4 "I have the body of an 80-year-old, but I'll be all right," Tudor quipped before his proposed start. Joseph Durso, "Darling and Tudor Meet in a Tie Breaker," *New York Times*, October 7, 1988, nytimes.com/1988/10/07/sports/darling-and-tudor-meet-in-a-tie-breaker.html.
5 The Dodgers' strategy paid off, as the NLCS did produce a Game Seven – and Hershiser hurled a shutout to send the Dodgers to the World Series.
6 Ron Darling postgame interview, ABC broadcast, October 8, 1988.
7 Lyle Spencer, "Oral History of Epic Mets-Dodgers 1988 NLCS," MLB.com, October 5, 2015, m.mlb.com/news/article/152995440/oral-history-of-epic-mets-dodgers-1988-nlcs/.
8 ABC News broadcast, October 8, 1988. According to the NLCS ABC broadcast, the Mets were aware Howell had been using pine tar on his glove in Game One, but broadcaster Al Michaels implied that since manager Davey Johnson waited until a 3-and-0 count became 3-and-2 on McReynolds, perhaps the Mets said nothing because they were winning. Dodgers pitcher Alejandro Peña may have been using pine tar in a previous game, as well.
9 Sam McManis, "Dodgers Lose Grip and Slip to 8-4 Loss: Mets Rally to Win After Howell Ejected," *Los Angeles Times*, October 9, 1988, articles.latimes.com/1988-10-09/sports/sp-5620_1_mets-rally.
10 Howell was suspended three games for the incident, and thus was available to pitch Game Seven – though his presence turned out to be unnecessary, as Hershiser went the distance.
11 NLCS ABC broadcast, October 8, 1988.
12 Joseph Durso, "THE PLAYOFFS; Bizarre Game Turns the Mets' Way," *New York Times*, October 9, 1988, nytimes.com/1988/10/09/sports/the-playoffs-bizarre-game-turns-the-mets-way.html.
13 Ibid.

METS SURVIVE EXCITING SIX-RUN NINTH-INNING RALLY BY PHILLIES

JULY 25, 1990: NEW YORK METS 10, PHILADELPHIA PHILLIES 9, AT VETERANS STADIUM

by Michael Huber

As July 1990 neared its end, the New York Mets were closing in on the first-place Pittsburgh Pirates, entering this contest only 1½ games back in the senior circuit's East Division. They were finishing a three-game series against the Philadelphia Phillies, who were stuck in fourth place, 10 games out of first. A crowd of 40,079 showed up at Veterans Stadium for the Wednesday night game, and they were treated to a match that "rocket[ed] from one extreme to the other."[1]

Jeff Parrett toed the rubber for the home team. He had been made a Phillies starter on July 3, after 39 appearances from the bullpen and despite his 4.94 earned-run average. New York countered with Sid Fernandez, a winner of three of his last four decisions. Fernandez had allowed only six earned runs in his last 26 innings pitched.

With two outs and Dave Magadan on second base in the opening frame, Phillies skipper Nick Leyva instructed Parrett to walk Darryl Strawberry intentionally, despite Straw's recent 3-for-26 stretch in his last seven games. That brought Kevin McReynolds to the plate. McReynolds lifted a pop fly into foul territory for the third out.

In the third inning, Howard Johnson worked a full count off Parrett before launching a triple into center field. Magadan then "zonked a two-run homer," giving New York a 2-0 lead.[2]

In the fifth, Leyva tried the walk-by-design strategy again when Strawberry batted with two outs and Johnson on third. Strawberry was intentionally passed for the second time. This time, however, Parrett hung a curveball and McReynolds "crushed it for a triple," increasing New York's advantage to 4-0.[3] On the next pitch, Mackey Sasser grounded to short for the third out. Parrett never came back to the mound. After the game, the 6-foot-4 right-hander told reporters that "he was certain that he was headed back to the bullpen."[4] But after three relief appearances in the following week for the Phillies, Parrett was traded to the Atlanta Braves for Dale Murphy and players to be named later.[5]

The sixth inning was the key for New York, when Phillies reliever Don Carman "was pelted for five runs on four hits."[6] Daryl Boston doubled between strikeouts by Tom O'Malley and Fernandez. Then, for the third time in the game, Leyva called for an intentional walk, this time to Johnson. Magadan singled, driving in Boston. Afterward, Leyva said, "I tried to match a lefty against a lefty but if he doesn't make a good pitch, it doesn't matter. Magadan found a hole to keep the inning alive."[7] After Magadan, Gregg Jefferies tripled, plating two more runs, and then Strawberry smashed his 25th home run of the season, a blast that "glow[ed] through the night like a re-entering space shuttle."[8] The ball landed 450 feet away in the center-field seats.[9] The Mets had now scored seven runs after two intentional walks.

New York still had a shutout going into the bottom of the seventh inning. According to the *Philadelphia Inquirer*, "as the Vet's organist played 'Take Me Out to the Ball Game,' some pacifists began trudging home – the Phillies trailed by nine."[10] How many fans would regret it as they were stuck in traffic, listening to the radio? The game was far from over. Fernandez started the inning by striking out Dickie Thon. Darren Daulton then lined a single to center. After Jim Vatcher flied to left for out number two, Dykstra singled, advancing Daulton to third. Tom Herr jumped on Fernandez's first pitch and singled to right, driving in Daulton. Dykstra motored to third. With Von Hayes at the plate, Herr stole second base, and on catcher Sasser's throwing error, Dykstra scored the Phillies' second run.

Wally Whitehurst relieved Fernandez in the bottom of the eighth. Charlie Hayes singled, and an out later, so did Thon. Tom Nieto hit the third single of the inning, and Hayes scored, making it 9-3.

The Mets added a run in the top of the ninth, when Sasser singled in McReynolds, who had doubled to deep center with one out. Little did the Mets know this would be the insurance run they needed. Going into the last half-inning, the Mets had a comfortable seven-run lead.

Philadelphia opened the bottom of the ninth with a record seven consecutive nobody-out singles.[11] None of them were hit hard. After single number 7, Mets manager Bud Harrelson called on John Franco to replace Julio Machado, who had replaced Whitehurst when Ricky Jordan reached on single number 5, a weak grounder to third. Jordan had been 0-for-4, all strikeouts. Machado had lasted for only two batters, allowing two-strike singles to Thon and Nieto. Whitehurst remarked after the game that the Phillies "hit three or four in a row that just got by someone."[12]

John Kruk, pinch-hitting for Vatcher, strode to the plate to face Franco, worked a full count and then drew a walk, once again loading the bases. Eight straight Phillies had now reached base and five of them had scored. Philadelphia had all the momentum.

Franco now had to face Dykstra and Herr, who had collected six of the Phillies' hits. The tying run was on second base with no outs. Dykstra swung at Franco's first offering and rolled a hard grounder to second baseman Keith Miller, who started a 4-6-3 double play. Thon scored, making it a one-run game, 10-9. With the Mets still clinging to the lead, Nieto was only 90 feet from home plate, but now there were two outs. The first pitch to Herr, who had led off the inning with a single, was a ball. Herr drove the next pitch toward short, but Mario Diaz snared the liner at eye level. The Mets had survived a six-run rally with no outs. The few hardy Phillies fans who had remained were surely emotionally spent, first to watch their team give up nine unanswered runs, and then fight back with so many consecutive singles, each one building their hopes a bit more, only to see it not be enough.

Bob Murphy, the Ford C. Frick Award-winning sportscaster for the Mets, made the radio call: "Here's the pitch on the way. Line drive – caught! The game is over! The Mets win it! A line drive to Mario Diaz and the Mets win the ballgame! They win the damn thing by a score of 10-9!"[13]

The "damn thing" featured 30 hits, 10 walks, and 18 strikeouts. A total of 33 players found their names in the box score, with all of the pinch-hitters, pinch-runners, and pitching changes. The Phillies had banged out 16 hits, but 14 of them were singles (Dykstra had two doubles to pace their attack). Fernandez earned his seventh victory for the Mets and his ERA dropped to 3.16, while Franco picked up his league-leading 23rd save. Franco remarked after the excitement, "It wasn't pretty, but we got it done. It was crazy. It was scary."[14]

After the game, Leyva was chagrined: "We had a chance to win that game. It was amazing. We don't quit."[15] He added, "To get two down, have the bases loaded and none out, you've got to win the game if you're at home."[16] New York fought its way into a tie for first the next day, but then toggled between first and second position in the National League East for the next five weeks, before finishing the 1990 campaign as runner-up in the division to the Pirates.

Sources

In addition to the sources mentioned in the Notes, the author consulted baseball-reference.com, mlb.com, and retrosheet.org.

Notes

1 Joseph Durso, "Mets Survive Late Scare and Hold Off the Phillies," *New York Times*, July 26, 1990: B9.
2 Michael Bamberger, "Phils Get 6 in 9th but Lose," *Philadelphia Inquirer*, July 26, 1990: 29.
3 Ibid.
4 Ibid.
5 For the players to be named later, Atlanta received Jim Vatcher on August 9 and Victor Rosario on September 4, while Philadelphia received Tommy Greene on August 9.
6 Bob Brookover, "Phils Get on Late Roll, but Still Fall to Mets," *Camden* (New Jersey) *Courier-Post*, July 26, 1990: 45.
7 Don Bostrom, "Mets Withstand Late Barrage of Singles 10-9," *Allentown* (Pennsylvania) *Morning Call*, July 26, 1990: 59.
8 Bill Conlin, "Better Half Arrived Late," *Philadelphia Daily News*, July 26, 1990: 79.
9 Durso.
10 Bamberger.
11 Ibid.
12 Bostrom.
13 "Mets Fans Share Their Memories of the July 25, 1990 Game," The Ultimate Mets Database. Found online at ultimatemets.com/gamedetail.php?gameno=4606&tabno=B. Accessed January 2018.
14 Durso.
15 Bamberger.
16 Bostrom.

WALK-OFF ENDS ANTHONY YOUNG'S 27-GAME LOSING STREAK

JULY 28, 1993: NEW YORK METS 5, FLORIDA MARLINS 4, AT SHEA STADIUM

By Kevin Larkin

Futility is defined as a "lack of effectiveness or success." Baseball has had many examples in its history. For one, the Chicago Cubs, who went over 100 years without winning a World Series. The Boston Red Sox endured 86 years without a title. It can also be evidenced in individual performance. A prime example occurred between May 6, 1992, and July 24, 1993, when Anthony Young couldn't win. In fact, he lost 27 consecutive games – surpassing the previous major-league high of 23, set by Cliff Curtis in 1910-11.

Over a year without a victory on the mound certainly that fits the futility definition. But Young's effectiveness wasn't totally lacking; if he had been on a slightly more respectable team, he'd never find his name in the record books.

The team he was on arguably better fit the definition than Young.

During the losing streak, Young did record some saves between July 1 and September 22, 1992.[1] But he just couldn't seem to get that elusive win. The streak included games started, as well as those in which he pitched in relief.[2]

On July 28, 1993, the Mets hosted the Florida Marlins in a night game at Shea Stadium. Sixteen of his 27 losses were suffered in front of a hometown Mets crowd. In 14 of the losses he was the starting pitcher; the other 13 came as he pitched in relief.[3]

The starters on the 28th were Bret Saberhagen for the Mets and Jack Armstrong for the Marlins. Saberhagen had twice previously won the Cy Young Award (1985 and 1989 with the Kansas City Royals) and had a record going into the game of six wins and seven losses. Armstrong had a record of 7-10 for the Marlins, who were in their first year of existence.

Saberhagen had an easy first inning, two fly outs to left field and a groundout to the shortstop, Tim Bogar. Armstrong had it a little tougher. He struck out leadoff hitter Ryan Thompson, then gave up a home run to Joe Orsulak. Future Hall of Famer Eddie Murray grounded out to third for the second out. Bobby Bonilla doubled to left field, and Jeromy Burnitz walked, but Jeff Kent grounded out, Armstrong to Orestes Destrade at first, which limited the damage to the solo home run by Orsulak.

Anthony Young's hard-luck 27-game losing streak from May 6, 1992 through July 24, 1993 can't be directly blamed on individual struggles. It certainly didn't help that the Mets were arguably the worst team in baseball during that span.

Saberhagen had his second straight 1-2-3 inning in the top of the second with a groundout by Gary Sheffield, Destrade's strikeout, and a groundout by Marlins catcher Benito Santiago. Armstrong also had a 1-2-3 inning, getting a pop fly and then two straight groundouts.

In the top of the third inning, Saberhagen got two straight fly outs before allowing a single to center field by Armstrong. He bore down and got Marlins center fielder Chuck Carr to hit a force-play grounder.

The Marlins did not score a run in the fourth inning after getting two straight one-out singles, by Jeff Conine and Gary Sheffield. Both runners were left stranded as Saberhagen got a fly out and then a strikeout. New York scored a run in its half of the fourth as Burnitz led off with a single, stole second with two outs, went to third on a wild pitch, and scored on a single by Tim Bogar to make the score 2-0, Mets.

Florida tied the game in the sixth inning when Carr singled to left field and Bret Barberie hit a two-run homer to tie the score at 2-2. Saberhagen got out of the inning without any further damage as Conine grounded out and both Sheffield and Destrade flied out to left field.

The Mets went ahead in the seventh inning, 3-2, on a two-out solo home run by Thompson, but the Marlins restored the tie in the top of the eighth inning when Barberie hit a one-out single to right field, went to third on Sheffield's single to left, and scored on Destrade's double to center field. (Sheffield tried to score but was thrown out at home, right fielder Darrell Whitmore to shortstop Walt Weiss to catcher Santiago.)

New York did not score in the bottom of the eighth, stranding Kent at first base with a single. Anthony Young, with an 0-13 record in 1993 and 27 straight losses dating back to May 6, 1992, replaced Saberhagen and Santiago greeted him with a single to right field. Catcher Todd Hundley's error on a bunt by Darrell Whitmore put runners on first and second. Walt Weiss reached on a fielder's choice and the bases were loaded with nobody out. It looked as though Young's losing streak might run to 28. But he got Edgar Renteria to ground into a double play, third base to catcher to first base. But Carr was safe at first on a bunt single, and Whitmore scored the go-ahead run. Young struck out Barberie and the Mets came up in the bottom of the ninth inning trailing, 4-3.

The Marlins' Bryan Harvey came in seeking a save, but pinch-hitter Jeff McKnight singled to right field on his first pitch and was sacrificed to second by Dave Gallagher. Ryan Thompson's pop fly fell safely beyond first base and McKnight scored the tying run. Thompson held first on Orsulak's fly ball to left field. But Murray lined a double to right field and Thompson legged it home with the winning run.[4] Anthony Young's losing streak was ended at 27 games. The victory was his only one in 1993; he finished the season 1-16.

In Young's 27 straight losses, New York scored a total of 71 runs while giving up 139 runs, certainly not a recipe for success. Young would pitch in the major leagues until June 19, 1996, when he was a member of the Houston Astros. He ended his major-league career with a record of 15 wins and 48 losses and a fairly decent 3.89 ERA.

Sources

Besides the sources cited in the Notes, the author also consulted Baseball-Reference.com and Retrosheet.org.

Notes

1 Anthony McCarron, "Where Are They Now? Former Met Anthony Young Emerges a Real Winner," *New York Daily News*, January 3, 2009
2 Rory Costello, "Anthony Young," SABR Biography Project, sabr.org, accessed December 25, 2016.
3 Ibid.
4 Jennifer Frey, "Besieged 465 Days, Young Finally Breaks Free," *New York Times*, July 29, 1993.

FIRST REGULAR-SEASON GAME BETWEEN THE METS AND THE YANKEES

JUNE 16, 1997: NEW YORK METS 6, NEW YORK YANKEES 0, AT YANKEE STADIUM

By Bruce Slutsky

The New York City subway system, established in 1904, brings millions of people each day to their respective destinations. New Yorkers are much more dependent on public transportation than residents of other cities. Ballparks including Ebbets Field, the Polo Grounds, Yankee Stadium, and Citi Field were located close to subway stations. The term "Subway Series" referred to regular-season or World Series games between two New York City teams.

For four decades after the Dodgers and Giants moved to the West Coast in 1958, there was a void in New York City baseball. There was a Subway Series every time the Dodgers and Giants played in the regular season, but big games happened when two New York teams met in the World Series. The last such World Series was in 1956, when the Yankees beat the Dodgers in seven games. After the Mets were born in 1962, they would occasionally play the Yankees in spring-training games in Florida.

George Steinbrenner just hated it when the Yankees lost to the Mets in a spring exhibition game. On one occasion Steinbrenner screamed at Billy Martin after a loss to the Mets. They took their confrontation to the trainer's room, where Martin splashed ice water on club President Gabe Paul, an innocent bystander.[1]

The Mayor's Trophy Game was started in 1946 as an exhibition with the Yankees playing the Dodgers or Giants.[2] Its aim was to raise money for the New York City Amateur Baseball Federation, which included sandlot baseball programs. It ended when the Dodgers and Giants moved to California in 1958, but was revived in 1963. Fans of both teams liked the matchup, but the series ended in 1983 as scheduling issues were cited as the reason for its demise. Over its 19-year run, more than $2 million was raised for the charities.

Instead of playing the game, the two clubs simply donated money to the organizations.

In 1997 for the first time, teams in the National and American Leagues would play one another in the regular season.[3] The motivation for this major change may have been to help bring back fans lost after the strike of 1994-95. During interleague play the designated-hitter rule would apply only in the American League ballpark. For the first five years of interleague play, each division played against the same division in the other league, in an effort to promote local rivalries. In later years interleague play was modified so that teams in different divisions would meet, but local rivalries would be continued.

Interleague play began on Friday, June 12, 1997, with a slate of four games. On this first weekend the Mets played the Boston Red Sox at Shea Stadium and the Yankees faced the Florida Marlins in Miami. Would this be a novelty, or would it continue for many years to come? The attendance for these first games were higher than earlier games that season.[4]

On this date the Yankees had a record of 36-27 and were in second place in the American League East trailing the Baltimore Orioles by seven games. The Mets were in third place with a record of 35-28, trailing the National League East-leading Atlanta Braves by 6½ games.

The first Mets-Yankees Subway Series game featured Dave Mlicki (Mets) and Andy Pettitte (Yankees) as the starting pitchers with Bobby Valentine (Mets) and Joe Torre (Yankees) as the managers. Butch Huskey was the first DH for the Mets. Since the game was played at Yankee Stadium before a crowd of 56,188, the Mets had to be considered the underdog. The winner of this three-game series would get bragging rights in the Big Apple for one year.

The Mets meant business as they scored two runs in the first inning, driven in by a double by John Olerud and a single by Butch Huskey. A third run was scored by Todd Hundley on a double steal. In the seventh inning, Olerud came through again, driving in two runs with a single to left field. Pettitte was ineffective as he allowed five earned runs and eight hits in seven innings. Bernard Gilkey drove in Matt Franco with the Mets' sixth run in the ninth inning off Yankees reliever Graeme Lloyd.

Journeyman pitcher Mlicki, who was at best mediocre earlier in the season, struck out eight and walked only two gaining a complete-game, 6-0 shutout. The Yankees got eight hits off Mlicki but were 0-for-11 with runners in scoring position. Three of their hits came in the bottom of the ninth, when Charlie Hayes singled (but was thrown out trying to reach second base), Mark Whiten singled (but was thrown out at second base on Chad Curtis's grounder to third base), and a single to center by Joe Girardi. That brought up Derek Jeter with two on and two outs. Jeter was called out on strikes.

Mlicki had a real sharp curveball that night and specifically remembered the last one he threw to Derek Jeter to end the game. Jeter, who took two third strikes, said, "Mlicki pretty much pitched perfect. Every time we had a runner in scoring position he pitched well."[5]

The Mets could brag about beating the Yankees in a "real game" for only one day as the Yankees won the next two. In 1997 there was only one three-game series at Yankee Stadium. In 1998 the subway series games were played at Shea Stadium. In succeeding years the series was expanded to four or six games with each team hosting a series. Of course, the ultimate subway series between the Mets and Yankees was the World Series of 2000, which the Yankees won in five games. Through 2017 the two teams have played 112 times, with the Yankees winning 66 and the Mets 46.

Interleague play and the subway series continue until at least 2018. In later years there was some discussion of the significance of each. In a 2011 interview, Dave Mlicki was surprised that the subway series was still such a big deal.[6]

Sources

In addition to the sources mentioned in the Notes, the author consulted baseball-reference.com and retrosheet.org.

Notes

1 Murray Chass, "After 40 Years, It's New York at New York," *New York Times*, June 15, 1997. Accessed January 14, 2018. nytimes.com/1997/06/16/sports/after-40-years-it-s-new-york-at-new-york.html.
2 Jim Snedeker, "The rise and Demise of the Mayor's Trophy Game," Ultimate Mets Database – Mayor's Trophy Games. Accessed January 13, 2018. ultimatemets.com/mayorstrophy.php.
3 "Interleague History," Major League Baseball. Accessed January 13, 2018. mlb.mlb.com/mlb/history/interleague/.
4 Associated Press, "Interleague Play's a Hit for Owners' Pocketbooks," DeseretNews.com, June 16, 1997. Accessed January 14, 2018. deseretnews.com/article/566660/Interleague-plays-a-hit-for-owners-pocketbooks.html.
5 Murray Chass, "The First Brag Belongs to Mlicki and the Mets," *New York Times*, June 16, 1997. Accessed January 13, 2018. nytimes.com/1997/06/17/sports/the-first-brag-belongs-to-mlicki-and-the-mets.html.
6 Jeff Bradley, "Bradley: As Mets Met Yankees in 1997, Dave Mlicki Stole Show When Spotlight Was Brightest," *Star-Ledger* (Newark) at NJ.com, May 21, 2011. Accessed January 13, 2018. nj.com/mets/index.ssf/2011/05/bradley_as_mets_met_yankees_in.html.

NOT QUITE DEAD AND BURIED

SEPTEMBER 13, 1997: NEW YORK METS 9, MONTREAL EXPOS 6 (11 INNINGS), AT SHEA STADIUM

By Steven C. Weiner

The walk-off home run is the most dramatic and exhilarating of all baseball plays. As in any written account of such a conclusion, the writer need not worry about spoiling the ending. On this day, the Mets beat the Montreal Expos in 11 innings on Bernard Gilkey's pinch-hit two-out home run. The *New York Times* reporter, Jason Diamos, captured the state of the team two innings earlier. "The Mets were dead and buried. They were done, plain and simple. They were ready for next year, beginning right now. But then came one of the more improbable bottom of the ninths in the team's 36 seasons."[1] With a comeback and a game-winning homer, their faint hopes for catching the Florida Marlins and a Wild Card berth remained alive entering the final two weeks of the season.

The Mets had lost a long and difficult 15-inning game to the Expos, 3-2, less than 24 hours earlier to remain 5 ½ games behind Florida. As *The New York Times* put it, "They seemed hung over, showing nothing on the mound, in the field or at bat as [the] game slowly moved along."[2] For eight innings, they had managed only one hit off Montreal starter Dustin Hermanson. It came on Carlos Mendoza's bloop single to left field in the bottom of the sixth inning – his first major-league hit.

Meanwhile, the Expos got off to a fast start and a 3-0 lead in the first inning against Jason Isringhausen. Mike Lansing hit a two-run homer, his 20th of the season, after Mark Grudzielanek singled. The Expos added two more in the fifth inning on David Segui's double and a single run in the eighth inning courtesy of Darrin Fletcher's sacrifice fly. Most, if not all, of the 24,208 fans at Shea Stadium thought that this lead was insurmountable.

Then came the bottom of the ninth. A tiring Hermanson yielded one-out singles to Butch Huskey and Carlos Baerga before Brian McRae flied out to deep right-center.[3] Hermanson was near the finish line, but ran out of gas against pinch-hitter Roberto Petagine. His 129th (and last) pitch of the game, on a 1-2 count, was lined to center field. Huskey and Baerga scored to cut the Expos' margin to 6-2.[4] Shayne Bennett replaced Hermanson, and faced one batter, Luis Lopez, who singled through the right-side hole. That compelled manager Felipe Alou to go to his closer, Ugueth Urbina, who secured

Bernard Gilkey's first year in New York (1996) resulted in 44 doubles—setting a single-season club record—as well as 30 homers, 117 runs batted in, and a .317 batting average.

his 26th save last night. A repeat was not to be. Matt Franco singled up the middle to load the bases. Carl Everett came to the plate in a run-producing slump – having driven in only three runs in the last 43 days.[5] He teased everyone on Urbina's first-pitch changeup with a deep shot that was 20 feet wide of the right-field foul pole. On a full count, Everett saw another Urbina changeup and straightened it out. It went deep off the base of the scoreboard in right and, just as suddenly, the score was tied.[6] After Urbina got Edgardo Alfonzo on a swinging strikeout, it was extra innings for the second game in a row. Six runs on six hits to knot the score at six – and more drama yet to come.

So what was Bernard Gilkey doing all this time? He played all 15 innings the night before, getting two hits in the loss, but slightly sprained his left ankle. He scratched himself from the starting lineup just before the late afternoon start. Diamos reported that Gilkey about the time of the sixth inning emerged from the Mets' training room where he had been submerged in a whirlpool.[7] Perhaps manager Bobby Valentine would use him as a pinch-hitter.

Mets closer, John Franco, also made an appearance. He managed to get out of the 10th inning by inducing a Vladimir Guerrero groundout to strand David Segui at third base. "They wanted to take me out after the 10th," Franco remarked. "I said no. They were either going to win with me or lose with me. When I went out to start the inning, Gilk told me to go out, finish this inning, and he was going to end it. And he sure enough did."[8] The Expos' 11th inning was much the same as the 10th. With one out and Ryan McGuire on second, Franco struck out Mark Grudzielanek looking, intentionally walked Mike Lansing, and got Jose Vidro on a ground ball.

Gilkey's time was approaching. Brian McRae led off the 11th inning by singling to left field off southpaw Steve Kline. Alberto Castillo sacrificed McRae to second base, Luis Lopez walked, and Matt Franco struck out on three pitches. Why had Valentine used a left-handed hitter against the southpaw? Diamos noted that "Valentine thought about pinch-hitting Gilkey right there, but didn't want to risk the chance of a double play because of Gilkey's ankle."[9] At that point, it was right-hander Mike Thurman who came in to face Gilkey, who was batting for John Franco. Gilkey took one pitch before hammering the next into the left field mezzanine seats. The improbable was complete. For Gilkey, this walk-off homer was the second of his career, five years after his first one.[10]

This remarkable comeback evoked memories of 1973. On July 17 of that year, the visiting Mets also erased a six-run deficit in the ninth inning – capped by Willie Mays' two-run single – for an 8-7 victory over the Atlanta Braves.[11] Jason Diamos recalled "Ya Gotta Believe" courtesy of Tug McGraw and the Mets run in 1973 to the National League flag. "For the Mets, who have nothing to lose, it's not a bad slogan to dust off right now."[12] History shows that New York fell short in the final two weeks of the 1997 season, but until they had no more outs on this day, they would not quite be dead and buried.

Sources

In addition to the references cited in the Notes, the author also accessed Baseball-Reference.com and Retrosheet.org.

Notes

1 Jason Diamos, "Down by 6-0 in 9th With One Strike Left, Mets Pull Out a Victory," *New York Times*, September 14, 1997: SP1.
2 Ibid.
3 Huskey's only hit of the game extended his hitting streak to 20-games. Over that period, he batted .363 with 29 hits.
4 That single was Roberto Petagine's only hit in 15 official at-bats for the entire 1997 season.
5 Marty Noble, "Playing Hardball," *The Sporting News*, September 29, 1997: 36.
6 Carl Everett's grand slam was his second of the season and he would hit eight grand slams over his 14-year major-league career, but none more dramatic. The irony was that his very next grand slam came in a Houston Astros uniform on June 20, 1999 in the Astros' 11-3 victory over Montreal. The Expos victim was none other than Ugueth Urbina.
7 Diamos.
8 Ibid.
9 Ibid.
10 Bernard Gilkey's only other walk-off home run in his 12-year major-league career came on July 29, 1992 at Busch Stadium in St. Louis. Gilkey hit a three-run home run off Dennis Martinez as the Cardinals beat the first-place Montreal Expos, 4-1.
11 Michael Strauss, "Mets Win on 7 in 9th, 8-7; Aaron Homers," *New York Times*, July 18, 1973: 25-26. Rusty Staub and John Milner each hit two-run homers off Carl Morton to cut the Braves' lead to 7-5. Adrian Devine replaced Morton and managed to get the second out on a grounder before the roof fell in on him, as well. A single by Don Hahn and a walk to Ed Kranepool positioned Jim Beauchamp to drive in the next run with a single to right field. Willie Mays pinch hit for Wayne Garrett, facing the next Expos pitcher, Tom House, and delivered a two-run single. After the seven-run, eight-hit ninth inning, Harry Parker retired the Braves 1-2-3 for the save and the Mets' improbable comeback victory.
12 Diamos.

METS KEEP PACE WITH CUBS AS PIAZZA, HUNDLEY HOMER

SEPTEMBER 16, 1998: NEW YORK METS 4, HOUSTON ASTROS 3, AT THE ASTRODOME

By Mike Wuest

In front of a crowd of over 24,000, the New York Mets stole a game from the Houston Astros that they desperately needed to win in order to keep their hopes of earning a wild-card berth alive.

The game, which took just over four hours to complete and saw the Mets take three of four from the Astros, kept the Mets (86-68) a half-game back of the Chicago Cubs (86-67) in the National League wild-card chase and came about in dramatic fashion thanks to late-inning home runs by future Hall of Fame catcher Mike Piazza and the man he replaced when he was traded to the Mets in a "perfect storm of things coming together" from the Florida Marlins, former catcher Todd Hundley.[1]

Both starting pitchers found success early in the game, as neither the Mets' Bobby Jones nor the Astros' Mike Hampton gave up any runs. However, each pitcher issued two walks, and Hampton committed a balk, giving the early innings slightly more excitement than they otherwise would have featured.

The high point of the first two innings for the Astros came when seven-time All-Star second baseman Craig Biggio stole second and third in the first inning. The two steals gave him 49 for the season to date and eclipsed his career high of 47 in 1997.

The Houston fans found more to get excited about as Mets starter Bobby Jones gave up two runs in the third inning after walking Biggio, getting right fielder Richard Hidalgo to ground out, then giving up a home run to Carl Everett. Everett's homer, to deep right field, was his 15th of the season.

After the home run, Jones settled down and, while he walked five batters, he did not give up another run during his eight innings pitched. He struck out five.

For the Astros, starter Mike Hampton had an interesting night, walking six and striking out four during his time on the mound. He never had a calm inning, allowing at least one baserunner each inning and giving up eight hits. He offset that by inducing four double plays, keeping the Mets off the scoreboard during his eight innings of work.

The most nerve-wracking inning for Hampton was the fourth, when an error by Astros shortstop Tim Bogar allowed Mets center fielder Brian McRae to reach base. After walking right fielder Butch Huskey, Hampton got two quick outs, striking out second baseman Carlos Baerga and inducing shortstop Rey Ordonez to ground out. However, he then walked pitcher Jones to load the bases for the leadoff hitter, left fielder Tony Phillips. Hampton got Phillips to ground out to short, ending the bases-loaded threat and keeping the Astros on top.

Neither Jones nor Hampton wound up with a decision for their work in the evening's game.

The action picked up in the top of the ninth inning when Astros closer Billy Wagner, in relief og Hampton, gave up a leadoff single to pinch-hitter Todd Pratt. Wagner struck out Tony Phillips and got Edgardo Alfonzo to fly out to right fielder Richard Hidalgo. But John Olerud hit a two-out single, setting the scene for Piazza, who, on a 2-and-2 count, took a pitch over the center-field wall for a three-run home run, his 32nd homer of the season, giving the Mets the lead. Wagner then struck out McRae to end the inning. This was Wagner's fourth blown save of the season.

In the bottom half of the inning, Mets reliever Dennis Cook got Ricky Gutierrez to fly out to right field before giving up a tying home run to Astros catcher Brad Ausmus. Ausmus's homer, which went to deep left field, was his sixth of the season. Cook then struck out both Tim Bogar and Billy Wagner to send the game to extra innings.

In the top of the 10th, Wagner gave up a leadoff single to Jermaine Allensworth, who moved to second on a throwing error by left fielder Moises Alou. Luis Lopez, a second baseman who was subbed into the game, bunted Allensworth to third. Allensworth held third as Rey Ordonez grounded to second, and Matt Franco, playing first base as a defensive replacement, struck out to end the inning, stranding Allensworth.

In the bottom of the 10th Mets reliever Greg McMichael walked three (one intentional) after two outs, but struck out Ricky Gutierrez to end the inning.

In the 11th, Sean Bergman took over for Wagner and got two quick outs, Tony Phillips on a fly ball to right field, and Edgardo Alfonzo on a groundball to second. Todd Hundley, the former Mets catcher who was relegated to the bench after Piazza was acquired from the Marlins, pinch-hitter for McMichael. Hundley swung on a 2-and-0 pitch and put his last home run as a member of the Mets into the stands to give the Mets the lead. Piazza struck out to end the inning.

In the bottom of the inning, Mets reliever Turk Wendell struck out Brad Ausmus, Dave Clark, and Russ Johnson on 16 pitches to end the game and give the Mets their 86th win of the season.

Said Hundley of his winning blast, "I knew when I hit it I got it. … I was just trying to hit the ball hard and not pull it off. My numbers in this place are brutal. I hate this place."[2]

The four-game series between the Mets and the Astros prompted Amazin' Avenue blogger to proclaim it "my favorite regular season series I have watched since being a fan."[3]

The win moved the Mets to 6-4 in their last 10 games. The Astros also moved to 6-4 over their last 10, but won the season series with the Mets, 5 games to 4. The Astros stood at 97-57 for the season and remained in first place in the National League Central Division.

Sources

In addition to the sources cited in the Notes, the author consulted Baseball-Reference.com and Retrosheet.

Notes

1 Anthony McCarron, "Eight Amazin' Days: Oral History of The Trade That Sent Mike Piazza From the Dodgers to the Marlins to the Mets," *New York Daily News*, July 22, 2016, nydailynews.com/sports/baseball/mets/amazin-days-oral-history-piazza-trade-route-mets-article-1.2721781. Accessed January 21, 2018.
2 Jason Diamos, "Baseball; Latest Script: Hundley and Piazza Both Do It," *New York Times*, September 17, 1998, nytimes.com/1998/09/17/sports/baseball-latest-script-hundley-and-piazza-both-do-it.html. Accessed January 21, 2018.
3 Daniel Convery, "A Torrid Summer Love Affair and Heartbreak: An Existential Love Letter to the 1998 Mets," SBNation.com, May 10, 2016, amazinavenue.com/2016/5/10/11653974/a-torrid-summer-love-affair-and-heartbreak-an-existential-love-letter. Accessed January 21, 2018.

MATT FRANCO SINGLES OFF MARIANO RIVERA FOR A WALK-OFF WIN

JULY 10, 1999: NEW YORK METS 9, NEW YORK YANKEES 8, AT SHEA STADIUM

By Kevin Larkin

The Mayor's Trophy games began in 1946 as a way for the three New York teams to meet on the playing field. It was an in-season exhibition game originally for the Yankees and Giants, with the Brooklyn Dodgers being added to the mix as well. The series ended in 1955 and was played one more year, 1957, and then discontinued after the Giants and the Dodgers moved to the West Coast. The Yankees finished the series with a record of 10 wins and 3 losses, the Giants had 1 win and 7 losses, and the Dodgers had a record of 2 wins and 3 losses.

From 1963 to 1979 and in 1982 and 1983 the Yankees and the Mets resumed the series with the final standings of this part of the series being Yankees 10 wins, Mets 8 wins, and one tie. George Steinbrenner, who bought the Yankees in 1973 from CBS, hated losing to the Mets and considered them a big threat to the Yankees in the view of New Yorkers.[1]

As the teams prepared to meet on July 10, 1999, the Yankees were in first place in the American League East by three games over the second-place Boston Red Sox. The Mets were in second place in the National League East, trailing the Atlanta Braves by four games. The starters for the teams on July 10 were left-hander Andy Pettitte for the Yankees and right-hander Rick Reed for the Mets.

Chuck Knoblauch led off for the Yankees and grounded out. After a single by Bernie Williams, Paul O'Neill hit a home run to put the Yankees up 2-0. Reed struck out Derek Jeter and walked Tino Martinez, then got Scott Brosius to fly to center field for the final out of the Yankees' half of the inning.

The Mets got a run back in their half of the inning when Rickey Henderson singled, stole second base, and scored on Mike Piazza's double to left field. At the end of the first inning, it was 2-1 Yankees.

In the third, Reed struck out Ricky Ledee, Jorge Posada, and his mound counterpart Andy Pettitte. For the Mets, Roger Cedeno walked with one out, stole second and then third, and scored on a sacrifice fly. After Reed lined out for the third out, the game was tied 2-2.

Bobby Valentine often called on Matt Franco in key pinch-hit situations. And often, he delivered—just like he did on July 9, 1999 against the Yankees.

It was a relatively easy inning for Reed and the Mets in the third; Knoblauch singled and was caught stealing after Williams and O'Neill made outs. Rickey Henderson walked for the Mets, but was picked off trying to steal second. Edgardo Alfonzo flied out to center. John Olerud walked and was forced at second base on a ball hit by Mike Piazza and the score remained tied.

Reed got the Yankees 1-2-3 in the fourth on two groundouts and a popout. The Mets got to Pettitte in the bottom of the inning when Benny Agbayani singled and scored on Robin Ventura's double. Cedeno sacrificed Ventura to third, and Ventura scored on Ordonez's fly to right field, and the Mets were on top, 4-2.

The Yankees lived up to their nickname of "Bronx Bombers" (a name given to the 1936 Yankees by sportswriter Dan Daniel of the *New York World Telegram*[2]) as Ledee and Posada hit back-to-back home runs to open the fifth inning and O'Neill homered to lead off the sixth inning. That gave the Yankees a 5-4 lead after the Mets offense could not muster any runs in either the fifth or sixth innings.

Pettitte made short work of the Mets in the bottom of the sixth inning, getting Ventura, Cedeno, and Ordonez to ground out. In the top of the seventh inning, Knoblauch hit the Yankees' fifth home run of the game to put the Yankees up, 6-4.

The Mets showed some muscle at the plate in the bottom of the seventh inning. Henderson doubled to right field with one out. Alfonzo lined out to right field, then John Olerud walked. Mike Piazza, the next Mets hitter, slammed the team's only home run of the game, giving the Mets a lead of 7-6. Piazza said, "That's about as well as you can hit a ball."[3]

In the Yankees' eighth, Scott Brosius walked to lead off. Chad Curtis flied out to center field. Posada hit his second home run of the game and the sixth for the Yankees, putting them up, 8-7.

The Yankees had a "ace up their sleeve" in the person of Mariano Rivera, who had taken over the closer role from John Wetteland. Rivera had so far saved 106 regular-season games. As of his last appearance, Rivera had allowed only eight runs in 33 appearances. He was as close to being automatic as possible.

The Mets did not score in the bottom of the eighth and the Yankees could not add to the lead in the top of the ninth. In the bottom of the inning it was "Enter Sandman,"[4] with Rivera coming in for the save opportunity. He got McRae to ground out but walked Henderson and gave up a double to Alfonzo, putting runners at second and third. Olerud's grounder was the second out of the inning. Mike Piazza was walked to load the bases with two outs. Matt Franco pinch-hit for Melvin Mora and hit a single to right field that scored Henderson and Alfonzo. Rivera took the loss on Franco's single. After the game Franco said, "Without a doubt this is the biggest moment of my career so far."[5]

The Mets finished the year in second place in the National League East with a record of 97 wins and 66 losses, 6½ games behind the division-winning Atlanta Braves. The Yankees won the American League East by four games over the Boston Red Sox and then went on to defeat the Rangers and Red Sox on the way to a World Series title by beating the Atlanta Braves.

Sources

In addition to the sources cited in the Notes, the author consulted Baseball-Reference.com and Retrosheet.org.

Notes
1 Harold Friend, "George Steinbrenner Was Right to Fear the Mets as Much as the Red Sox," bleacherreport.com, bleacherreport.com/articles/1035255, January 23, 2013.
2 sportingcharts.com/dictionary/mlb/bronx-bombers.
3 Brian Heyman, *Courier News* (Bridgewater, New Jersey), July 11, 1990: 140.
4 The heavy-metal rock band Metallica had released the song "Enter Sandman" in 1991 as the first song on their fifth album. It quickly became a hit and was played at Yankee Stadium when Mariano Rivera came into a game.
5 James Diamos, "Piazza an All-Star Starter as Ordonez Hopes for Bid," *New York Times*, July 7, 1999: D3.

WIN OR GO HOME: RINSE, REPEAT

OCTOBER 3, 1999: NEW YORK METS 2, PITTSBURGH PIRATES 1, AT SHEA STADIUM

By Seth Moland-Kovash

As September 1999 ended, Bobby Valentine's New York Mets saw themselves looking up at a very high hill. Bobby Cox's Atlanta Braves were too far ahead to catch in the National League Eastern Division, at eight games ahead of the second-place Mets with three games to play. But the wild card was still a possibility – a narrow possibility, but a possibility. As the final weekend of the season began, the Mets at 93-66 were looking up not only at the far-distant Braves (101-58) but also at a tie situation atop the NL Central featuring the Cincinnati Reds, led by Jack McKeon, and Larry Dierker's Houston Astros for the National League wild card. Both the Reds and Astros sat at 95-64. At the end of play on September 30, the Reds and Astros had a two-game lead on the Mets for that final postseason spot with each team having only three games remaining. It would take a miracle for the Mets to play on.

That weekend, the Mets were set to close out the season at home against the Pittsburgh Pirates (78-80) who were led by Gene Lamont. Meanwhile the Reds were in Milwaukee to face Jim Lefebvre's 72-86 Brewers and the Astros were to play host to the 76-83 Los Angeles Dodgers, who were led by Davey Johnson. On Friday and Saturday, the Mets went 2-0, the Astros went 1-1, and the Reds were 0-2. Heading into Sunday, the Mets created a tie with the Cincinnati Reds for the NL wild card.

The Mets were led by All-Star catcher and eventual Hall of Famer Mike Piazza along with third baseman Robin Ventura, second baseman Edgardo Alfonzo, and first baseman John Olerud. The Mets threw in veterans like aging future Hall of Famer Rickey Henderson and Bobby Bonilla along with many others to fill out the outfield. On the pitching side, the staff was led by ace Al Leiter and closer Armando Benitez.

For Sunday's finale, the Mets were going out behind veteran starter Orel Hershiser. Hershiser, at 40 years old and in his only season with the Mets, posted a fielding independent pitching (FIP) rate of 4.63. This was respectable, but nowhere near the dominance of the 1980s Dodgers' Hershiser. Meanwhile the Pirates took the field behind 24-year-old rookie Kris Benson, who posted a FIP of 4.14 in his first year, good enough for fourth place in National League Rookie of the Year voting.

The game started at 1:40 in front of 50,111 spectators[1] on a lovely early fall day in New York with scattered clouds and a warmer-than-average game time temperature of 70 degrees. The Reds game in Milwaukee was being delayed because of rain.

The Pirates played small ball in the top of the first inning, which began with a five-pitch walk to left fielder Al Martin. After a sacrifice and a nonproductive groundout, Martin found himself on second base with two outs with cleanup hitter Kevin Young coming to the plate. Young, with a 1999 OPS of .908 and 105 RBIs coming into the game, was a threat to cash in the opportunity. Martin helped him out by stealing third on the second pitch of the at-bat. Young did not disappoint, lining the ball into center field for an RBI single. But that was all the Pirates could produce in the first.

The pitchers settled in and traded scoreless innings through the top of the fourth. In the bottom of the fourth, the Mets got something going thanks to an error by Kevin Young at first base allowing John Olerud to reach. Olerud would later score on a double by center fielder Darryl Hamilton,[2] and the game was tied. The middle innings continued with no further damage.

In the top of the sixth inning, Valentine began to pull the managerial strings. After Hershiser gave up a one-out double to Al Martin, lefty Dennis Cook came in to face the switch-hitting Abraham Nunez and lefty Brant Brown. After Nunez struck out, Pirates skipper Lamont swapped switch-hitting Adrian Brown in for Brant Brown. Adrian Brown earned a walk and Valentine came back out. This time he went to Pat Mahomes with the tough assignment of facing Kevin Young with men on first and second to keep the game tied. In a six-pitch at-bat, Mahomes won out, getting Young to swing and miss for the final out of the top of the sixth and preserve the tie.

Benson faced his own trouble in the bottom of the sixth, loading the bases on two singles (by Ventura and Hamilton) and a walk to Rey Ordonez. Utilityman Matt Franco pinch-hit for the pitchers' spot with the bases loaded and two outs. Franco popped out in foul territory to Pirates third baseman Aramis Ramirez to end the inning.

Both pitching staffs kept things quiet through the top of the ninth with no more major scoring chances. The Pirates would lean on Benson through seven innings and Jason Christiansen for a mostly quiet Mets eighth inning. The Mets, on the other hand, followed Mahomes with Turk Wendell for the seventh and eighth innings and to start the top of the ninth. After a two-out double switch brought Armando Benitez in to pitch for the Mets and Shane Halter to play right field, Benitez struck out Ramirez, ending a ninth-inning threat.

The bottom of the ninth opened with Greg Hansell being brought on to face the 9-1-2 places in the Mets' batting order. Bobby Bonilla, the 36-year-old former All-Star, pinch-hit for Halter to start the inning. Bonilla had had only 140 plate appearances thus far and had only a .584 OPS. Bonilla grounded out to first base and Melvin Mora[3] came to the plate. Mora got something started with a single to right field. Alfonzo followed with another single and Mora took third base on the ball hit to right. The Pirates put the still-dangerous John Olerud on first base intentionally. The bases were now loaded with one out for Mike Piazza. Despite Piazza's 0-for-4 so far, things would seem to be looking good for the Mets, with their All-Star leader at the plate with the opportunity to win the game.

Pirates manager Lamont brought in bullpen regular Brad Clontz[4] to face Piazza. Clontz, a side-armer, had a good career track record against Piazza, with Piazza entering the plate appearance 1-for-6 lifetime. With his first pitch to Piazza, Clontz uncorked a wild pitch! He threw a slider that cut way too much for catcher Joe Oliver to handle. The ball sailed "nearly into the Mets' dugout,"[5] allowing Mora to score from third and the Mets to win in one of the more bizarre walk-off wins in team history.

After the celebration, attention turned to Milwaukee, where the Reds also won, finishing off the Brewers, 7-1, in a game marked by a rain delay of nearly six hours.[6] Thus the 1999 season ended with the Mets and Reds tied at 96-66. The Mets beat the Reds the next day, 5-0, with Leiter going the distance and giving up only two hits. They would then go on to beat the Arizona Diamondbacks three games to one in the National League Division Series before succumbing to the Atlanta Braves in six games in the National League Championship Series. All those extra games were able to happen because of the persistence of that Mets team, the legs of Melvin Mora, and a wild one thrown by Brad Clontz.

Sources

In addition to the sources cited in notes, the author also used Baseball-Reference.com and Retrosheet.org.

Notes

1 This was the Mets' 10th biggest crowd of the year.
2 Hamilton had come over from the Colorado Rockies as the centerpiece of a July 31 five-player deal and had paid off for the Mets, hitting for a .339/.410/.488 slash line.
3 Mora had come into the game in the seventh inning as a pinch-runner/defensive replacement for the future Hall of Fame speedster Rickey Henderson. Henderson injured his knee in the seventh legging out a single to right. Mora was a rookie speedster who would have some very good years later in his career for the Baltimore Orioles. His introduction to the big leagues had been rough, however, as he had an on-base percentage of just .278 in his 39 plate appearances in 1999.
4 Clontz had appeared in 55 games up to this point for the Pirates, with only 49⅓ innings pitched as he was often used in specialized roles. In that time, he had been quite effective, earning a 4.74 FIP and an ERA+ of 170.
5 Wallace Mathews, "Mets' Wild Ending Gets Piazza Off the Hot Seat," *New York Post*, October 4, 1999.
6 Kevin Kernan, "Soggy Reds Slosh Way to Playoff," *New York Post*, October 4, 1999.

BACK FROM THE BRINK, RESOURCEFUL METS WIN

OCTOBER 5, 1999: NEW YORK METS 8, ARIZONA DIAMONDBACKS 4, AT BANK ONE BALLPARK

GAME ONE OF THE 1999 NATIONAL LEAGUE DIVISION SERIES

By Joel Rippel

Even though they were making their first postseason appearance in more than a decade, the New York Mets were ready for the pressure of Game One of their National League Division Series against the Arizona Diamondbacks.

Four must-win games over the previous four days had prepared them for the postseason.

"Since we've been through it in the last few days, it's not going to get any harder from here," Mets pitcher Kenny Rogers said. "We already felt like we were at the bottom, and I think it prepared us for the playoffs. We were basically in a playoff atmosphere for the last four days."[1]

With less than two weeks left in the regular season, the Mets trailed NL East Division-leading Atlanta by one game and had a four-game lead over the Cincinnati Reds in the wild-card race. The Mets then slumped with a seven-game losing streak that left them two games behind in the wild-card race going into the final weekend of the regular season.

The Mets regrouped to sweep a three-game series from Pittsburgh at Shea Stadium – winning two of the games by one run –to finish in a tie with Cincinnati for the wild-card spot. In a one-game tie-breaker – the second consecutive season a one-game playoff decided the NL wild-card spot – the Mets defeated the Reds in Cincinnati to earn their first postseason berth since 1988.

The four consecutive victories salvaged a postseason berth for the Mets after an early-season slump had almost derailed the season. An eight-game losing streak in late May and early June had left them one game under .500 and led to the firing of three coaches. But the Mets recovered and had the best winning percentage in the NL over the next two months.

"We've come back from devastating things twice," said Mets pitcher Orel Hershiser.[2]

The first game of the Division Series featured the Mets, playing their third game in three different cities in less than 72 hours, and the well-rested Diamondbacks, managed by former Yankees manager Buck Showalter. The Diamondbacks, the first expansion team to

Perhaps the most underrated player in franchise history, Edgardo Alfonzo led the team in both 1999 and 2000 while batting .292 for his Mets career.

reach the playoffs in its second year of existence, had won the NL West with a 100-62 record, 14 games ahead of second-place San Francisco. The Diamondbacks, who had gone 65-97 in their inaugural season, had clinched the division title on September 24, with nine games remaining in the regular season.

For the second time in two days, Edgardo Alfonzo provided the spark for the Mets. Alfonzo, who had homered in the first inning of the Mets victory over the Reds in the tiebreaker, hit a home run on Randy Johnson's sixth pitch of the game to stake the Mets to a 1-0 lead. Alfonzo, who had hit 27 home runs (a franchise single-season record for home runs by a second baseman), then capped the evening with a grand slam with two outs in the ninth inning to lift the Mets to an 8-4 victory.

Mets manager Bobby Valentine, managing in the playoffs for the first time after 1,704 regular-season games, praised his team's resiliency: "Well, you know, they are not just going on adrenaline. We have a lot of talent and a lot of strength and plenty of endurance."[3]

After Alfonzo's first-inning home run, the Mets extended their lead to 3-0 in the third inning on John Olerud's two-run home run – the first home run surrendered by Johnson to a left-handed hitter in two years.

The Diamondbacks, who won seven of the nine regular-season meetings with the Mets, got on the scoreboard in the bottom of the third on Jay Bell's sacrifice fly, but the Mets restored their three-run lead in the fourth when Robin Ventura led off with a double, went to third on a bunt single by Shawon Dunston, and scored on a sacrifice bunt by Rey Ordonez.

As Johnson settled down with four shutout innings, the Diamondbacks forged a tie. Erubiel Durazo's solo home run in the bottom of the fourth pulled the Diamondbacks within 4-2. They tied it in the sixth when Bell led off with a single to right and Luis Gonzalez followed with a two-run home run to chase Mets starter Masato Yoshii.

Ventura opened the top of the ninth with a single to right. Ventura remained at first when Johnson caught Roger Cedeno's bunt attempt, but Ordonez singled to left and Melvin Mora coaxed a walk to load the bases and end Johnson's night.

The first hitter to face reliever Bobby Chouinard was Rickey Henderson. Diamondbacks third baseman Matt Williams made a diving stop on Henderson's groundball and threw home to force Ventura. With two outs Alfonzo stepped to the plate and hit Chouinard's 3-and-1 offering just inside the left-field foul pole to make it 8-4.

"I didn't know if it was a foul or fair ball," said Alfonzo, who had a team-high 191 hits and batted .304 with 108 RBIs during the regular season. "I was waiting, and they said it was fair."[4]

In the bottom of the ninth, Armando Benitez, the third Mets reliever, retired Durazo, Steve Finley, and Hanley Frias in order (on two fly outs and a popup) to save the victory. Dennis Cook, Turk Wendell (the winning pitcher), and Benitez combined for 3⅔ innings of one-hit shutout relief.

For Johnson, it was his sixth consecutive postseason loss – a major-league record. Going into the start, Johnson, whose postseason record fell to 2-6, was tied with Joe Bush (1914-1923) and Doyle Alexander (1973-1987) with five consecutive postseason losses. Johnson threw 138 pitches as he allowed eight hits and seven runs in 8⅓ innings. Johnson, who struck out 364 during the regular season (the fourth highest in major-league history), struck out 11.

Johnson was the first of three Arizona left-handed starting pitchers the Mets would face in the series. The Mets, who were 97-66 (counting the victory in the tiebreaker), were just 22-18 against left-handed starters in the regular season.

"I don't think anybody on our team necessarily thinks that we're a .500 team when we play against a left-hander," Ventura said. "Those numbers don't mean a whole lot once you're here."[5]

Sources

In addition to the sources cited in the Notes, the author also consulted Newspapers.com and Retrosheet.org.

Notes

1 Dan Bickley, "This loss bad omen for D-Backs," *Arizona Republic* (Phoenix), October 6, 1999: C2.
2 Kit Stier, "Built to Win Now, Mets Do Just That," *Journal News* (White Plains, New York), October 5, 1999: 7K.
3 Bickley.
4 Associated Press, "Alfonzo's Slam Lifts Mets," *Minneapolis Star Tribune*, October 6, 1999: C4.
5 Bickley.

JOURNEYMAN TODD PRATT SLAMS METS INTO NLCS

OCTOBER 9, 1999: NEW YORK METS 4, ARIZONA DIAMONDBACKS 3, AT SHEA STADIUM
GAME FOUR OF THE 1999 NATIONAL LEAGUE DIVISION SERIES

By Cosme Vivanco

On January 26, 1997, the New England Patriots and the Green Bay Packers played in Super Bowl XXXI in front of a jam-packed Louisiana Superdome. At a South Florida Domino's Pizza, a full crew was processing about a thousand orders in a three-hour period to football fans anxious to see the two best football teams in the NFL battle for supremacy. The shift manager for that evening was a former major-league baseball player named Todd Pratt. In his former life, Pratt played four seasons in the big leagues, hitting just nine home runs in total. After being released by the Seattle Mariners, Pratt went unsigned. He would step away from the game he loved to work as an instructor at Bucky Dent's baseball school.

While working as an instructor, Pratt met a local entrepreneur who persuaded him that teaching baseball wasn't a feasible means of income. "So I spent a summer there and the guy who used to feed the kids there was a young entrepreneur, and owned 20 Domino's in South Florida. Actually 20/20 Pizza was his business. And he was asking me what I was going to do with my life and I said I don't know what I'm going to do yet. He told me, well, you can't be doing this, you've got to get serious about something and he said why don't you come work for me," Pratt said.[1] To a reasonable person, going from playing major-league baseball to managing a Domino's Pizza was an incredible fall from grace. But Todd Pratt never saw it that way.

"If I had to go back to it, I could," Pratt said. "There's nothing wrong with managing a pizza parlor."[2]

On October 9, 1999, Todd Pratt found himself in another high-pressure situation – only this time he was back doing what he loved: playing major-league baseball.

The 1999 New York Mets finished the regular season by losing eight of their last 12 games. During that stretch they went 1-8 against the Atlanta Braves and Philadelphia Phillies. The Mets finished with a 96-66 record, good enough to tie with the Cincinnati Reds for the NL wild-card. On Monday, October 4, the day after the season ended, the Mets and Reds played a tiebreaker at Cincinnati's Cinergy Field to determine the wild-card winner. The Mets, behind a two-hit shutout from left-handed pitcher Al Leiter, clinched the wild card with a 5-0 victory.

In their second season of existence, the Arizona Diamondbacks made a dramatic leap from their inaugural campaign. They signed left-handed ace Randy Johnson out of free agency and, true to form, he paid off on their investment. Johnson led all National League pitchers with a 2.48 ERA and 364 strikeouts while walking only 70. Johnson's incredible season led him to the first of his four consecutive Cy Young Awards. The Diamondbacks went from 65 wins in 1998 to 100 in 1999. They ran way with the NL West title by 14 games.

The Mets and the Diamondbacks battled in the National League Division Series, with the winner to advance to the National League Championship Series. The first two games, in Phoenix, were split. New York won the first game, beating the Diamondbacks and Randy Johnson, 8-4. In the second game, Todd Stottlemyre's solid pitching and Matt Williams's bat engineered the Diamondbacks to a 7-1 victory to even the series. During the offday between Games Two and Three, Mets All-Star catcher Mike Piazza received a cortisone shot to alleviate the pain from a sore left thumb that had been bothering him since late September. Instead of relief, Piazza woke up in horror to find his thumb swollen in a grotesque manner. Doctors told Piazza it would take 48 to 72 hours for the swelling to go down.

Met-rospectives

The prospect of not having their best bat in the lineup was a tough pill for the Mets to swallow. But they managed to make their way through a tough final stretch to earn their first postseason trip since 1988. For Mets backup catcher Todd Pratt, the road back to the majors was an arduous journey. He had to make the dramatic jump from understudy to caretaker of the Mets pitching staff for the rest of the series.

The series shifted to New York for Game Three, which the Mets won with ease, 9-2. They were one game away from winning their first postseason series since the 1986 World Series. For the upstart Diamondbacks, a win in Game Four and the series would back to Arizona for a deciding Game Five with the best pitcher in the National League, Randy Johnson, ready to go.

Something had to give.

Game Four of the NLDS took place on Saturday, October 9, 1999, in front of a crowd of 56,177 at Shea Stadium. The weather was perfect for a Saturday afternoon, 65 degrees and not a cloud in the sky. The Mets sent out Al Leiter, while the Diamondbacks answered with fellow left-hander Brian Anderson. For 3½ innings the two starters were locked in a scoreless pitchers' duel. In the bottom of the fourth, Mets second baseman Edgardo Alfonzo hit a home run off Johnson to give New York a 1-0 edge. With a no-hitter going into the top of the fifth inning, Leiter got Diamondbacks third baseman Matt Williams to fly out to left. Leiter's no-hitter was broken up by first baseman Greg Colbrunn, who tied the game on a home run to left. In the bottom of the sixth, Mets leadoff hitter Rickey Henderson led off with a single. With one out, first baseman John Olerud singled to left and Henderson moved to third. Benny Agbayani singled to right off Brian Anderson to score Henderson and give the Mets the lead once again at 2-1.

In the top of the eighth, Mets manager Bobby Valentine replaced Henderson in left with Melvin Mora as a defensive substitution. With two outs, Leiter walked Turner Ward and gave up a single to shortstop Tony Womack. Armando Benitez relieved Leiter with the Mets an inning away from heading to the NLCS, but Jay Bell's double to left scored both Ward and Womack, and the Diamondbacks were now in the driver's seat with a 3-2 lead. In the bottom of the eighth, Diamondbacks manager Buck Showalter made a defensive switch of his own by moving Tony Womack from shortstop to right field.

The move backfired as Womack dropped a deep drive by Olerud that put runners in scoring position at second and third. Roger Cedeno's fly ball drove in Alfonzo with the tying run. The drama in the eighth didn't cease. Mets third-base coach Cookie Rojas was ejected for shoving left-field foul-line umpire Charlie Williams. Rojas believed that a line drive by Todd Pratt was fair but the replays showed that it was foul by barely an inch. The emotion was reaching a fever pitch. The thoughts of facing Randy Johnson were dancing in the heads of Mets players.

The Arizona Diamondbacks were looking to climb the next ladder in their quest to win the World Series.

With the tight contest reaching the bottom of the 10th inning, Pratt, who was 0-for-7 so far in the NLDS, slugged a 1-and-0 pitch from Diamondbacks closer Matt Mantei over the center-field fence, securing a 4-3 Mets victory over Arizona that catapulted them into the National League Championship Series. The crowd of 56,177 at Shea Stadium went into a fit of euphoria while Mets players were basking in the glory after being considered left for dead toward the end of the regular season.

"We have something special going," Mets manager Bobby Valentine said. "It's a special group of guys. It's going to take a good effort to stop us. The next team is going to play against some ghosts because they said we were dead. I don't know if that team has ever played against ghosts."[3]

Diamondbacks skipper Showalter was struggling to find the words to describe the backbreaking end to a fantastic year. "Unless you've been through … the words to describe this. … My vocabulary is not that good. You win 101 games, whatever, and then you're a spectator."[4]

On a beautiful Saturday afternoon in New York City, Pratt made the most of his second act and propelled himself into baseball lore. And while his teammates thought of him as the hero of the day, Pratt was all too modest. "I am going to kiss my wife, give my son a high-five, and then probably I will be back on my computer playing computer games," he said. "Hey, I could have easily been the goat today."[5]

Sources

In addition to the sources cited in the Notes, the author consulted Baseball-reference.com and retrosheet.org.

Notes

1 Matthew Brownstein, "MMO Exclusive: Former Mets Catcher Todd Pratt," MetsMerizedOnline.com, April 25, 2017.
2 George Vescey, "Todd Pratt Can Stand the Heat," *New York Times*, October 12, 1999.
3 William Gildea, "Mets Look a Little Amazin' in Series Win," *Washington Post*, October 10, 1999.
4 Ibid.
5 Wallace Matthews, "The Journeyman Arrives; No-Name Pratt Now NY Hero," *New York Post*, October 10, 1999.

AFTER FIVE HOURS AND 46 MINUTES ... IT'S BACK TO GEORGIA

OCTOBER 17, 1999: NEW YORK METS 4, ATLANTA BRAVES 3, AT SHEA STADIUM
GAME FIVE OF THE 1999 NATIONAL LEAGUE CHAMPIONSHIP SERIES

By Brian Wright

They spent nearly three weeks walking a tightrope.

By losing eight of nine in a crucial late September stretch – including five times to Atlanta – the Mets went from one game behind the Braves in the National League East standings to eight back. And with it came an unwelcome sense of déjà vu. In 1998, five straight defeats to end the regular season left the Mets one game short of the National League wild card. The only difference in their week-plus meltdown of '99 was that the Mets had time to rectify it. They were two games behind the Cincinnati Reds, but with just three games to play. Chipper Jones, who used his otherworldly performance at New York's expense as a springboard to being named the 1999 National League MVP, was leaving his division rivals for dead. "Now all the Mets' fans can go home and put their Yankees stuff on," he said.[1]

But the Braves would soon realize how many lives the Mets had remaining.

A home sweep of Pittsburgh in the final three games of the regular season coupled with two Reds defeats put New York and Cincinnati in a tie for the final playoff spot and forced a one-game tiebreaker at Cinergy Field. Behind Edgardo Alfonzo's first-inning homer and Al Leiter's nine innings of brilliance on the mound, the Mets prevailed, 5-0. It was off to Arizona for the Division Series, where the Mets split two with the Diamondbacks. New York took Games Three and Four at Shea, the latter on Todd Pratt's walk-off home run.

Some 20 days since the Braves presumably wiped the Mets out of the playoff picture, they were battling for the right to go to the fall classic. But that battle became relatively one-sided, as Atlanta edged New York in each of the first three games to take a commanding series advantage that no team had ever overcome. The Mets, continuing to teeter on the brink, staved off elimination in Game Four with a bottom-of-the-eighth-inning rally.

That drama, though, had nothing on what would transpire the next day and night. A two-run first-inning homer by John Olerud (who delivered Game Four's winning single) off Greg Maddux was countered by a pair of Braves scores in the top of the fourth. From there, the bats went silent. New York manager Bobby Valentine, operating with no margin for error, called on a bevy of bullpen help – beginning with Orel Hershiser. Eleven years earlier, as a Los Angeles Dodger, Hershiser almost single-handedly killed the Mets' pennant hopes. Now, he tried to prolong them – with 3⅓ shutout innings in relief of starter Masato Yoshii.

Robin Ventura launched 18 grand slams throughout his big league career. But it's the grand slam that wasn't that remains his most memorable moment.

Met-rospectives

Seven more New York pitchers followed. Atlanta skipper Bobby Cox used five relievers to back Maddux, who was replaced for a pinch-hitter in the top of the eighth. The 2-2 deadlock persisted into extra innings. As darkness fell over Shea Stadium, so did the rain. Stranded runners (who eventually totaled 31 for both sides) piled up. Run-scoring opportunities went by the wayside – never more so than in the top of the 13th. Chipper Jones appeared to be adding to his "Mets villain" status with a base hit to right field. Keith Lockhart, running on the pitch, attempted to score from first. But Melvin Mora prevented Jones's hit from bouncing to the fence and initiated a relay that got Lockhart out at home by a wide margin.

The Braves broke through in the top of the 15th against Octavio Dotel with the likelihood of finally breaking the Mets' spirits in the process. Lockhart tripled home Walt Weiss from second base to put Atlanta ahead, 3-2. As the rain intensified, the chances dwindled for New York to keep its season alive. That three-week-long tightrope had seemingly frayed to its last straining threads. Three more outs and the Mets' hypnotic, thrilling journey would officially be finished. The Braves thought they had left the Mets for ruin when they pummeled them in late September, when they took a one-run lead in the eighth inning of Game Four, and again tonight.

But then came another encounter with ghosts of miracles past.

To shut the door in the bottom of the 15th, Cox passed on using perhaps his most reliable starting pitcher throughout the regular season, Kevin Millwood, and stayed with a relatively untested Kevin McGlinchy for a second frame. The 22-year-old right-hander battled leadoff hitter Shawon Dunston for nine minutes, 12 pitches, and six foul balls before Dunston singled up the middle. Matt Franco, pinch-hitting for Dotel, worked a walk. Alfonzo, in his ever-understated way, sacrificed both runners 90 feet farther.

With a base open, Olerud – still the lone man responsible for the entirety of the Mets' scoring – got an intentional pass. Pratt, who entered the game when Mike Piazza's strained left forearm wouldn't allow him to continue past the 14th, somehow had the chance to reprise the dramatics of eight days earlier. Yet he played a lesser role here. The rattled McGlinchy walked in the tying run on five pitches.

Bases remained full for a man quite comfortable with this RBI-rich scenario. Robin Ventura, pained yet not sidelined, could send everyone home (and both teams south) with an addition to his 18 career grand slams. "It's different when the bases are loaded and the guy has already walked a guy," said Ventura, who had been 1-for-18 up to this point in the NLCS. "He can't really fool around and throw a bunch of pitches in the dirt. So I'm just trying to get a ball in the air so the guy can score."[2]

Ventura sent McGlinchy's 2-and-1 offering to deep right-center. Deep enough to certainly score the winning run. And, then, deep enough to clear the right-center-field fence. "He scalded that ball," Pratt said. "I knew we had won the game just the way the ball came off the bat. It was just classic for him to come through."[3]

The longest game (at the time) in major-league postseason history, at 5 hours and 46 minutes, had reached a spectacular conclusion. But then came an unusual postscript.

After Ventura touched and rounded first base, he incessantly waved over-enthusiastic teammates away so he could round the bases. But their exuberance was too much to allow their hero to savor a home-run trot. Instead, they mobbed Ventura before he reached second. "As long as I got to first base, I don't care," Ventura said. "It means we won."[4] Because of the human basepath blockade and because he never touched any of the remaining bases, the "Grand Slam Single" was forever cemented in franchise lore. But whether the final score read 4-3 instead of 7-3 was of little consequence to the joyous Mets. They had risen from the dead once more with another life to spare.

"I've been in long games," a mentally drained Valentine said. "But not games where every pitch meant so much."[5]

Sources

In addition to the references cited in the Notes, the author also consulted Baseball-Reference.com, Retrosheet.org, and Ultimatemets.com

Notes

1 "For Braves' Jones, a Personal Link to Shea Stadium." *New York Times*. August 18, 2008: 1.
2 "After 15 Pitchers and 15 Innings, Mets Live." *New York Times*. October 18, 1999: 1.
3 Ibid.
4 *Essential Games of Shea Stadium, 1999 NLCS Game Five*. MLB Official DVD, A&E Home Video, 2008.
5 Ibid.

WALK-OFF WALK IN NLCS ENDS METS' SEASON

OCTOBER 19, 1999: ATLANTA BRAVES 10, NEW YORK METS 9 (11 INNINGS), AT TURNER FIELD

GAME SIX OF THE 1999 NATIONAL LEAGUE CHAMPIONSHIP SERIES

By Jack Zerby

The 1999 New York Mets were no strangers to walk-off wins.1 They had engineered eight of them in the regular season, then walked off on a Todd Pratt home run to close out the Arizona Diamondbacks in four games in the Division Series and advance to the National League Championship Series against the Atlanta Braves. There, they had kept their season alive with a 15-inning, 4-3 walk-off win at Shea Stadium on October 17. That win didn't even the series – the Braves still led three games to two on the strength of victories in the first three games – but for the second game in a row it staved off elimination as the teams returned to Atlanta for Game Six.

Although the Mets had led the National League East Division as late as the morning of August 22, they had had to beat the Cincinnati Reds on the road in an October 4 wild-card tiebreaker game to even make the playoffs.2 The Braves were and had been dominant in the division.3 They won 103 games in the 1999 regular season, taking the division by 6½ games over the Mets; they'd won nine of the 12 games against New York. After losing the first game of their divisional playoff to the Houston Astros, Atlanta eliminated the Astros in three straight, then took three more in a row against the Mets in the League Championship Series. Then the Mets' survival mode kicked in as they won consecutive one-run games, capped by the 5-hour 46-minute walk-off epic two nights before.

Shawon Dunston, Pratt, and Robin Ventura had been the heroes of the season-saving Game Five walk-off. "We feel like we've scored a breakthrough that will hopefully carry over," Mike Piazza enthused. We've put a little pressure on [the Braves] and hopefully they'll come out pressing. We feel like if we can win [Game Six], we have a better than even chance of winning the next night."4 Reliever John Franco echoed, "How can you not like your chances with what we've done? We've played two unbelievable games, and we keep coming back. That does something for you."5

The Mets had "blown out their entire bullpen and two starters in another miracle win,"6 and New York manager Bobby Valentine tabbed lefty Al Leiter for the Game Six start "because the other possible starters, Kenny Rogers, Octavio Dotel, and Orel Hershiser, had each thrown at least two innings in Game Five."7 Leiter was pitching on three days of rest, having gone seven solid innings in Game Three, yielding the only run of the game – unearned – in the top of the first inning.8 He was 33, in his 13th season, the first nine of them mostly undistinguished in the American League. He'd led the Mets starters with 213 innings pitched and said he was ready to go, even on short rest. "You bet I want [the start]. You alter your routine based on the situations that come up. I don't have much experience on three days' rest but I've been mentally preparing myself for it."9

Graced with a starting staff that included future Hall of Famers Tom Glavine, John Smoltz, and Greg Maddux, Atlanta manager Bobby Cox had yet another ace in the hole for Game Six. In his third season, 24-year-old righty Kevin Millwood had gone 18-7 with a 2.68 ERA in 228 innings for the 1999 Braves and had handled the Mets with relative ease through 7⅓ innings in Game Two, getting the win.

A national television audience joined the Tuesday-night crowd of 52,335 filling Turner Field and saw Rickey Henderson nick Millwood for a leadoff single. But Millwood then methodically retired Edgardo Alfonzo, John Olerud, and Piazza in order to thwart any Mets hopes for a fast start that would keep their momentum going. The fast start, though, came in the Braves' half when Leiter, seeming "as tattered as a worn coat," and with "no command of his pitches, sending them swerving in all directions,"[10] faced six hitters without getting an out and saw four runs score before Pat Mahomes replaced him and gave up a fifth Leiter run on a sacrifice fly.

The Mets' Game Six dream was quickly clouded by the wrong side of a 5-0 score, and they garnered only three more harmless hits through the fifth inning, advancing a runner only as far as second base. But Mahomes, then Turk Wendell, held the Braves as well. Through five, the score remained 5-0, Atlanta.

New York came to life against Millwood in the sixth inning. Alfonzo doubled, Olerud singled, and Piazza scored Alfonzo with a sacrifice fly. Ventura doubled Olerud to third base and Darryl Hamilton singled them both home to close the score to 5-3. That chased Millwood. Cox brought in well-traveled lefty swingman Terry Mulholland,[11] who walked pinch-hitter Benny Agbayani but got out of the inning when Rey Ordonez drilled a shot at shortstop Walt Weiss; it became an unassisted double play.

Wendell ran into trouble in the Braves' half of the sixth on a hit batsman, a single, a sacrifice, and an intentional walk to load the bases with one out. He got the second out in a force play at the plate, then departed in favor of Dennis Cook. Pinch-hitter Jose Hernandez greeted Cook with a two-run single to boost the Atlanta lead to 7-3. Cox then called on Smoltz, 11-8 in 29 starts during the regular season, to hold the lead. But he faltered, giving up doubles to pinch-hitter Matt Franco and Henderson that plated a run, a long out by Alfonzo that moved Henderson to third, a scoring single by Olerud, and a dramatic two-run home run by Piazza that forged a 7-7 tie through seven innings.

Lefty Mike Remlinger put out the seventh-inning fire but gave up a run in the Mets' eighth on pinch-hitter Melvin Mora's single. Amazingly, New York had an 8-7 lead with veteran lefty John Franco coming to the mound. He retired Andruw Jones, but Eddie Perez, who would be named MVP of the Championship Series, singled. Otis Nixon ran for Perez and stole second before Brian Hunter brought him home with a single that tied the game, 8-8.

The closers, John Rocker for the Braves and Armando Benitez[12] for the Mets, each worked scoreless ninth innings. That wasn't the case in the 10th, however, as the Mets, still fighting for the chance to play another game, got to Rocker for an unearned run to take a 9-8 lead.

But Benitez couldn't close the deal. Veteran Ozzie Guillen, signed by the Braves for infield depth early in the 1998 season, pinch-hit for Weiss and singled in Andruw Jones, who had led off the inning with a single and moved to second on a walk worked by pinch-hitter Ryan Klesko.

Tied again, Cox had veteran Russ Springer ready in the Atlanta bullpen. The slender righty had pitched a scoreless inning in Game Five and delivered again, retiring Olerud, Dunston as a pinch-hitter for Benitez, and Ventura to goose-egg the Mets in the top of the 11th inning.

Valentine had already used seven pitchers and had few options. He sent out lefty Kenny Rogers,[13] who had faced seven batters two nights before. Gerald Williams greeted him with a double and advanced to third on Bret Boone's sacrifice. With Chipper Jones, known to Mets fans as "Lar-ry," a taunting chant based on his given name, and Brian Jordan next in the order, Valentine elected to walk them both, loading the bases with one out and yet another dangerous hitter, but a more undisciplined swinger, Andruw Jones, up. Jones refused to flail, worked the count to 3-and-2, and "finally, 4 hours 25 minutes after the game began, Rogers threw the fourth ball to end the season."[14]

It was 10-9, Atlanta, with Springer getting the win that put Atlanta in the World Series; Rogers took the crushing loss.

The walk-off walk loss[15] ended what had been for the Mets "an enthralling story line for much of the second half of the season, but this, like Game Five, became a battle of attrition and weariness. And it finally caught up with an otherwise extraordinarily resilient team."[16]

Valentine, whose job security had been in question due to "the pressure of nearly missing the playoffs,"[17] returned to manage the Mets in 2000. That team, boosted by Leiter's 16-8 record, Benitez's 41 saves, and the acquisition of starting pitcher Mike Hampton from the Houston Astros, won the National League pennant. Although their team fell to the cross-city Yankees in five games, Mets fans had their "Subway Series," just a year late.

Sources

In addition to the sources cited in the Notes, the author also used the Baseball-Reference.com and Retrosheet.org websites for box scores, player, team, and season pages, pitching and batting logs, and other material pertinent to this account. The reference to the taunting chants of "Lar-ry" aimed at Chipper Jones by Mets fans throughout his career comes from personal recollection as a longtime follower of the Braves.

Notes

1 Merriam-Webster defines "walk-off" as ending a baseball game immediately by causing the winning run to score in the bottom of the last inning. Merriam-Webster.com/dictionary/walk-off, accessed February 10, 2017.

2 To get to a 96-66 regular-season record and the deadlock with Cincinnati that necessitated the tiebreaker game, the Mets had needed two of their 1999 walk-off wins in their final regular-season series, against Pittsburgh on October 1 and 3.

3 The Braves came from "worst to first" to win the 1991 NL West, then repeated in 1992 and 1993. Realigned to the NL East for 1994, they were six games behind Montreal when a players strike ended that season on August 11. No divisional winners were determined for 1994 and there were no playoffs or World Series. The Braves won the NL East again when play resumed in 1995 and every season through 2005. The 14-year run produced five World Series appearances, but only one championship, in 1995.

4 Ross Newhan, "Banged Up Piazza Plays Through Pain," *Los Angeles Times*, October 19, 1999: B1.

5 Jason Reid, "Mets' Wild Ride Returns to Atlanta," *Los Angeles Times*, October 19, 1999: B1.

6 Chris Baldwin, *Gannett Newspapers*, "Al Leiter Ready to Go for Mets in Game 6," *Morris County* (New Jersey) *Daily Record*, October 18, 1999: D4.

7 Ibid.

8 Leiter had mastered Cincinnati, 5-0, with a complete-game two-hitter in the October 4 tiebreaker game.

9 Baldwin, "Al Leiter Ready."

10 Judy Battista, "Subway Series Dies Hard; Mets Lose It All on a Walk," *New York Times*, October 20, 1999, nytimes.com/1999/10/20/sports, accessed February 15, 2017.

11 Mulholland had come to the Braves from the Chicago Cubs at the July 31, 1999, trade deadline. He was 36 years old; Atlanta was already his seventh major-league organization after his 1986 debut with the San Francisco Giants. His 20-season major-league odyssey ultimately took him through 6 trades, 10 free agencies, and 11 organizations before he retired at age 43 in 2006. Mulholland pitched 2,575⅔ innings in 685 games and won 124 games against 142 losses in his journeyman career.

12 Benitez, acquired by New York from the Baltimore Orioles during the 1998-99 offseason, had 22 saves in 1999; John Franco had 19.

13 The Mets had acquired Rogers in a trade with the Oakland Athletics on July 23, 1999. He was 5-1 in 12 starts for New York, his only sojourn in the National League during a 20-year career. He left as a free agent at the end of the season, signing with the Texas Rangers.

14 Battista, "Subway Series Dies Hard."

15 New York's only other walk-off loss in the 1999 season was on June 30 against the Florida Marlins.

16 Battista.

17 Ibid.

METS SCORE 10 RUNS IN EIGHTH INNING VERSUS BRAVES

JUNE 30, 2000: NEW YORK METS 11, ATLANTA BRAVES 8, AT SHEA STADIUM

By Thomas J. Brown Jr.

The Mets and the Braves had become intense rivals towards the end of the 1990s. The 1999 season ended with the two teams playing an intense league championship series that the Braves won in six games. With the Mets fortunes rising, the Braves finally returned to Shea Stadium on June 30, 2000. It was Fireworks Night at Shea and the 52,831 fans that came out for the game saw many more fireworks than they expected.[1]

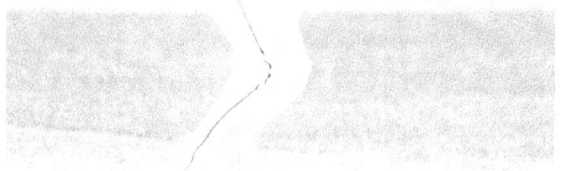

Mike Piazza arguably remains the greatest hitting catcher and the most prolific home run producer among those who played the grueling position.

The Braves jumped out to the lead in the top of the first inning. Quilvio Veras hit a leadoff single off Mike Hampton. After Andruw Jones lined out to center field, Brian Jordan singled to left. A passed ball by Mike Piazza allowed both runners to advance. Andres Galarraga was then hit by a pitch to load the bases. Hampton walked Javy Lopez to score Veras. Although it looked like the Braves might blow the game open, Hampton got Bobby Bonilla to ground into a double play that ended the inning.

The Braves continued to rattle Hampton in the third inning. A leadoff single by Veras was followed by another single by Jones. Hampton walked Galarraga to load the bases. Lopez then singled to left field. Veras and Jones scored on the hit. Galarraga also scored when Piazza was not able to handle Benny Agbayani's throw to home plate. Although Lopez ended up at second base on the play and moved to third on a wild pitch, Hampton was able to finish the inning with no more damage. Bonilla ground out to third base and Trent Hubbard eventually struck out.

Braves starter Kevin Millwood held the Mets to one earned run through seven innings. He scattered several singles over the first six innings. Eventually the Mets were able to get on the scoreboard with a trio of singles in the seventh inning. Both Todd Zeile and Jay Payton hit singles. After Agbayani struck out swinging, Matt Franco pinch hit for Hampton. He hit a single to right field. Mets fans suddenly had some hope that the Mets might stage a comeback victory.[2]

Unfortunately the Braves quickly dashed those hopes in the top of the eighth when Brian Jordan hit a three run home run off Eric Cammack who had taken over for Hampton. The Braves now had what appeared to be an overwhelming 8-1 lead.

Heading into the bottom of the eighth, it appeared as if Fireworks Night would be a fizzle although most fans were still sticking around, willing to see any sort of fireworks that night.[3] Braves manager Bobby Cox brought in Don Wengert to pitch the eighth inning. He replaced Millwood who had been taken out of the game for a pinch hitter in the top of the inning. Derek Bell led off with a line drive single to center field. Edgardo Alfonzo hit a fly ball to deep centerfield for the first out. Piazza then singled. An error by shortstop Rafael Furcal allowed Bell to move to third and Piazza to second. Robin Ventura then ground out to second base for the second out. Bell scored on the play making the score 8-2.

Although things were still looking bleak for the Mets, the excitement was just beginning. Zeile hit a single that scored Piazza. The score was now 8-3. Another single by Payton brought Kerry Ligtenberg into the game to replace Wengert. Ligtenberg immediately walked Agbayani to load the bases. Mets manager Bobby Valentine sent Mark Johnson to the plate to pinch hit for Cammack. Ligtenberg walked Johnson to score Zeile. The score was now 8-4 and the bases were still loaded. Ligtenberg walked the next batter, Melvin Mora, to score another run and the score was 8-5. Cox now brought in Terry Mulholland to replace Ligtenberg while Valentine sent Joe McEwing into the game to pinch run for Johnson.

Unfortunately, Mulholland fared no better than any of the other Braves pitchers. Bell came to the plate for the second time in the inning and Mulholland walked him on four straight pitches to score the Mets sixth run of the inning. Alfonzo hit a single to left field that scored both McEwing and Mora. Now the Mets were tied with the Braves and the crowd was on their feet. The fireworks had finally started.

With runners on first and second, Piazza came to the plate for the second time that inning. Most of the crowd was ready for what happened next. Piazza hit the first pitch for a line drive home run over the left field wall. It happened so fast that Mets announcer Gary Cohen barely had enough time to make his "It's outta here!" call.[4] With one swing of the bat the Mets were up 11-8 and Shea Stadium erupted.

Armando Benitez was brought in to pitch the ninth inning and finish the game for the Mets. Benitez always had trouble pitching 1-2-3 innings and this was no exception. Two of the first four batters he faced reached base.[5] After leadoff batter Lopez fouled out to first baseman Zeile, Keith Lockhart was brought in to pinch hit for Bonilla. He singled on a ground ball. Benitez got Hubbard to strike out swinging for the second out. Then he walked Furcal to put runners on first and second. Benitez finally ended the game and earned the win when he got Wally Joyner to fly out to center field.

Shortly after the game ended, the Mets put on their advertised fireworks show. But the planned show took a back seat to the fireworks of the eighth inning. Many Mets fans describe this comeback victory as one of the ten best games in the franchise's history. It was a game that had a memorable eighth inning that Valentine described as "one of the most unlikely innings I've ever seen."[6]

Sources

In addition to the sources cited in the Notes, the author also used the Baseball-Reference.com, Baseball-Almanac.com, and Retrosheet.org websites for box score, player, team, and season pages, pitching and batting game logs, and other material pertinent to this game account.

Notes

1 Ed Leyro, "June 30, 2000: 10-Run Rally Capped By Piazza Blast," MetsMerizedOnline.com, June 30, 2009.
2 Ed Leyro, "10 Years Later: The 10-Run Rally Still Amazin' To Me," MetsMerizedOnline.com, June 30, 2010.
3 Ed Leyro, "June 30, 2000: 10-Run Rally Capped By Piazza Blast."
4 Mark Simon, "Mike Piazza's 10 Most Memorable Home Runs for the Mets," ESPN.com, January 7, 2016.
5 Ed Leyro, "June 30, 2000: 10-Run Rally Capped By Piazza Blast."
6 Jon Blau, "Shea Moment No. 8: 10-run Eighth," MLB.com, September 23, 2008.

FRANCO SAVES THE DAY, METS EVEN SERIES

OCTOBER 5, 2000: NEW YORK METS 5, SAN FRANCISCO GIANTS 4, AT PACIFIC BELL PARK
GAME TWO OF THE 2000 NATIONAL LEAGUE DIVISION SERIES

By Paul Hofmann

The 2000 National League Division Series against the NL West champion San Francisco Giants and the wild-card New York Mets was the first postseason series played at Pacific Bell Park. The Bayfront stadium was opened in April of that year. The Giants finished with a 97-65 regular-season record, 11 games ahead of the Los Angeles Dodgers. Meanwhile, the Mets finished with a record of 94-68, narrowly edged out by the Atlanta Braves for the NL East title. With the teams separated by just three games, the best-of-five series shaped up to be an intriguing matchup between evenly-matched squads.

The Giants won the opener, in San Francisco. Backed by an Ellis Burks three-run homer that capped a four-run third inning, right-hander Livan Hernandez coasted to a 5-1 victory. The Mets found themselves in a must-win position to avoid returning to New York down two games to none.

A capacity crowd of 40,430 jammed Pac Bell Park for Game Two, a matchup between a pair of veteran southpaws. Al Leiter, 16-8 during the regular season, was given the start for the Mets while Shawn Estes (15-6) took the hill for the Giants. Estes delivered the first pitch at 5:07 P.M. under clear skies, a comfortable game-time temperature of 62 degrees and a 10-mph breeze blowing out to right field. The weather was ideal for an October evening in San Francisco.

The starters tossed scoreless first innings. Estes walked Mike Piazza, while Leiter retired the Giants in order. Estes helped the Mets out when he struggled with his control in the top of the second. After hitting Robin Ventura, the left-hander walked Benny Agbayani and Mike Bordick to load the bases. With two outs, right fielder Timo Perez singled to center to drive in two Mets runs. The Giants answered with a run of their own in the bottom of the inning when Jeff Kent led off with a single to right, stole second, and scored on Burks' double to short left field.

Piazza led off the top of the third with a single and advanced to second when Agbayani singled two outs later. However, the Mets rally fizzled when Jay Payton grounded out to short. The Giants also threatened but failed to score in the bottom half of the frame when Estes drew a four-pitch walk off Leiter. After Calvin Murray struck out, Bill Mueller sent a high chopper deep in the hole at shortstop. Estes, going in standing up, beat the throw from Bordick but immediately came up hobbling and fell off the bag. Edgardo Alfonzo applied the tag for the second out and Estes came up lame and limped off the field. The threat never materialized and the left-hander was done for the remainder of the series.

Kirk Rueter, the Giants fifth starter, was summoned to relieve Estes in the top of the fourth inning. Another veteran left-hander, Rueter – nicknamed Woody for his resemblance to the *Toy Story* character – was on top of his game and turned in an excellent performance. He scattered three hits in 4⅓ innings. The closest thing to a Mets threat came in the top of the sixth, when Bordick stroked a one-out single. The Mets shortstop was quickly erased when Leiter tried to advance him into scoring position but instead bunted into an inning-ending double play.

Leiter was equally as effective on the mound. Following Mueller's third-inning infield single, the left-hander breezed through the next five innings. He looked to be in complete control as he allowed only three Mets to reach base.

Ventura's fly ball to right to lead off the top of the eighth wrapped up Rueter's stint. Right-handed Doug Henry relieved Rueter and issued a one-out walk to Agbayani, who was lifted in favor of pinch-runner Joe McEwing. Henry induced Jay Payton to hit into a 1-4-6-3 inning-ending double play.

Henry, who was set to lead off the bottom of the eighth, was pinch-hit for by utilityman Felipe Crespo. The versatile Crespo was retired on a foul pop fly to third before Murray singled to left and Mueller hit a sharp grounder to short that resulted in yet another inning-ending double play.

The score remained 2-1 Mets going into the top of the ninth when right-hander Felix Rodriguez entered the game with the task of keeping the game within striking distance. After Rodriguez struck out Bordick and Leiter, Perez picked up his third hit of the night with a single to left field. That brought Edgardo Alfonzo to the plate. After Rodriguez fell behind 2-and-0 to Alfonzo, the Mets second baseman blasted a two-run homer to left-center to increase the Mets' lead to 4-1. With the ease with which Leiter was mowing down the Giants, the two insurance runs appeared to put the game out of reach.

Barry Bonds led off the bottom on the ninth with a double to right-center, prompting Mets manager Bobby Valentine to lift Leiter in favor of Armando Benitez. Despite his outstanding season, in which he saved 41 games while striking out 106 batters in only 76 innings, Mets fans were accustomed to holding their breath when the right-hander was called upon to close out a game. Benitez had blown five saves during the year and struggled in the last month of the season with a 4.50 ERA.

Benitez got ahead of Jeff Kent 0-and-2 before the Giants first baseman laced a groundball deep in the hole at shortstop. Although Bordick was able to field the ball cleanly, Kent was able to beat the throw to first as Bonds wisely held at second. That brought the tying run to the plate. Benitez and the Mets were given a short-lived reprieve when Burks hit a pop fly to right on the first pitch. With the Giants down to their last two outs, manager Dusty Baker sent J.T. Snow to the plate to hit for second baseman Ramon Martinez. Snow, the Giants regular first baseman, wasn't in the starting lineup to allow for another right-handed bat in the lineup against Leiter. After getting ahead 2-and-1 in the count, Snow hit a high arching shot down the right-field line that just cleared the 25-foot wall in right field, tying the game 4-4. Benitez retired the next two batters, but the damage was done. After the game, Benitez credited Snow. "I give him my hat," Benitez said.[1]

But these Mets were resilient. In the top of the 10th inning, with two outs, pinch-hitter Daryl Hamilton doubled off Rodriguez and Payton followed with an RBI single to plate Hamilton and put the Mets back on top, 5-4.

Benitez returned to the mound in the bottom of the 10th and surrendered a leadoff single to pinch-hitter Armando Rios. Valentine had seen enough and yanked a rattled Benitez in favor of 40-year-old former closer John Franco. The left-handed veteran, now serving in a situational setup role, was called upon to do what he had previously done 420 times in his 17-year career – save a ballgame. This time the stakes were a bit higher.

Marvin Benard, pinch-hitting for Murray, was the first batter to face Franco. The left-handed-hitting Bernard sacrificed Rios to second with a deftly-placed bunt to the first-base side. Mueller followed with a sharp grounder to shortstop. Though the ball was hit in front of him, Rios inexplicably tried to advance to third and was thrown out, causing Fox play-by-play man Thom Brennaman to comment, "Boy, you have to wonder what in the world Armando Rios is thinking about there."[2] The Giants were now down to their final out, but as if someone had scripted the scenario in advance, up to the plate came the Giants' best player and most polarizing figure, Barry Bonds.

Facing the most dangerous hitter in the baseball, Franco fell behind 2-and-0 and 3-and-1 to Bonds. The Giants slugger took a slider for strike two before fouling off a high fastball he couldn't quite catch up to. On the seventh pitch of the at-bat, Bonds was caught looking at a 3-and-2 changeup that plate umpire Gary Cederstrom ruled a strike.[3] Questioned about the 3-and-2 pitch selection after the game, left-hander Franco left little doubt. "I've been making a living for 17 years getting people out on my changeup," he said. "What better time to throw it?"[4] Thanks to the peculiarities of official scoring, Franco preserved the victory for Benitez as the series shifted back to Shea tied at a game apiece.

Sources

In addition to the sources cited in the Notes, the author also consulted Baseball-Reference.com.

Notes

1 Sean Deveney, "Standing Room Only," *The Sporting News*, October 16, 2000: 15.
2 Mets at Giants Game Two 2000 NLDS Live Clips, Retrieved from youtube.com/watch?v=2rG8cZTjfSg.
3 2000 NLDS Gm2: Franco Freezes Bonds, Mets Even Series. Retrieved from youtube.com/watch?v=w85HX4rc-vw.
4 "Quick Hits: Players Who Provided Special Postseason Moments. Change Is Eternal: John Franco," *The Sporting News*, October 16, 2000.

BENNY'S BLAST ENDS PLAYOFF DRAMA IN 13TH

OCTOBER 7, 2000: NEW YORK METS 3, SAN FRANCISCO GIANTS 2 (13 INNINGS), AT SHEA STADIUM
GAME THREE OF THE 2000 NATIONAL LEAGUE DIVISION SERIES

By Rory Costello

This game started at 4:20 on a crisp fall afternoon.[1] It ended 5 hours and 22 minutes later on a dramatic home run by Benny Agbayani into the "picnic area" bleachers in left-center. The capacity crowd of 56,270 had the ballpark moving on its foundation as the popular Hawaiian's teammates carried him off the field.[2]

Agbayani was fortunate even to be with the Mets to start the 2000 season. He had options left to be sent back to the minors, whereas his close friend and fellow outfielder Jay Payton did not. Agbayani got a reprieve, however, when the Mets carried 10 pitchers rather than 11 early on. He stayed because Darryl Hamilton had toe surgery and got more playing time after the Mets released Rickey Henderson in May.

"[Mets manager] Bobby Valentine told me things have a way of working out," Agbayani said afterward. "I didn't understand that. Now I do."[3]

This was a battle full of tension. Giants starting pitcher Russ Ortiz took a no-hitter into the sixth inning, and the Mets had to come from behind. San Francisco closer Robb Nen, who'd blown just five of 46 save opportunities in 2000 – and none since July 2 – gave up a clutch two-out hit in the eighth. Also, both sides squandered many opportunities. "These are always nerve-racking," Mets catcher Mike Piazza said. "A lot of guys really couldn't swallow out there."[4] New York's starter, Rick Reed, said, "I was on the bench and I said to someone, 'You can hear a pin drop.'"[5]

The Shea crowd got raucous early, though. The game was only two pitches old when the scoreboard flashed that in the other NLDS, the St. Louis Cardinals had completed their sweep of the Atlanta Braves, who'd knocked the Mets out of the playoffs in 1999. The fans did a derisive tomahawk chop.[6]

Reed – called the "poor man's Greg Maddux" because he relied on location, not speed – held San Francisco scoreless through three innings. After Bill Mueller's two-out double in the third, the Mets intentionally walked fearsome Barry Bonds, who had hit 49 homers in the regular season. Jeff Kent then grounded out.

Hawaiian-born Benny Agbayani became a cult figure at Shea Stadium with his underdog status.

San Francisco scored twice in the fourth. Ellis Burks and J.T. Snow started with singles. After Rich Aurilia fouled out, Bobby Estalella's single brought Burks home. Ortiz tried to sacrifice, but Snow was forced out at third. Ortiz beat the throw to first, though, and Marvin Benard followed with the Giants' fourth single of the inning, scoring Estalella.

Mueller flied out, and after that, Reed and five relievers – Dennis Cook, Turk Wendell, John Franco, Armando Benitez, and Rick White – threw nine scoreless innings. "We were out in the bullpen just feeding off of each other," said White.[7] It wasn't easy, though; San Francisco got the leadoff man on first base five times. On average, two of those runners should have scored.[8] The Giants stranded 16 altogether.

Ortiz began the game with a 4-0 career record and a 2.83 ERA against the Mets.[9] But he didn't make it out of the sixth. After Mike Bordick drew a leadoff walk on four pitches, Hamilton, batting for Reed, singled for the Mets' first hit. Bordick went to third and then scored on Timo Pérez's single. A big inning did not develop, though. Edgardo Alfonzo grounded one up the middle; Pérez, running with the pitch, beat the flip to second and prevented a double play. With runners in scoring position, Giants manager Dusty Baker called for an intentional walk to slugger Piazza. The strategy worked perfectly: Lefty reliever Alan Embree entered and got Robin Ventura to ground into a 4-6-3 DP. Embree's day was done after just two pitches.

The Giants' first threat to add an insurance run came in the seventh. Lefty Cook walked Benard and Mueller sacrificed successfully, bringing up Bonds. He grounded out to first baseman Todd Zeile, moving Benard to third. Valentine then brought in Wendell for a righty-righty matchup against Kent. Wendell struck him out.

Burks walked to lead off the eighth, but Wendell stayed out of trouble, striking out Snow and Aurilia and getting Estalella to ground out. The Mets then tied it. Doug Henry, who'd pitched a 1-2-3 seventh, hit Bordick with a pitch. Lenny Harris, the lifetime leader in pinch hits, batted for Wendell. He forced Bordick out at second, barely avoiding a double play – in fact, first-base umpire Brian Gorman got the close call wrong.[10] After Pérez popped out, Baker brought in Nen with a four-out save in mind. But Harris stole second and Alfonzo doubled. "I don't try to think about how nasty [Nen] is," said Alfonzo.[11]

"Fonzie's entire career, it seems like he does the big thing that gets us to the point where we have a chance to win," said Valentine. "And then someone else does something right at the end."[12] Alfonzo went no further, though, because Piazza struck out.

Franco, the 40-year-old lefty who'd moved from closer to setup man for Benitez in 1999, then came on. Again the Giants' first batter, shortstop Ramón Martinez, singled. Franco retired the next three, though, ending with a strikeout of Bonds, who later groused about plate umpire Jerry Crawford. Franco, who'd slipped a changeup past Bonds to end Game Two, shook off Piazza and went with fastballs this time. "You have to get the feeling that Barry Bonds has seen enough of John Franco," wrote the *New York Daily News*.[13]

In the bottom of the ninth, Payton singled with two outs and stole second. Nen pitched around Zeile and walked him; he then whiffed Bordick on three pitches. So, for the second time in the series, extra innings ensued. New York City Mayor Rudy Giuliani, well-known as a Yankees fan, thereupon left for the game at Yankee Stadium. It was then 7:55.[14]

Kent singled off Benitez to start the 10th and took second as Burks grounded out. The Mets then put Snow on intentionally – not a surprise, because he'd hit a three-run homer off Benitez in the bottom of the ninth to tie Game Two. Benitez got two flyouts, and the big Dominican flamethrower struck out the side in the 11th.

Meanwhile, Felix Rodríguez pitched two scoreless innings for San Francisco. He set the Mets down 1-2-3 in the 10th, which featured "a bit of intrigue. … Crawford walked toward a small camera that rested on the padding against the backstop, about waist-high. Valentine, suspected by some of using electronic equipment to steal opponents' signals, sauntered out of the dugout. And as if to prove nothing was sinister, he took a white towel and covered the camera. An inning later, the camera was gone."[15]

Rodriguez threw 36 pitches as he worked out of trouble in the 11th. Piazza singled to lead off and Joe McEwing pinch-ran. Ventura singled, and Rodríguez then survived two long at-bats. Agbayani flied out on the ninth pitch after failing to get a sacrifice bunt down, and Payton struck out on the 10th pitch. He had fouled off seven deliveries, breaking three bats in the process.[16] Zeile walked on four straight balls to load the bases, but pinch-hitter Todd Pratt flied out. The game went on.

Staffs weren't 12 and 13 men deep back then. When White entered in the 12th, the Mets had just fifth starter Glendon Rusch left. Again the Giants put the leadoff man aboard as Bonds walked – "I got a little too picky with him," said White.[17] After striking out Kent and Burks, White walked Snow too. However, Doug Mirabelli flied out.

Baker then brought in his sixth pitcher, rookie southpaw Aaron Fultz. With two out, Alfonzo singled, as did McEwing, but Alfonzo overran second base. He "seemed stunned, holding his foot on the bag a full 20 seconds after … Kent tagged him out."[18]

White escaped another jam in the 13th. He struck out Calvin Murray, but Martinez and Mueller singled around Benard's strikeout – the Giants' 17th of the game. That brought up the ever-dangerous Bonds, but he popped White's first pitch, a fastball away, to second. "If he had dove into it and hit it the other way, it might have gone out of the park," said the pitcher.[19]

Indeed, though the night had grown chilly, the wind was blowing out to left.[20] With one out in the home half, Fultz left a 1-and-0 fastball up, and Agbayani – hitless in his first five at-bats – took the mistake deep to end it. As he began his trip around the bases, he flipped his black bat skyward. Rounding first, he flashed the Hawaiian shaka "hang loose" sign.[21] The gesture has various meanings – including thanks.

"My approach was ... I'm going to hit the ball hard," said Agbayani. "I had to redeem myself. . . that was the redemption right there."[22] He added, "Nothing could compare to this. Nothing."[23]

Notes
1 Murray Chass, "Good Omen at Start Augurs Victory in 13," *New York Times*, October 8, 2000.
2 For discussion of how big crowds at Shea caused this movement, likened to the sensation of an earthquake, see Michael S. Schmidt, "Shea, Rattle and Roll," *New York Times*, October 20, 2006.
3 Tyler Kepner, "Agbayani Makes His Bid for Mets' Mr. October," *New York Times*, October 8, 2000.
4 Ben Walker, "Agbayani's Homer in 13th Propels Mets," Associated Press, October 8, 2000.
5 Kepner, "Agbayani Makes His Bid for Mets' Mr. October."
6 Chass, "Good Omen at Start Augurs Victory in 13."
7 Roger Rubin, "For Rick, Playoff Spotlight White Hot," *New York Daily News*, October 8, 2000.
8 According to a study of major-league data from 1952 through 2009, 37.8 percent of leadoff batters who reached first base eventually scored. "The Leadoff Walk," fangraphs.com, September 15, 2010.
9 Walker, "Agbayani's Homer in 13th Propels Mets."
10 T.J. Quinn, "Benny Blast Is a Giant Lift," *New York Daily News*, October 8, 2000.
11 Steve Popper, "Rookie Is Left to Explain the Pitch That Got Away," *New York Times*, October 8, 2000.
12 Kepner, "Agbayani Makes His Bid for Mets' Mr. October."
13 Roger Rubin, "Franco Gets Best of Bonds – Again," *New York Daily News*, October 8, 2000.
14 Chass, "Good Omen at Start Augurs Victory in 13."
15 Walker, "Agbayani's Homer in 13th Propels Mets."
16 Kepner, "Agbayani Makes His Bid for Mets' Mr. October."
17 Chass, "Good Omen at Start Augurs Victory in 13."
18 Kepner, "Agbayani Makes His Bid for Mets' Mr. October."
19 Chass, "Good Omen at Start Augurs Victory in 13."
20 Mark Kriegel, "Benny Blast Is a Giant Lift," *New York Daily News*, October 8, 2000.
21 Andre Marchand, "Mets' Hawaii Five-O Deep Sixes Frisco," *New York Post*, October 8, 2000.
22 Dan O'Neill, "Agbayani's Homer Gives NY a Late Win," *St. Louis Post-Dispatch*, October 8, 2000.
23 Kriegel, "Benny Blast Is a Giant Lift."

METS ADVANCE TO NATIONAL LEAGUE CHAMPIONSHIP SERIES

OCTOBER 8, 2000: NEW YORK METS 4, SAN FRANCISCO GIANTS 0, AT SHEA STADIUM
GAME FOUR OF THE 2000 NATIONAL LEAGUE DIVISION SERIES

By Alan Cohen

Per Bobby Valentine, on the eve of what was to be the most important game of Bobby Jones's baseball life, Jones's wife, Kristi, spoke briefly with the Mets manager. Kristi said to Valentine, "Is Bobby pitching tomorrow?" After Valentine said, "Yes, he is," Kristi said, "You won't be sorry. He'll pitch the game of his life."

I also thought Bobby was the guy to go in this game since the beginning of the series. He's a pro. Look it up in the dictionary and you'll see his picture beside the word 'pro.'"

In the game's aftermath, Kristi slightly contradicted the Valentine accounting, saying that she had spoken with Valentine and after being assured that her husband would pitch the game said "Oh yeah, he's definitely ready. It's a guaranteed win. Guaranteed."

"I'm so happy for Bobby Jones. I'm so proud of him. To go out and pitch the best game of his life and dismiss all the critics who thought it was a bad decision. He went out and nailed it."

– Al Leiter

The New York Mets, after losing the first game of the Division Series to the Giants, had won the next two games and were poised to clinch the series as they opposed the San Francisco Giants at Shea Stadium in front of 56,245 onlookers. The Mets' pitcher was Bobby Jones. The Mets had two fellows named Bobby Jones on the roster. This was the guy who had gone 11-6 during the regular season with a 5.06 ERA. Bobby J. Jones was the Mets' first-round draft pick in 1991 and had first pitched for them in 1993. He had a 74-56 record over eight seasons. During the final innings of the game, the large crowd was chanting, "Bobby, Bobby!" At game's end, in the Mets' clubhouse, his teammates would be chanting as one, "Bobby Jones, Bobby Jones, Bobby Jones," after the California native and Fresno State alumnus had hurled a one-hitter, as the Mets won 4-0 to advance to the NLCS and face the St. Louis Cardinals.

Jones, after being named to the All-Star team in 1997 (15-9), had been slipping and spent parts of the 1999 and 2000 seasons in the minor leagues. with the Mets' Triple-A squad in Norfolk, Virginia. His trip to Norfolk for two weeks during June 2000 came after he started the season with a 1-3 record in eight starts with the Mets and posted a 10.19 ERA in 32⅔ innings. He accepted the temporary reassignment (two starts) as the Mets would not be needing him as a starter during that time, and he knew that he had to work on his mechanics if he was to help the Mets advance to the postseason. After returning to the Mets, he went 10-3 the rest of the way. Down the stretch he won three of his last four starts as the Mets gained the NL's wild-card berth.

The Giants' pitcher was Mark Gardner, another Fresno State alumnus and a good friend of Jones. The 12-year veteran (eight years Jones' senior) had gone 11-7 for the Giants in 2000 with a 4.05 ERA.

The ceremonial first pitch was thrown out by a man best remembered as having coined the phrase "Ya Gotta Believe" during the Mets pennant run in 1973 – Tug McGraw.

The big name in the Mets offense was Mike Piazza. Most of the supporting cast was not that well known beyond New York, but it was that supporting cast that played a big role in putting the Mets in position to advance further in the postseason. Benny Agbayani had had career highs in games played (119), batting average (.289), extra-base hits (35), and RBIs (60). On this Sunday afternoon, he was stationed in left field. After a game-winning 13th-inning homer in Game Three, he went 2-for-4 in Game Four, and although neither of his hits figured in the scoring, the crowd gave him a standing ovation when he was removed for a pinch-runner after doubling to lead off the ninth inning.

On this day, it was Robin Ventura's time to shine. He had come to the Mets in 1999 after 10 years with the Chicago White Sox and had performed exceptionally well during his first year in Queens, batting .301 with 32 homers and 120 RBIs. All were career highs. He finished sixth in the MVP balloting and received his sixth Gold Glove. But in 2000, Ventura went into what amounted for him to a yearlong slump, batting only .232. But still fresh in the minds of Mets fans was Ventura's final at-bat in Game Four of the prior season's NLCS with the Braves. In the bottom of the 15th inning with the Mets trailing 2-1 and facing elimination, Ventura hit a bases-loaded fly ball over the center-field fence. Euphoric Met fans mobbed Ventura midway between first base and second, and he was credited only with a game-winning single.

A year later, with two out in the first inning on October 8, 2000, Ventura got a chance to touch all the bases. Piazza walked, and Ventura slammed a homer off the lower right-hand corner of the big scoreboard in right field. The Mets had all the runs that Bobby Jones would need.

Then Jones went to work, pitching four perfect innings, striking out Barry Bonds in his first two trips to the plate, before Jeff Kent broke up the perfecto with a leadoff fifth-inning double over a leaping Ventura, who barely touched the ball as it eluded his outstretched glove. After recording two outs, Jones walked the bases full, bringing up Gardner. Giants manager Dusty Baker chose not to send up a pinch-hitter, and Jones retired Gardner on a popup.

Ventura, in the joyous clubhouse after the game, took extra time to point out the value to the team of second baseman Edgardo Alfonzo. Fonzie didn't just pop on the scene. In 1999, he had batted .304 with 27 homers and 108 RBIs, winning the Silver Slugger Award and finishing eighth in the MVP balloting. In 2000, he was named to the All-Star team and batted a career-high .324. On this day, he came to bat in the fifth inning with rookie Timo Perez on base.

Perez was a late-season addition to the Mets lineup, filling in for the injured Derek Bell, at a time when it seemed like many players were filling in for injured somebodies, and played in 24 September games batting .286. In the playoffs, he was an igniting spark. He went 3-for-5 in the Game Two win, drove in the Mets' first run in Game Three and, with one out in the fifth inning, doubled to right field, sending Jones to third base. Jones had reached safely after striking out, as the pitch bounded past catcher Doug Mirabelli of the Giants. The stage was set for Alfonzo. The Mets second baseman doubled to complete the Mets scoring, and Jones, after toweling himself off, returned to the mound.

Jones retired the last 13 batters he faced to complete his masterpiece. After Bonds flied out to center fielder Jay Payton for his team's last out, the celebration began.

In the Giants' clubhouse, manager Dusty Baker said, "He was changing speeds and getting strike one and had the 'atem' ball working pretty good. We just couldn't find any holes. We had a couple of near home runs. First inning, we hit three bullets."

The Mets went on to defeat the Cardinals in the NLCS and advanced to the World Series against the Yankees in New York's first Subway Series since 1956, losing to their crosstown rivals in five games.

Jones had starts in both the NLCS and World Series, but he did not come close to matching his performance against the Giants. In the NLCS, he started the fourth game but left in the fifth inning. His mates had staked him to an 8-3 lead, but after the first three batters reached base and the Cardinals cut the lead to 8-4, he was removed from the game. The Mets went on to win 10-6. In the World Series, Jones started the fourth game and left after five innings with the Mets trailing 3-2. There was no further scoring in the game, and Jones was tagged with the loss.

In the partying in the clubhouse after Jones's masterpiece, his 4-year-old son, perched atop the shoulders of teammate Ventura, doused his dad with champagne, prompting Jones to say, "After I went through in the beginning of the season, to battle back and do something in the postseason – it meant a lot."

Sources

In addition to the sources cited in the Notes and Baseball-Reference.com, the author used

Marchand, Andrew. "Mets Ride Jones All the Way to St. Louis – Bobby Nearly Perfect in Ousting Giants," *New York Post*, October 9, 2000.

O'Connell, Jack. "Bonds Isn't Money: Postseason Struggles Continue as Giants Bow Out," *Hartford Courant*, October 9, 2000: C-8.

THE METS PUNCH THEIR TICKET TO A SUBWAY SERIES

OCTOBER 16, 2000: NEW YORK METS 7, ST. LOUIS CARDINALS 0, AT SHEA STADIUM
GAME FIVE OF THE 2000 NATIONAL LEAGUE CHAMPIONSHIP SERIES

By Joe Schuster

The New York Mets came into the 2000 National League Championship Series against St. Louis facing a number of challenges.

For one, the Cardinals had had an easier time in their best-of-five division series, against Atlanta, than the Mets had against San Francisco. Despite pitcher Rick Ankiel's meltdown as the St. Louis starter in Game One, when he failed to get out of the third inning, walking four and throwing five wild pitches, St. Louis had swept the Braves, outscoring them 24-10.

On the other hand, the Mets' series against the Giants had been more taxing. The Giants took the first game, 5-1, and while the Mets won the next three, it was not easy. Games Two and Three went into extra innings before right-hander Bobby Jones clinched the series with a nifty 4-0, one-hit shutout in the decisive fourth game. Beyond that, they lost right fielder Derek Bell when he injured his right ankle in Game One going after a Barry Bonds line drive.[1]

As *The Sporting News* put it, "While the Giants and the Mets were knocking the drool out of each other, the Cardinals were at ease, their only concern being the removal of Korbel stains from polyester. … So as the Mets and Braves were resorting to whoever was able to stand, the Cardinals had their feet up, resting. … It's a ragged bunch of New Yorkers being sent [to the NLCS]."[2]

This is not to say that the Cardinals did not have their own raggedness, largely due to injury. While the Mets were missing Bell, St. Louis was down several components of the team that had won the National League Central. Sixteen-game winner Garrett Stephenson tore a ligament in his pitching elbow in Game Three of the Division Series (he would miss the entire 2001 season), Gold Glove catcher Mike Matheny sliced two tendons in his right hand in a September accident with a hunting knife, and slugger Mark McGwire was reduced to pinch-hitting after developing tendinitis in his right knee in early July, keeping him either on the bench or the disabled list for the last three months of the season and the playoffs.

There was, however, another factor that eventually determined the outcome of the league championship series: The Mets simply played better ball.

While they made three errors in Game One, they overcame them to win the game, 6-2, and then won Game Two, 6-5, by exploiting three Cardinals errors and another poor outing by Ankiel, who lasted but two-thirds of an inning. While St. Louis took Game Three 8-2 behind an eight-inning stint by starting pitcher Andy Benes, the Mets scored seven in the first two innings of Game Four against 20-game winner Darryl Kile and put themselves on the brink of the World Series with a 10-6 victory.

For Game Five, Mets manager Bobby Valentine sent southpaw Mike Hampton to the mound as the Mets' starting pitcher. The team had acquired Hampton from Houston in a December 1999 deal that had also brought them Bell in exchange for three players, gambling that Hampton, who would leave as a free agent after the season, could be the piece the team lacked the previous season when it lost the NLCS to Atlanta. With the Astros in 1999, Hampton had his career-best season, going 22-4 and finishing second in the Cy Young Award voting to Randy Johnson. For the Mets in 2000, he had not been quite as good but he did go 15-10 and his 3.14 ERA ranked fifth in the league. In the division series, he'd been the losing pitcher in Game One, but in the opening contest of the NLCS he had thrown seven shutout innings for the victory.

Met-rospectives

For the visiting Cardinals, manager Tony La Russa tapped right-hander Pat Hentgen, whom the team had also acquired in an offseason deal, in November 1999, when they sent three players to Toronto for Hentgen and reliever Paul Spoljaric. St. Louis released him in spring training.) The deal was also, according to some, "a gamble" as Hentgen, who had won the 1996 American League Cy Young Award, was coming off two mediocre seasons (1998 and '99) when he'd gone a combined 23-23 with an ERA of just under 5.00.[3] While he did not approach his Cy Young form, posting a 4.72 ERA, he managed to go 15-12 and had generally pitched well over the last half of the season, going 6-4 in his last 10 decisions. However, in his final two starts he had been "abysmal" in the words of a *St. Louis Post-Dispatch* sports writer, allowing 11 runs on 16 hits in nine innings; partly because of that, La Russa had not used him in the playoffs at all to that point and he came in on 16 days' rest.[4]

Unfortunately for St. Louis, Hentgen's rustiness showed in Game Five and, compounded by sloppy Cardinals defense and Hampton's best outing of the year, the game was never truly a contest.

After Hampton retired the Cardinals in the first, surrendering only a leadoff single to Fernando Vina, the Mets batted around in the bottom of the inning, aided by wildness by Hentgen and two errors. Timo Perez, in the lineup in place of Bell, led off with a single, then stole second, ending up on third when catcher Carlos Hernandez threw the ball into center field trying to nab him. Perez scored on a single by Edgardo Alfonzo that just got past Cardinals shortstop Edgar Renteria and, after Mike Piazza walked, Robin Ventura singled, driving in Alfonzo and sending Piazza to third. Piazza scored on a fielding miscue when Todd Zeile hit what appeared to be double-play ball to Vina, but he bobbled it and then made what a *Post-Dispatch* sportswriter described as a hurried flip of the ball from his glove to Renteria for the first out, then first baseman Will Clark dropped Renteria's throw, making Zeile safe at first and scoring Piazza.[5] The Mets threatened to add even more when Hentgen walked Benny Agbayani and Jay Payton singled, but Mike Bordick popped out and Hampton fanned.

Hentgen got through the next two innings without further damage but the Cards were unable to put together any offense, as Hampton allowed only a third-inning single by Hentgen (his only career postseason hit) and another in the fourth, by Clark, the Cardinals' last hit in the game.

In the fourth, Hentgen ran into trouble that ended his night. After Hampton flied out leading off, Perez lined a ball off Hentgen's foot that went for an infield single, although it could have been charged as an error when Clark again dropped a throw from Renteria.[6] Piazza doubled and Ventura walked, bringing up Zeile. On a 2-and-2 pitch, "Zeile crushed a fastball that cut through the chilly air and caught the wind, crashing in to the wall in right center and clearing the bases."[7] Zeile's double sent the crowd of 55,695 into a roar that culminated, with their anticipation of the first all-New York World Series in more than four decades, in anti-Yankee chants.[8] That was all for Hentgen as La Russa replaced him with Mike Timlin.

From that point, the Cardinals managed only a sixth-inning walk to Placido Polanco, and the action on the field took an ugly turn. In the seventh, La Russa sent Ankiel to the mound, a move a *Post-Dispatch* writer characterized as an "indignity" as Ankiel suffered "more wildness and humiliation. The kid threw two more wild pitches [the second scoring the Mets seventh run] and walked two Mets before LaRussa ended the farce."[9]

The Cardinals frustration boiled over the next inning when St. Louis reliever Dave Veres threw first one pitch up and in to Payton and then a second one that hit him in the face, opening a cut; Payton charged the mound and the benches cleared but after a brief spate of shoving, the game resumed.[10]

An inning later it was over. The Cardinals went down in order in the ninth and when pinch-hitter Rick Wilkins lofted a fly ball to Perez in center, Hampton thrust his fist into the air and was picked up by a jubilant Ventura as their teammates swarmed the field. Hampton's three-hit shutout, combined with his Game One effort, gave him 16 scoreless innings against St. Louis in the series and earned him the NLCS Most Valuable Player Award.

For the Mets, it meant a ticket to their first World Series since their 1986 victory over the Boston Red Sox.

Sources

In addition to the publications listed in the endnotes, the author also referred to Retrosheet, Baseball Reference, and the SABR Biography Project.

Notes

1 Sean Deveney, "Standing Room Only," *The Sporting News*, October 16, 2000: 14, 15.
2 Deveney.
3 Mike Eisenbath, "Former Cy Young winner Hentgen, Spoljaric join Cards," *St. Louis Post-Dispatch*, November 12, 1999: D1.
4 Mike Eisenbath, "Hentgen has waited weeks to get the ball, but he isn't angry about it," *St. Louis Post-Dispatch*, October 16, 2000: C8.
5 Rick Hummel, "Cards Go Five and Out as Hampton Slams Door," *St. Louis Post-Dispatch*, October 17, 2000: 35.
6 Bernie Miklasz, "Baseball's Best Fans Must Cope Again with Unhappy Ending," *St. Louis Post-Dispatch*, October 17, 2000: 35.
7 Tyler Kepner, "7 Train Awaits: Mets Reach World Series," *New York Times*, October 17, 2000: A1.
8 Ibid.
9 Miklasz.
10 Joe LaPointe, "Payton's Blood Spills, Then Champagne Flows," *New York Times*, October 17, 2000: D2.

SUBWAY SERIES 2000 – ACT THREE

OCTOBER 24, 2000: NEW YORK METS 4, NEW YORK YANKEES 2, AT SHEA STADIUM

GAME THREE OF THE 2000 WORLD SERIES

By Kevin Larkin

For the first time since 1956, the major leagues had a Subway Series,[1] pitting the New York Yankees against the New York Mets. At the start of the season there was nothing etched in stone that would suggest the Yankees and the Mets would meet for a World Series title. The Yankees, who were trying to clinch their third World Series title in a row and fourth in five years, stumbled into October baseball after a rather long September losing streak, and a scare in the first round of the playoffs against the Oakland Athletics. The Mets were wild-card winners and if the truth be known they had an easier time making it to the Big Show than the Yankees, as they beat the Giants and the Cardinals to make it to the World Series.

In Game One at Yankee Stadium, the Yankees won on a single by Jose Vizcaino in the bottom of the 12th inning that scored Tino Martinez and gave the Yankees a 4-3 victory. This game set a record for the longest World Series game ever at 4 hours 51 minutes.

Game Two was also played at Yankee Stadium and was notable for two events. The first occurred in the first inning when Mike Piazza's bat shattered as he struck a pitch from Roger Clemens. There was a history between the two as a pitch by Clemens had hit Piazza in the head in July. A piece of the bat bounded toward Clemens; he picked it up and threw it in the general direction of Piazza, who was running down the first-base line. Both benches cleared, but order was restored and the game resumed. (The ball struck when the bat shattered went foul.) Then in the top of the ninth inning the Mets were trailing, 6-0, and scored five runs off Jeff Nelson and Mariano Rivera to make the final score 6-5, Yankees.

In Game Three, at Shea Stadium, there was a battle of right-handers, Orlando Hernandez (known as "El Duque") for the Yankees and Rick Reed for the Mets. Reed made quick work of the Yankees in the first inning, with the only issue a two-out walk to David Justice after which Bernie Williams took a called third strike. It was an even quicker inning for "El Duque" as he struck out the side.

In the second, Reed struck out Martinez and Jorge Posada, and gave up a two-out double to Paul O'Neill, but struck out Scott Brosius, leaving O'Neill at second base. Robin Ventura led off the Mets second with a home run for a 1-0 lead, but Hernandez struck out Todd Zeile, Benny Agbayani, and Jay Payton, giving the Cuban right-hander six strikeouts.

Hernandez struck out to open the Yankees third and Jose Vizcaino grounded out. Derek Jeter singled and scored the tying run on a double by David Justice. Williams grounded out to end the inning. For the Mets, Reed singled with one out, but was left stranded as Timo Perez flied out to left field and Edgardo Alfonzo popped out to the second baseman.

Tino Martinez led off the Yankees fourth with a single and with one out he scored on Paul O'Neill's triple. Reed hit Scott Brosius to put runners on first and third with one out. Brosius went to second on Hernandez's bunt (O'Neill held third) but Vizcaino was caught looking at a third strike. The Yankees had a leadoff single by Jeter in the fifth inning but could not score and the Mets could not score in the bottom of the inning after Mike Bordick hit a one-out single to center field.

In the sixth, Reed set the Yankees down in order. In the bottom of the inning the Mets tied the score. Piazza doubled on a fan interference call, Ventura walked, and Todd Zeile's double to left field scored Piazza and sent Ventura to third base. Benny Agbayani walked to load the bases with no outs, but Hernandez got out of the inning by whiffing Payton and Bordick and getting Darryl Hamilton,[2] batting for Reed, on a force-play grounder to shortstop.

Turk Wendell replaced Reed on the mound for the Mets to begin the seventh inning and struck out Hernandez and Vizcaino before walking Jeter. Through seven innings the Yankees and the Mets pitchers had combined for 22 strikeouts, three short of a World Series record.[3] Dennis Cook then relieved Wendell and hit David Justice with a pitch, but ended the inning by striking out Williams.

Hernandez retired the Mets in order in the seventh. Tino Martinez walked to open the Yankees eighth. Mets reliever John Franco replaced Cook and got Posada to ground into a 5-4-3 double play. O'Neill singled to center field but was left stranded when Glenallen Hill, batting for Brosius, flied out to right field.

In the Mets eighth, Zeile singled to center field with one out and Agbayani sent him home with a double to left that gave the Mets a 3-2 lead. After the game Zeile said, "We all felt that things would be different once we got back to Shea because of how we've played here all season."[4] Joe McEwing ran for Agbayani. Payton singled and McEwing went to third. After Lenny Harris came to the plate to hit for Bordick, Mike Stanton replaced Hernandez on the mound for the Yankees. Bubba Trammell then batted for Harris and hit a fly ball to center field that scored McEwing. Kurt Abbott batted for Franco and struck out, but the Mets had a 4-2 lead going to the top of the ninth inning.

Mets pitcher Armando Benitez came in looking to close out the game. Chuck Knoblauch batted for Stanton and singled to give the Yankees a baserunner with nobody out. But Benitez was up to the task. He retired pinch-hitter Luis Polonia on a fly to center field and got Jeter to take a called third strike. With David Justice batting, Knoblauch went to second on defensive indifference, but Justice popped out to second baseman Alfonzo for the final out.

The defeat broke the Yankees' 14-game World Series winning streak, the longest streak in championship play among the major sports.[5] They led the Mets two games to one, but Mets manager Valentine said, "It seems like light years difference between 3-0 and 2-1. ..."[6]

Sources

In addition to the sources cited in the Notes, the author consulted Baseball-Reference.com and Retrosheet.org.

Notes

1 A Subway Series is commonly defined as one in which two teams from the same city play each other.
2 Of Agbayani, manager Bobby Valentine said, "He was not supposed to be in the lineup. We're here because of him. He is one of the key players on the team." Associated Press, *Rochester* (New York) *Democrat and Chronicle*, October 25, 2000: 36.
3 Chris Haft, "Pitching Stars; Tied 2-2 After 7," *Cincinnati Enquirer*, October 25, 2000: 39.
4 Jason Reed, "Zeile Steps Into Spotlight," *Los Angeles Times*, October 25, 2000: 187.
5 Buster Olney, "Mets Top Hernandez 4-2, and Get Back Into Series," *New York Times*, October 25, 2000: 1.
6 Ibid.

NEW YORK CITY'S FIRST BASEBALL GAME AFTER 9/11

SEPTEMBER 21, 2001: NEW YORK METS 3, ATLANTA BRAVES 2, AT SHEA STADIUM

By Thomas J. Brown Jr.

New York City was still reeling from the devastation of the attacks on the World Trade Center on September 11, 2001. With that experience still fresh in everyone's memory, the New York Mets played the Atlanta Braves 10 days later, on September 21, 2001. Mike Piazza would later reflect that "[p]eople wanted to find refuge in baseball, in a crowd, in baseball. It has the tendency to ease your pain a little bit."[1]

After the events of Tuesday, September 11, Commissioner Bud Selig canceled all games through the end of the week and announced that the season would resume on Saturday, September 17. To make up for the lost time, the entire season would be pushed back one full week.[2] Once the season resumed, the Mets played three games against the Pirates in Pittsburgh. Their game against the Atlanta Braves would be the first baseball game in New York after the attacks and no one

After rumors and speculation kept him out temporarily, Mike Piazza finally earned induction into the Hall of Fame in 2016.

was sure how to approach this game. Howie Rose, one of the Mets announcers, recalled what his bosses told him: "This is unlike any game we've ever done. Make sure you don't get too excited about anything. Don't emote. This is a night of healing, not of celebration."[3]

The Mets and the Braves had fought each other competitively in the National League East for many years. But this night would be different. Both teams took the field before the game and honored all the first responders and others who had rallied to help the region recover from the shock of September 11. Braves manager Bobby Cox said of the opening ceremony, "[The Mets] weren't the enemy after all, for about 10 minutes."[4]

Coming into the game, the Mets had been playing well. They had been 13½ games out of first place on August 15. But they finally started to play well as a team right before September 11. By September 21, the Mets were just five games behind the Braves after sweeping all three games in Pittsburgh.

Jason Marquis was chosen to start the game for the Braves and Bruce Chen was given the start by Mets manager Bobby Valentine. Once the Mets took the field, the two teams settled down to play baseball and for that evening, spectators and those watching on television allowed baseball to help them to come together following 9/11's catastrophic events.

The game was scoreless through the first three innings; the only hits were a double by the Mets' Piazza in the bottom of the second inning and a single by the Braves' Rey Sanchez in the top of the third inning. The Braves took a 1-0 lead in the top of the fourth inning. After Julio Franco flied out to right field, Chipper Jones singled. He came home with an unearned run when Ken Caminiti doubled to right field and catcher Piazza couldn't handle the throw to the plate by Matt Lawton.

The Mets tied the game in the bottom of the inning. After Edgardo Alfonzo flied out to center field, Piazza hit his second double of the game. He moved to third on a single by Robin Ventura and scored on Tsuyoshi Shinjo's sacrifice fly to right field. Todd Zeile followed with a double but Ventura was able to advance only to third base. Marquis got Jay Payton to ground out to end the threat,

The score remained tied until the eighth inning. Valentine brought in John Franco, who was born and grew up in New York City, to pitch the top of the inning. After getting the first two batters out, he walked Julio Franco. Cox sent Cory Aldridge in to run for Franco. Jones's hit a single that moved Aldridge to second. That chased John Franco in favor of closer Armando Benitez for the Mets. The first batter Benitez faced, Brian Jordan, doubled into the gap in left-center and Aldridge scored to give the Braves a 2-1 lead.

Cox brought in Steve Karsay to face the Mets in the bottom of the eighth inning. The right-hander had grown up only a few miles from Shea Stadium in Queens.[5] Karsay got the first batter, Lawton, to ground out to short. Then he walked Alfonzo, and Desi Relaford pinch-ran. When Piazza came to bat, Rose told the TV audience, "Here's the man the Mets want up in this spot, down a run, late in the game."[6] Karsay threw a fastball for a strike and Piazza took the pitch without swinging. Then Karsay threw another fastball and Piazza smashed this one to left-center. Andruw Jones chased the ball but in vain as it left the park.

As Piazza rounded the bases, the crowd of 41,235 cheered "USA, USA!"[7] After the game he said, "[I]t was almost like a blur to me, it was almost like a dream, sort of surreal. I'm just so happy I gave the people something to cheer. There was a lot of emotion. It was just a surreal sort of energy out there. I'm just so proud to be a part of it tonight."[8] Karsay got the next two batters, Ventura and Shinjo, out but the damage was done. The Mets left the inning with a 3-2 lead and New Yorkers had something to cheer about.

Benitez stayed in the game to pitch the ninth inning. After giving up a single to Javy Lopez, he struck out pinch-hitter B.J. Surhoff. The next batter, Keith Lockhart, grounded into a double play to end the game.

The Mets finished the season with an 82-80 record to finish in third place in the National League East. But they played with heart during the final six weeks of the season. The Mets put together a 25-6 run during that time, which included winning five straight games once baseball resumed play after 9/11.[9] Even more importantly, the Mets gave the region something to cheer about on the evening of September 21 and helped a city continue to heal as fans came together to cheer the home team.

Sources

In addition to the sources cited in the Notes, the author also used the Baseball-Reference.com, Baseball-Almanac.com, and Retrosheet.org websites for box score, player, team, and season pages, pitching and batting game logs, and other pertinent material.

Notes

1 "Piazza's Healing Home Run," MLB.com video presentation, accessed October 5, 2016.
2 Rob Neyer, "How Major League Baseball Responded to 9/11," SB Nation.com, accessed October 6, 2016.
3 Mike Vaccaro, "How Sept. 21, 2001, Unfurled at Shea – when Piazza made NY smile," *New York Post*, July 16, 2016.
4 "Piazza's Healing Home Run."
5 Ken Rosenthal, "What I'll Never Forget About Baseball's Return to New York After 9/11," Fox Sports.com, accessed October 6, 2016.
6 "How Sept. 21, 2001, Unfurled at Shea."
7 Steve Politi, "One Swing of the Bat Showed the Healing Power of Sports After 9/11," CNN.com, accessed October 7, 2016.
8 Ibid.
9 Ken Rosenthal, "What I'll Never Forget."

DAVID HAS THE WRIGHT STUFF:
WALK-OFF HIT POWERS METS TO COMEBACK WIN

MAY 19, 2006: NEW YORK METS 7, NEW YORK YANKEES 6, AT SHEA STADIUM

By Mark S. Sternman

Overcoming an early four-run deficit, the Mets rallied for a walk-off 7-6 win against the Yankees on May 19, 2006, after a classic confrontation between two of the biggest names in New York baseball during the early years of the twenty-first century.

The fireworks began long before the two teams even took the field. "A large transformer fire broke out … on the Grand Central Parkway in Queens, shutting down parts of the highway and snarling traffic for hours as baseball fans headed to … Shea Stadium. … At least three lanes were closed in both directions, and traffic had to be diverted … for several hours as firefighters worked."[1]

On paper, the pitching matchup favored the visitors. "The Mets' starting pitcher was Jeremi González, a 31-year-old right-hander who two weeks ago was at Class-AAA Norfolk after five undistinguished seasons with the Cubs, the Devil Rays, and the Red Sox. That's not exactly what [Mets owner] Fred Wilpon had in mind as the ideal opponent for the left-hander Randy Johnson, the Yankees' struggling future Hall of Famer."[2]

Mets manager Willie Randolph did not seem too concerned about his team taking on Johnson. "His velocity is down …" Randolph said. "Before, lefties were trying to get out of the lineup with hangnails. You don't see as much of it now because he's come back to the pack a little bit. But he's still tough."[3]

The Bronx Bomber bats boomed from the beginning of the ballgame. Johnny Damon doubled and scored on a single by Derek Jeter. Jeter stole second ahead of a Jason Giambi walk. Alex Rodriguez singled home Jeter. Giambi went to third, but Jose Valentin, normally an infielder, pegged out the needlessly aggressive A-Rod at second. Against a drawn-in infield, Jorge Posada grounded out, and Gonzalez needed just one more out to escape the onerous opening frame. But Robinson Cano doubled to score Giambi, and Bernie Williams doubled to plate Cano. The Yanks led 4-0. Gonzalez walked Melky Cabrera intentionally before fanning Johnson.

In a typical performance in a season where he would have an ERA of exactly 5.00, Johnson nearly gave the lead away immediately. Granted, he did not have a top-notch defensive alignment behind him, especially in the outfield: "Williams ha[d] one start in left field since 1992. Damon [was] playing with a cracked bone in his right foot. Cabrera … is so shaky that [Yankees manager Joe] Torre said he would rather not use him in left anymore."[4]

Doing the one thing a pitcher does not want to do with a big lead, Johnson walked leadoff hitter Jose Reyes. Paul Lo Duca singled Reyes to third. Facing future Yankee Carlos Beltran, Johnson gave

Fittingly named team captain in 2013, David Wright made seven All-Star teams before spinal stenosis severely hindered his career.

up a gopher, and the Yankees lead went from 4-0 to 4-3 in a flash. Carlos Delgado followed with a single, meaning both New York teams had the first four men in their batting orders reach, but the Big Unit rebounded to get out of the first with the one-run lead.

After a 1-2-3 top of the second, the Mets threatened in the bottom of the inning. Johnson, with Kelly Stinnett in for Posada behind the plate (the Yankees' star catcher had to leave because of tightness in his back), again walked the leadoff hitter, Valentin. Gonzalez sacrificed him to second, and, with two outs, Valentin stole third, but Lo Duca could not deliver the tying run.

The Yanks padded their lead in the top of the third. A walk to A-Rod, a single by Stinnett, and a fly ball by Cano sac fly put the Yankees up 5-3. Cabrera and Johnson followed with singles, so Damon came up with a chance to blow the game wide open, but flied harmlessly to Valentin.

After Johnson retired the first two batters in the bottom of the third, David Wright singled and another future Yankee, Xavier Nady, homered. Shea, normally a graveyard for offense, had seen 10 runs in three innings, as the teams went to the top of the fourth tied, 5-5.

A double by Jeter knocked out Gonzalez to start the fourth. Darren Oliver relieved and plunked Giambi, but recovered to fan Rodriguez. The substitute Stinnett singled again to score Giambi. Williams beat out a hit to shortstop Reyes. It was the second straight inning the Yankees loaded the bases with two outs on an infield hit to Reyes, and for the second straight time the Yankees left the bases loaded when Cabrera could not come through.

Johnson staggered through the fourth but preserved the 6-5 lead. Again with two outs, Reyes singled for the Mets and stole second. Lo Duca walked. Beltran, with two baserunners on again, flied out this time.

Oliver had an easy fifth, which allowed the Mets to tie the game in the bottom of the inning. With one out, Wright singled. He advanced on Nady's grounder to second and scored on Kaz Matsui's single. Valentin reached on A-Rod's error, but Chris Woodward, batting for Oliver, grounded to first.

The relief corps quelled the offense. For the Mets, Aaron Heilman retired nine Yankees in a row and Billy Wagner got them in order in the ninth. Heilman struck out three; Wagner struck out the side swinging in the ninth. "Heilman ha[d] requested a return to the starting rotation, but he is being impeded by his own success," a *New York Times* sportswriter commented. "The better he does in relief, the more he means to the Mets. 'All I want is the opportunity,' said Heilman, who lowered his earned-run average to 1.48. 'In the same respect, I want to go out and do my job however I can help the team.'"[5]

For the Yankees, Scott Proctor faced the minimum number of batters in the sixth and seventh innings. He did walk Reyes in the sixth, but Stinnett gunned down the speedy runner trying to steal. Kyle Farnsworth had a 1-2-3 eighth. Mariano Rivera, arguably one of the best closers, would surprisingly turn in the poorest relief effort in this game.

Joe Torre tended not to use Rivera in road tie games, but one of three injuries during the game resulted in the unusual move: Besides "Posada … Farnsworth [had to leave after an inning] because of a lower-back problem, and … Williams hurt his buttocks."[6]

Rivera yielded a double to Lo Duca with one out but fanned Beltran for the second out. The Yanks faced a choice – have Rivera go after Delgado or Wright. Rivera walked Delgado intentionally, and Wright walked off the Mets with a single to deep left field, scoring Lo Duca and giving the Mets a gratifying 7-6 win over their crosstown rivals. "Wright used every inflection of body language, not to curl the ball around a foul pole, but to push it over the head of Yankees' center fielder Johnny Damon," the *New York Times* noted. "When the ball bounced against the warning track, Wright celebrated as if he had just won Game 6 of the 1975 World Series."[7]

After the game, Wright shifted the credit to his teammates. "The bullpen did an unbelievable job," he said. "When you get that momentum swing, you feel like something good will happen. You could feel the momentum shifting."[8]

Wright knew well the challenges entailed in hitting Rivera. In a 2013 interview, Wright observed, "He basically dominates you with one pitch. Everybody says the same thing. He'll tell you what's coming and you're still not going to hit him. … He's the best to ever do it and I've seen firsthand how dominating he can be."[9]

Nearly a decade after the game, Wright talked about how much he enjoyed the moment. "I was 23 years old at the time and getting a chance to get a walk-off hit against arguably the greatest closer of all time, that's pretty exciting," Wright said in 2015. "I remember my parents came in that day, so my parents got a chance to see me get the hit against Mariano – definitely one of my great memories from the Subway Series."[10]

Thanks to Wright and his mates, for one day, at least, the Mets ruled New York baseball.

Notes

1 "Transformer Fire Clogs Traffic," *New York Times*, May 20, 2006.
2 Dave Anderson, "Two Teams Grope for Help Amid Avalanche of Injuries," *New York Times*, May 20, 2006.
3 Pat Borzi, "Latest Lima Effort Is No Laughing Matter," *New York Times*, May 19, 2006.
4 Tyler Kepner, "Mounting Injuries Trump Wright's Outing," *New York Times*, May 19, 2006.
5 Lee Jenkins, "Heilman Continues to Show Why He Could Start," *New York Times*, May 20, 2006.
6 Tyler Kepner, "Surgery for Pavano; Setbacks for Outfielders," *New York Times*, May 20, 2006.
7 Lee Jenkins, "Wright's Body Language Says It All for the Mets," *New York Times*, May 20, 2006.
8 Tyler Kepner, "For Mets, a Perfect Ninth," *New York Times*, May 20, 2006.
9 Mark Simon and Katie Sharp, "One Mo time: Rivera vs. Mets" espn.com/blog/new-york/mets/post/_/id/67871/one-mo-time-rivera-vs-mets (accessed July 26, 2017).
10 Anthony McCarron, "Yankees vs. Mets: The Daily News' 15 most memorable Subway Series moments," *New York Daily News*, September 17, 2015.

BELTRAN'S WALK-OFF ECLIPSES DELGADO'S 400TH CAREER HOMER

AUGUST 22, 2006: NEW YORK METS 8, ST. LOUIS CARDINALS 7, AT SHEA STADIUM

By Mike Wuest

The New York Mets outslugged the St. Louis Cardinals to win their 76th game of the season by a score of 8-7 in front of just under 50,000 fans at home in Shea Stadium. The win pushed the Mets' lead in the National League East to 13½ games, ahead of the second-place Philadelphia Phillies. The Cardinals, meanwhile, saw their lead over the Cincinnati Reds in the National League Central drop to just one game.

The victory gave the Mets (76-48) the best record in the National League. The Cardinals (66-58), at 66 wins, sat second overall in the NL, 10 games behind the Mets.

Mets starter John Maine came into the game feeling good about his chances to walk away with a win, seeing as how earlier in the season he had pitched four straight outings without allowing a run, including a shutout. This game started well for Maine, too; he retired the first nine batters he faced. Another shutout was not to be, however, as he saw his earned-run average jump almost a full run, from 2.68 to 3.58, after allowing seven runs to the Cardinals in the next two innings. Maine struck out five and walked two during his five innings of work for the Mets.

All seven of the runs charged to Maine came off the bat of All-Star slugger Albert Pujols, who hit two home runs against Maine – a three-run shot in the fourth inning, and a grand slam one inning later. The pair of round-trippers gave Pujols 38 homers and 105 runs batted in. After the game he was characteristically laconic about his fantastic day at the plate (2-for-4, 2 homers, 7 RBIs): "It doesn't matter. It's not about me."[1]

Cardinals starter Jeff Weaver fared little better. Making his eighth start for the Cardinals after being traded from the Los Angeles Angels of Anaheim, Weaver gave up four earned runs in five innings. The first run came on Carlos Delgado's 399th career home run, a line drive in the bottom of the second inning. In the bottom of the fifth, Weaver put Mets hitter Ricky Ledee aboard with a six-pitch walk, Jose Reyes reached on an error by left fielder Chris Duncan and Paul Lo Duca singled to load the bases. Ledee was out at the plate on Carlos Beltran's grounder to Weaver, but Delgado took a 3-and-1 pitch deep to plate four runs, his second home run of the game and the 400th of his career. The grand slam gave the Mets a 7-5 lead. Delgado finished the day 2-for-4 with two home runs and

Carlos Beltran set the franchise single-season home run mark with 41 in 2006.

five runs batted in. Asked after the game to compare his day to that of Pujols, Delgado responded, "This isn't a man-to-man matchup."[2]

Reliever Guillermo Mota came on for the Mets in the top of the sixth. After giving up a single to Cardinals center fielder Juan Encarnacion, who stole second on Mota's first pitch to Preston Wilson, Mota struck out Wilson and Ronnie Belliard, and got Cardinals catcher Yadier Molina to ground out.

The bottom of the sixth went slightly worse for Cardinals reliever Adam Wainwright. He gave up a leadoff single to the Mets' Endy Chavez and walked Chris Woodward. The runners advanced on pinch-hitter Jose Valentin's sacrifice, and Chavez scored on speedy shortstop Jose Reyes' grounder to second. Lo Duca's grounder to shortstop ended the sixth with the Cardinals clinging to a 7-6 lead.

In the seventh, reliever Pedro Feliciano replaced Mota. So Taguchi grounded out, but back-to-back walks to Aaron Miles and Chris Duncan chased Feliciano with Pujols coming up. Chad Bradford got Pujols to ground into an inning-ending 6-4-3 double play, however, and kept the Mets deficit at one run.

In the Mets's seventh, reliever Randy Flores retired three fearsome Mets hitters, Beltran (groundball to shortstop), Delgado (fly ball to left), and third baseman David Wright (liner to deep right) in order. The top of the eighth was also scoreless. Bradford got Scott Rolen to fly out, gave up a double to Encarnacion, walked pinch-hitter Timo Perez intentionally, then got Ronnie Belliard to hit into an 5-4-3 double play.

In the bottom of the eighth, the Mets threatened to tie the game. Reliever Tyler Johnson hit Michael Tucker with his first pitch. Endy Chavez bunted Tucker to second, and Johnson was pulled for Braden Looper. Chris Woodward's grounder in front of the plate moved Tucker to third. Mets manager Willie Randolph sent up ageless wonder Julio Franco to pinch-hit for pitcher Bradford. But Franco, playing in his 22nd major-league season, struck out looking.

The top of the ninth inning went as well as it could for Mets reliever Aaron Heilman, who struck out Yadier Molina and So Toguchi and got Aaron Miles to ground out to first. Now the Mets had three outs to try to win the game or send it to extra innings. As it turned out, they needed just one out.

Cardinals closer Jason Isringhausen retired Reyes on a grounder to second, but gave up a single to Paul Lo Duca. Beltran, who signed a $119 million contract with the Mets before the 2005 season[3] precisely for moments like these, was next up in the batter's box and he took Isringhausen's first pitch to him over the right-field wall for a two-run walk-off homer that extended the Mets' winning streak to five games.

Said Beltran after the game, "Walk-off is a great feeling."[4] Willie Randolph agreed, and added, "Beltran is my MVP, that's for sure."[5]

Sources

In addition to the sources cited in the Notes, the author also consulted Baseball-Reference.com and Retrosheet.

Notes

1 Associated Press, "Cardinals vs. Mets – Recap - August 22 2006," ESPN.com espn.com/mlb/recap?gameId=260822121. Accessed December 3, 2017.
2 Ibid.
3 Associated Press, "With $119 Million Deal Comes Stadium Tour – January 12, 2005," ESPN.com. espn.com/mlb/news/story?id=1964440. Accessed December 3, 2017.
4 Associated Press, "Cardinals vs. Mets - Recap – August 22, 2006."
5 Brian Lewis, "Good times – Beltran Walkoff, Delgado Slam Cap Amazin' Day," *New York Post*, August 23, 2006, nypost.com/2006/08/23/good-times-beltran-walkoff-delgado-slam-cap-amazin-day/. Accessed December 3. 2017.

A FATIGUED COMEBACK

MAY 17, 2007: NEW YORK METS 6, CHICAGO CUBS 5, AT SHEA STADIUM

By Gregory H. Wolf

The New York Mets had good reason to be tired when they took the field at Shea Stadium at 1:10 on Thursday afternoon to wrap up their four-game series with the Chicago Cubs. About 12 hours earlier, manager Willie Randolph's squad had left the diamond after an 8-1 victory that began more than three hours late due to inclement weather. That win improved the Mets' record to an NL-best 25-14 and pushed them back into first place, a half-game ahead of the Atlanta Braves.

With the spectacle of the Mets-Yankees interleague series about to take over Gotham for the coming weekend, Randolph, himself a former five-time All-Star second baseman for the Bronx Bombers, decided to give some of his players a day off. "There were so many regulars missing," opined sportswriter Ben Shpigel of the *New York Times*, "that some Mets who wandered by did not know which understudy was playing where."[1] Taking a seat on the pine were five former All-Stars, including three-quarters of the infield – shortstop Jose Reyes, second baseman Damion Easley, and third baseman David Wright – as well as catcher Paul Lo Duca and center fielder Carlos Beltran. Another past All-Star, Moises Alou, was also missing, having been placed on the disabled list the day before because of a quadriceps injury. "We've got the strongest bench in baseball," joked Shawn Green, who, along with slugger Carlos Delgado, occupied their customary third and fourth positions in the batting order.[2]

The Cubs (18-20), in third place in the NL Central, six games behind the streaking Milwaukee Brewers, might have breathed a sigh of relief when they saw the Mets lineup. But as beat writer Paul Sullivan of *Chicago Tribune* noted, "[M]isery happens, especially when the Cubs invade New York."[3] Losers of five of their last seven games, the North Siders were also without a major component of their offense, slugger Derrek Lee, who missed his third straight game with neck pain. "Without Lee," wrote Sullivan," the lineup looks average."[4]

Shea Stadium was packed with 42,667 partisan fans who took advantage of a spring afternoon with temperatures in the mid-60s and skies partly cloudy. To their delight, 24-year-old southpaw Jason Vargas set down the all nine Cubs batters in the first three innings. Vargas, who had just been called up from Triple-A New Orleans because starter Orlando Hernandez landed on the DL with shoulder bursitis, was making his first appearance for New York since being acquired from the Florida Marlins in an offseason trade. His teammates welcomed him back to the big club by shaving his head.[5]

The Cubs' 25-year-old right-handed starter, Angel Guzman, winless in six decisions in his career, benefited from a 6-4-3 double play to

David Wright became the Mets' all-time hits leader in September 2012, surpassing Ed Kranepool.

erase Endy Chavez's leadoff single and then overcame a rough third (a hit batter and a walk) to keep the game scoreless.

In the fourth, the Cubs struck first when Aramis Ramirez connected for a two-out single to drive in Angel Pagan, who had singled and stole second.

After putting two men on base in three of the first four innings, the Mets tied the game in the fifth. Chavez followed the Pagan method by singling and swiping second base. When Ruben Gotay doubled to right field, it was even at 1 apiece. Gotay moved to third on Green's single, but Delgado grounded back to Guzman who initiated a timely inning-ending twin killing.

Vargas had yielded only two hits through five innings, but stumbled in the sixth, surrendering a two-run round-tripper to Pagan, his second of the season, and another two-run blast to Ramirez, his 10th of the campaign, to give the Cubs a 5-1 lead. With just one out, Randolph seemed committed to resting his players, including his staff, no matter what the outcome. The bullpen remained silent and Vargas calmed down to retire the next two batters.

Suffering from what the *Tribune* called "hamstring cramps," Guzman did not return for the sixth.[6] Relievers Michael Wuertz and Will Ohman hurled three hitless innings to put Guzman in position to pick up his maiden victory, but that day would have to wait (in fact, he waited two more years).

Reliever Ambiorix Burgos took over for Vargas to start the eighth and held the Cubs hitless for two innings to set the stage for one of the Mets' most exciting and least expected come-from-behind victories.

Among the Achilles heels of the Cubs was its bullpen. Coming into this game, relievers had sported a dismal 2-10 record and seven blown saves. Skipper Lou Piniella called on closer Ryan Dempster, a 30-year-old right-hander coming off a lackluster 2006 campaign (1-9, 4.80 ERA with 24 saves). However, with a sturdy 2.37 ERA in 19 innings thus far in 2007, Dempster was one of Piniella's few bright spots in relief.

David Newhan ignited the Mets' comeback by leading off with a line-drive single. New York's first stroke of lucked occurred when Cubs right fielder Matt Murton snared Ramon Castro's short fly and then, according to the *Tribune*, failed to double up Newhan, who had almost reached second base.[7] Carlos Gomez followed with a single, which drew Piniella from the dugout to calm down his closer. It didn't help. Dempster walked pinch-hitter Beltran to load the bases, then issued another free pass, to Chavez, to force in Newhan as the Shea faithful were on their feet. Representing the winning run, Gotay stepped to the plate. With just three hits in 19 at-bats entering the afternoon, Gotay admitted candidly, "I thought I was going to be pinch-hit for." Gotay wasn't, and whacked a single to short left – just "beyond the outstretched glove" of shortstop Cesar Izturis, according to the *New York Times*, bringing Gomez home and pulling the Mets to within two runs.[8]

Piniella had enough. He yanked Dempster in favor of Scott Eyre, a 35-year-old rubber-armed LOOGY[9] with left-hander Shawn Green at the plate. Randolph, who recognized the shift in momentum, made his chess move by sending in the right-handed David Wright to bat for Green, who was no longer the threat that he once was in his 15th and final big-league season. In the first pinch-hit scenario in his career, Wright connected on Eyre's first offering for a single to drive in Beltran and put the Mets only one run behind. With the bases loaded and one out, to the plate stepped Delgado. Although he was mired in a season-long slump with just three home runs and a .217 batting average, the 35-year-old Delgado was still considered one of the most feared sluggers in the NL, having averaged 36 round-trippers per year over the last 11 seasons. "[W]e got the bases loaded down by four, but with only one out," said the Puerto Rican native. "[Dempster] wasn't throwing strikes and I said we've got a chance."[10] Delgado connected on Eyre's 1-and-0 fastball, sending a screeching grounder between first and second into right field, easily scoring Chavez and Gotay for a dramatic 6-5 victory in 2 hours and 31 minutes.

Delgado's hit "brought the Mets out of their dugout as they were a high school team," wrote sportswriter Harvey Araton of the *New York Times*.[11] The club's 11th comeback victory already in the early season made Burgos the winner, while collaring Dempster with his second loss. The win also marked the Mets' biggest ninth-inning comeback since they scored five runs against the Philadelphia Phillies' Curt Shilling on May 23, 1999.

While the Mets celebrated and gradually turned their eyes to their series with the Yankees, Lou Piniella of the Cubs fumed about another bullpen meltdown. "These guys have to do it," said the feisty skipper.

Named for the man who was most influential in bringing a National League franchise to New York, Shea Stadium also housed the New York Yankees in 1974 and 1975 while Yankee Stadium was undergoing renovation.

"I don't know what else to say."[12] Dempster, who was charged with five runs while recording just one out, had little to add. "I just lost the game. Not much more to say."[13]

Sources

In addition to the sources cited in the Notes, the author also consulted Baseball-Reference.com, Retrosheet.org, and SABR.org.

Notes

1 Ben Shpigel, "Mets' Makeshift Lineup Jells in Ninth," *New York Times*, May 18, 2007: D4.

2 Ibid.

3 Paul Sullivan, "Not-So-Sweet Charity; Dempster, Eyre Give Up 4-Run Lead as Mets Rally for 5 in 9th," *Chicago Tribune*, May 18, 2007: 4, 3.

4 Paul Sullivan, "Letter From the Cubs Beat," *Chicago Tribune*, May 18, 2007: 4, 14.

5 Kevin Devaney Jr., "No Win, but Vargas Feels He Fits In," *Journal News* (White Plains, New York), May 18, 2007: 5C.

6 Sullivan, "Not-So-Sweet Charity."

7 Ibid.

8 Shpigel.

9 LOOGY is an acronym for "left-handed, one-out only guy."

10 Kevin Devaney Jr., "Subs Super in Mets' Victory," *Journal News* (White Plains, New York), May 18, 2007: 5C.

11 Harvey Araton, "Sometimes It's Hard to Tell Which Team Is Really Up," *New York Times*, May 18, 2007: D1.

12 Sullivan, "Not-So-Sweet Charity."

13 Ibid.

SANTANA PITCHES METS' FIRST NO-HITTER

JUNE 1, 2012: NEW YORK METS 8, ST. LOUIS CARDINALS 0, AT SHEA STADIUM

By Thomas J. Brown Jr.

The evening of June 1, 2012, will be remembered as the night 50 years of frustration ended for the New York Mets. Johan Santana went through the St. Louis Cardinals' lineup all evening on the way to the Mets' first no-hitter. He walked five and struck out eight in the historic 8-0 victory. It was a triumph that marked the end of Mets' no-hit futility that went back to the start of the franchise in 1962.[1]

Santana had missed the entire 2011 season due to shoulder surgery. His return had been challenging. Mets manager Terry Collins said before the game that he had planned to limit Santana to a maximum of 110 to 115 pitches that night. Santana finished with a career-high 134. "I just couldn't take him out," Collins said after the game.[2]

Santana started strong, collecting three strikeouts in the first two innings. He kept the Cardinals in check while allowing three batters to hit fly balls to the deeper reaches of the outfield. But beyond the two walks, both surrendered in the second inning, the Cardinals never came close to getting a runner in scoring position.

The Mets scored in the bottom of the fourth inning as Adam Wainwright gave up three hits and a deep fly ball to the heart of the Mets batting order. Kirk Nieuwenhuis led off the inning with the Mets' first hit, a single up the middle. David Wright then doubled and runners were on second and third. Lucas Duda flied to deep right-center and Nieuwenhuis scored. Daniel Murphy tripled to right field and Wright trotted home. Wainwright got out the next two batters but the Mets led 2-0.

Santana continued to pitch masterfully. He walked the leadoff batters in the fourth and fifth innings. But each time he settled down and retired the Cardinals. He collected two more strikeouts, raising his total to five.

It almost ended in the sixth inning. Carlos Beltran, making his return to New York after being traded away the season before, led off and pulled a pitch from Santana down the left-field line. The ball appeared to hit the foul line but third-base umpire Adrian Johnson called it foul. "I saw the ball hitting outside the line, just foul," said Johnson after the game.[3] If it had been fair, Beltran would have had

Citi Field features an exterior façade reminiscent of Ebbets Field and the Jackie Robinson Rotunda at the main entrance, honoring the first African -American player in the major leagues.

a double and the no-hitter would have been over. After the foul call, Beltran grounded out. Santana kept his focus and struck out Matt Holliday. Allen Craig fouled out to first to end the inning.

The Mets built on their lead in the sixth inning. Wainwright gave up another single to Nieuwenhuis, then walked Wright. Duda stepped to the plate and hit another fly ball; this time it cleared the center-field fence. Three runs scored and the Mets led 5-0.

After keeping his no-hitter going on the umpire's call, Santana almost saw it end again in the top of the seventh. Left fielder Mike Baxter, who grew up in Queens, just minutes away from Citi Field, made a fantastic catch to save the no-hitter. Yadier Molina hit a line drive to deep left. Baxter ran at full speed and did not slow down as he stepped on the warning track. He extended his glove and made the catch just before his body violently slammed into the wall. He fell but managed to hold on to the ball. He subsequently left the game due to a bruised shoulder.[4]

In the bottom of the seventh inning Omar Quintanilla led off with a single. After Santana sacrificed him to second, Wainwright walked Andres Torres, who had replaced Baxter in left field. Cardinals manager Mike Matheny pulled Wainwright and called in Sam Freeman from the bullpen. Freeman walked Nieuwenhuis to load the bases, then walked Wright to force in a run. Duda struck out, but Murphy singled to left and Torres and Nieuwenhuis scored. Ike Davis grounded out but the Mets were up 8-0.

In the dugout during the Mets' seventh, Collins told Santana it would be his call to stay in the game or come out. Santana had no plans to remove himself.[5] After the game he said: "Tonight he was not going to take me out of the game. No chance."[6]

Johan Santana battled arm trouble and other injuries during his Mets tenure, but he summoned the strength to do what no other pitcher in team history had done: throw a no-hitter.

Santana continued his march toward the no-hitter in the eighth inning. After Tyler Greene flied out to left field and pinch-hitter Shane Robinson struck out, the crowd of 27,069 began shouting "Johan! Johan! Johan!"[7] When Santana gave up his fifth walk, to Rafael Furcal on his 118th pitch, Collins came to the mound. But it was a quick conversation. Santana got former teammate Beltran on a liner to second to end the inning.[8]

While the Mets batted in the bottom of the eighth inning, Santana sat away from his teammates at the end of the dugout, awaiting his chance at history. He had already surpassed the 108 pitches that he threw on May 8, his previous season high.[9] No one on the team bothered him as he waited for his chance to go out and make Mets history.

The ninth inning arrived and Mets fans were on their feet. Matt Holliday lined Santana's first pitch to center fielder Andres Torres for the first out. The tradition-starved Mets fans stood and roared as if Santana had just ended the inning.[10] When Allen Craig popped out to Nieuwenhuis in short left, the noise grew even louder. And when David Freese, the 2011 World Series most valuable player, struck out swinging, the crowd went wild.

Santana's teammates stormed the mound and a celebration erupted on the field and in the stands. Santana said in a postgame news conference that he had never thrown a no-hitter at any level. "I don't think I've ever even thrown a no-hitter in video games," he said.[11]

After Santana finished his interviews with the Mets announcers, he walked into the locker room where his teammates were waiting with champagne. "What a night for the Mets. Nobody better than Johan," Baxter said of the two-time Cy Young Award winner.[12]

The Mets finally had that elusive no-hitter. Their all-time ace Tom Seaver had come close, throwing five one-hitters during his years with the Mets. After 50 years and 8,019 games, the Mets finally had one for the record books. "I know how much this means to New York and to the New York Mets," Santana said, humbled at his accomplishment.[13]

Sources

In addition to the sources cited in the Notes, the author also used the Baseball-Reference.com, Baseball-Almanac.com, and Retrosheet.org websites for box-score, player, team, and season pages, pitching and batting game logs, and other pertinent material.

Notes

1 Gabe Lacques, "Johan Santana Ends Mets' 50-Year Wait for a No-Hitter," *USA Today*, June 2, 2012.
2 Andrew Marchand, "Johan Santana Tosses No-Hitter," ESPN.com, June 2, 2012.
3 Tim Rohan, "Santana, Pushing Past Pitch Count, Throws Mets' First No-Hitter," *New York Times*, June 2, 2012.
4 Marchand.
5 Ibid.
6 Lacques.
7 Marchand.
8 Ibid.
9 Lacques.
10 Rohan.
11 Marchand.
12 Rohan.
13 Ibid.

FOR FLORES, THERE'S (LIFE AFTER) CRYING IN BASEBALL: UNWANTED WILMER'S WALK-OFF BOOSTS METS OVER NATIONALS

JULY 31, 2015: NEW YORK METS 2, WASHINGTON NATIONALS 1, AT CITI FIELD

By Mark S. Sternman

Shown sobbing just days earlier after receiving word of a trade from his beloved Mets, Wilmer Flores, who remained in Queens after the transaction fell through, stroked an even more dramatic than usual walk-off homer to power New York over Washington by a 2-1 score in 12 innings.

Of the storybook tale, columnist Phil Mushnick opined, "Just when it seems time to swear off sports as a business predicated on doing one-way bad business, something happens to cause a reconsideration. … Nationals-Mets, start to finish, did the trick."[1]

Two days before this game, Flores, originally signed by the Mets nearly eight years earlier, cried on the field when he learned that the only professional organization for which he had ever played had traded him to the Brewers. But New York did not consummate the transaction due to concerns about the condition of Carlos Gomez's hip.

The day before his heroics, Flores talked about how he had to move on past his publicly painful humiliation. "I didn't want to make that scene out there," he said after Thursday's [game]. "I couldn't help it. … What happened yesterday, it's in the past. Now we've got to play."[2]

Flores certainly came to play with both his bat and his glove. His blast put an explanation point on the end of the nearly four-hour contest that saw little in the way of offensive production. The two teams used nine pitchers who yielded only 11 hits. The starting pitchers – Gio Gonzalez for the Nationals and Matt Harvey for the Mets – each gave up but one run, albeit in vastly different fashions.

Harvey started with a perfect top of the first. "The second batter, Yunel Escobar, hit a sharp grounder to second base, and Flores dived to his left and threw to first for the out. The crowd exploded and gave him a standing ovation."[3]

Leadoff hitter Curtis Granderson singled for New York, but a strike-out-caught-stealing double play bookended by the arms of Gonzalez and Washington catcher Jose Lobaton snappily erased the threat by the Mets.

Harvey also had a 1-2-3 second, and New York again got its leadoff hitter on thanks to a walk to Juan Uribe. Gonzalez retired the next three hitters to keep the game scoreless through two innings.

After Uribe reached, neither team had a baserunner until the bottom of the fourth. With two outs and none on, Gonzalez got wild, walking Uribe for the second time and walking Travis d'Arnaud as well. Flores beat out a grounder to short that plated Uribe from second, giving the Mets a 1-0 lead and Flores the first RBI of his memorable day. Gonzalez issued his third walk of the inning by

Yoenis Cespedes chats during batting practice prior to Game Three of the 2015 World Series.

passing Juan Lagares before fanning Eric Campbell to end the frame with a trio of New Yorkers stranded.

Harvey had retired the first 15 Nats in a row through five innings. The Mets threatened again with two outs in the bottom of the fifth. Ruben Tejada singled, and Daniel Murphy doubled him to third. Washington manager Matt Williams hooked the inefficient Gonzalez, who had needed 105 pitches to get only 14 outs, in favor of Tanner Roark. The reliever retired Uribe to keep the Nationals within a run.

With one out in the sixth, Lobaton singled off Harvey for Washington's first baserunner. Roark tried to sacrifice the catcher to second but struck out bunting. The failure to execute this fundamental play hurt the Nationals. Anthony Rendon's single moved Lobaton to third rather than scoring him, and Washington still trailed 1-0 after Harvey retired Escobar.

Roark set down New York in order in the bottom of the sixth, and the Nationals threatened again in the top of the seventh thanks to a leadoff double by Jayson Werth. But Harvey bore down against Bryce Harper, Ryan Zimmerman, and Ian Desmond to leave Werth at second.

After another clean inning by Roark, who faced seven hitters and got them all (including four strikeouts), Washington rallied to tie the score. With two outs and none on, Clint Robinson hit for Roark and Harvey hit Robinson. Danny Espinosa pinch-ran. Rendon singled Espinosa to second, and Escobar hit a clutch RBI single on Harvey's 109th and final pitch of the game. Tyler Clippard kept the game deadlocked by coming in and fanning Werth.

Aaron Barrett replaced Roark. Tejada had a leadoff single but could not score in the bottom of the eighth.

In the top of the ninth with one out, Clippard walked Zimmerman and Desmond, the only two free passes the Nationals would earn all game. With the save situation gone, manager Terry Collins brought in Jeurys Familia, the closer for the Mets, who escaped the jam by striking out Michael Taylor "before Eric Campbell snagged Jose Lobaton's sinking line drive in left field."[4]

The New York and Washington bullpens both did great work. With an easy ninth, Barrett ended up getting the final six batters he faced to send the game into extra innings. Likewise, Familia faced five Nationals and escaped unscathed. Felipe Rivero got New York in order in the bottom of the 10th and the bottom of the 11th; Hansel Robles and Carlos Torres did the same against the Nationals in the top of the 11th and 12th innings, with the final five Washington hitters of the game striking out.

Harper, the fourth National to fan, struck out looking. The tempestuous star complained about the call, causing home-plate umpire Jerry Meals to eject the Washingtonian. Even though a team's best player really should do all he can to stay in a tight game, Harper still tried to defend his indiscretion after the game: "He called a strike," he said. "I don't know. He'd been doing it all night. I told him what I said and that was it. … I'm sticking up for my team and myself at the same time. He was bad all night. I didn't get up the next inning so nothing hurt."[5]

Having already pitched two full innings, Rivero stayed on for the bottom of the 12th to face Flores "though Casey Janssen, Drew Storen and Jonathan Papelbon, the Nationals' deadline acquisition, had not yet pitched. Nationals manager Williams said two relievers were unavailable, but he would not specify who."[6]

Nearly traded days earlier, Flores played the storybook hero. Having not hit a round-tripper since June 12, he hit a walk-off home run to left-center field to give New York the win. The crowd gave him its fourth standing ovation.[7]

"I am sitting here looking at some guys who are outstanding writers – outstanding – and you can't write that. You guys couldn't come up with that. … Unbelievable," Terry Collins said. "Can it happen to a better person in a bigger situation than that? We're all thrilled for him."[8]

"Words can't really describe what has been going through his head and us as a team the last couple days," Harvey said. "For tonight to happen the way it did, it's pretty unreal."[9]

The man the Mets did not want delivered a sweet home victory to New York over the team's fiercest divisional rival. With the win, the Mets pulled to within two games of the Nationals for the division lead. Better yet, New York had a major reinforcement on the way, having acquired Yoenis Céspedes from Detroit earlier that day just before the trade deadline. With an old hand having come to the rescue and a new star heading to Queens, the Mets looked poised to make some playoff noise in 2015.

Wilmer Flores delivered perhaps the most important hit of the 2015 season. After his walk-off, the Mets took off and soon dispensed with the Washington Nationals in the NL East chase.

Met-rospectives

Notes

1 Phil Mushnick, "Just When Sports Is at Its Darkest, Here Comes Wilmer Flores," *New York Post*, August 2, 2015.
2 Roger Rubin, "Mets' Flores Ready to Move On After Trade Story Caused Tears," *New York Daily News*, July 31, 2015.
3 Rob Harms, "Wilmer Flores Swaps Tears for Cheers With Walk-Off Home Run," *New York Times*, August 1, 2015.
4 Mike Puma, "Unbelievable! Flores Dries Tears for Walk-Off HR in Thriller," *New York Post*, July 31, 2015.
5 James Wagner, "Bryce Harper Ejected in 11th Inning of a Crucial Game for Arguing a Called Strike Three," *Washington Post*, August 1, 2015.
6 Chelsea Janes, "Extra Dramatic: Nationals Fall to Mets in 12 Innings, 2-1," *Washington Post*, August 1, 2015.
7 This claim comes from Gary Cohen of SportsNet New York. See the archived video of the home run at youtube.com/watch?v=UmL4rNYmJ9U (accessed February 28, 2018).
8 Peter Botte, "Wilmer Flores, Nearly Traded, Hits Walk-Off HR in Mets Win," *New York Daily News*, August 1, 2015.
9 Mike Fitzpatrick, Associated Press, "Fan Favorite Flores Homers in 12th, Mets Beat Nationals 2-1," *Washington Times*, August 1, 2015.

NIEUWENHUIS HOME RUN CAPS METS' COMEBACK WIN

SEPTEMBER 8, 2015: NEW YORK METS 8, WASHINGTON NATIONALS 7, AT NATIONALS PARK

By Steven C. Weiner

As the July 31, 2015, nonwaiver trade deadline[1] got closer, it became apparent that the race for the National League East Division title was going to be a two-team affair, the New York Mets and the Washington Nationals. Speculation began months before as to who would contend for a postseason position and be buyers as the deadline loomed, what they might need to solidify their position, and what players might be available at what cost.

Each team made a major move as the deadline approached. On July 28, the Nationals traded minor leaguer Nick Pivetta to the Phillies for their closer, Jonathan Papelbon, and cash. The deal was not without controversy. Drew Storen was 29-for-31 in save opportunities at the time of the trade, but Nationals general manager Mike Rizzo was clear: "Papelbon is our ninth-inning pitcher."[2]

Minutes before the trade deadline, the Mets obtained Yoenis Cespedes from the Detroit Tigers in exchange for Michael Fulmer and Luis Cessa. Although Cespedes was a very accomplished defensive outfielder, it was clear that the Mets obtained the power hitter for his offense, having scored the fewest runs of any team in baseball through late July.[3] In addition to the Cespedes trade, the Mets also made deals to obtain Kelly Johnson, Juan Uribe, and Tyler Clippard to strengthen their infield depth and add a bullpen arm. In total, the Mets had given up five minor leaguers for their new acquisitions. It was clear that the Mets were serious about contending for a postseason spot for the first time since 2006.[4] Fans could eagerly anticipate what impact these players would have down the stretch of the race for the postseason.

Nine Mets-Nationals games remained on the schedule, including three at Citi Field beginning the very night of the trade deadline. Recent records in this rivalry revealed little regarding what was about to happen. The Nationals won 15 of the 19 games played against the Mets in 2014 and held a 6-4 record thus far in 2015, as well as a three-game lead in the National League East standings. The first game of the three-game series ended in dramatic fashion when Wilmer Flores hit a walk-off home run off Felipe Rivero in the bottom of the 12th inning for a 2-1 Mets victory. By the time the weekend was over, the Mets had swept the Nationals out of New

Matt Harvey's first full big-league season was highlighted by getting the starting nod in the Citi Field-hosted All-Star Game and a 2.27 ERA. After undergoing Tommy John surgery, he won the 2015 NL Comeback Player of the Year.

Met-rospectives

York and into a first-place tie in the NL East standings. Their early September series in Washington loomed large.

As the teams readied for their three-games series at Nationals Park starting September 7, the Mets held a four-game lead in the division race. In the month since their last meeting, the Mets had run off a seven-game winning streak while the Nationals had a six-game losing streak.

In the first game, the Mets got off to a 3-0 lead on solo home runs by Michael Conforto, Kelly Johnson, and Yoenis Cespedes off Max Scherzer. The lead was wiped out in the fourth inning when the Nationals scored five runs, including a grand slam by Wilson Ramos. The Mets tied the score at 5-5 in the sixth inning when Cespedes, who had doubled, scored on Travis d'Arnaud's sacrifice fly. The Mets scored three runs in the seventh inning that included an RBI double by Cespedes and led for good, 8-5. All that was left was to have Jeurys Familia strike out the side in the ninth inning for his 37th save. Mets' comeback victory number one was in the books!

For the second game in the series, the pitching matchup was set, the Nationals' Jordan Zimmermann (12-8, 3.38 ERA) versus the Mets' Matt Harvey (12-7, 2.60 ERA). Harvey, in his first full season back from Tommy John surgery, was in the middle of an innings-limit controversy that involved his agent Scott Boras, Dr. James Andrews, who performed the surgery, and the Mets.[5]

The game didn't start well for Harvey. Singles by Anthony Rendon and Yunel Escobar set the stage for consecutive RBI singles by Clint Robinson and Ian Desmond for a 2-0 Nats lead. In the top of the second, David Wright hit a solo home run to left for the Mets to cut the lead in half. Bad back and all, Wright was playing in only his 20th game of the season. The Nationals answered immediately and manufactured a run. Michael Taylor walked, was sacrificed to second by Jordan Zimmermann, and scored on Anthony Rendon's RBI single.

The Nationals' lead remained at 3-1 until the bottom of the sixth inning. Escobar singled and Robinson walked. When Harvey was unable to cleanly field a sacrifice bunt by Desmond, the bases were loaded. Taylor hit a hot grounder up the middle that skipped over the glove of center fielder Cespedes and all four runners scored. Cespedes seemed disconsolate over his error despite the encouragement of his teammates and coaches in the dugout after the inning ended.[6] Was the Mets' 7-1 deficit insurmountable in what was now a bullpen game?

Nationals relief pitcher Blake Treinen started the top of the seventh inning by yielding a single to David Wright. Treinen retired the next two batters and then things fell apart for the Nationals relievers. A walk to Wright and an RBI single by Wilmer Flores, and Treinen was done. Felipe Rivero walked his only two batters and was replaced by Drew Storen. Yoenis Cespedes cleared the bases with a double down the left-field line and suddenly the Mets trailed by just one run at 7-6. Storen proceeded to walk Daniel Murphy, advance the runners on a wild pitch, and walk the next two batters (forcing in a run) before getting the third out on a lineout. The Mets had tied the score, 7-7, on three hits and six walks in the inning.

In the top of the eighth inning, Kirk Nieuwenhuis became the latest Mets hero when he crushed a two-out solo home run to deep right center off Papelbon for an 8-7 Mets lead. Tyler Clippard retired the Nationals in order in the eighth and Jeurys Familia got Escobar to ground into a double play in the ninth with two runners on base to close out his 38th save. Remarkably, Mets' comeback victory number two was also in the books!

On the field just before the third game of the series, *New York Times* sportswriter Tim Rohan noted that "the Nationals had to smile as they posed for their annual team picture, coming off two of their most dispiriting losses of the season."[7] Again, the Nationals took a lead into the late innings of the game. Stephen Strasburg retired 21 of the first 25 batters he faced and entered the eighth inning with 12 strikeouts and a 2-1 lead. Mets starter Jacob deGrom was equally effective with nine strikeouts in seven innings of work. In the eighth inning, Kelly Johnson hit a leadoff homer off Strasburg and the score was tied at 2-2. Two batters later, Strasburg was replaced by Drew Storen after Curtis Granderson singled. Yoenis Cespedes promptly hit his 32nd home run of the season off Storen and the Mets led 4-2. The Nationals got the score to 4-3 on Bryce Harper's second home run of the game, off Tyler Clippard, but the Mets got that run back with a run off Jonathan Papelbon in the ninth inning for a 5-3 lead. Mets' comeback victory number three was in the books when Jeurys Familia again closed out the Nationals for his 39th save of the season. For the series, the Mets got exactly the offense they expected when they acquired Cespedes on July 31: six hits in 14 at-bats, three doubles, two home runs, and seven RBIs.

The Mets left Washington and continued building a winning streak to eight games and expanding their division lead to 9½ games. The remaining regular-season schedule, ending with a three-game series against the Nationals at Citi Field, soon became irrelevant. They clinched the National League East title on September 26 with a 10-2 win over the Cincinnati Reds at Great American Ball Park.

The Nationals never recovered from two consecutive three-game sweeps by the Mets. In fact, on the day after the Mets' clinching victory, Jonathan Papelbon started a dugout fight with Bryce Harper in the Nationals' home-season finale against the Philadelphia Phillies and was suspended by the Nationals for the balance of the season. "Of course, the ruckus started in the Nats' favorite inning for disasters involving relievers: the eighth."[8] By the time early October came around, Nationals manager Matt Williams had been fired.

The Mets won the division title in convincing and emphatic fashion against their principal competition. It would be rather subjective to suggest that any one of the Mets' three consecutive comeback wins against the Nationals in early September was the decisive game. Nonetheless, according to the Elias Sports Bureau, the Mets' 8-7 comeback victory on September 8 was their largest comeback this late in a game since 2001, serving to break whatever spirit remained for the Nationals.[9] Now it was time for some postseason baseball in New York!

Author's note

This author watched the three-game series from three different locations within Nationals Park. That didn't make any difference in the outcome, a Mets' sweep! Thomas Boswell, *Washington Post* columnist, captured the sentiment perfectly with a question. "Who wants to endure moments like this series that send thousands of fans to the Metro with expressions of glazed, disbelieving pain that we usually reserve for real-life miseries?"[10] Not me!

Sources

In addition to the sources cited in the Notes, the author also accessed Baseball-Reference.com and Retrosheet.org.

Notes

1 The nonwaiver trade deadline has been July 31 since 1986. For the previous six decades, the deadline date was June 15. The outrage in baseball circles surrounding Babe Ruth's historic $100,000 sale from the Red Sox to the Yankees in 1920 played a role in establishing restrictions on player swapping between teams. For additional discussion see: Jacob Pomrenke, "Many Twists and Turns in History of MLB Trading Deadline," July 27, 2011, sabr.org/latest/many-twists-and-turns-history-mlb-trading-deadline.

2 "Nationals Make Deal for Phillies Closer Jonathan Papelbon," ESPN.com, July 28, 2015, accessed January 22, 2018, espn.com/mlb/story/_/id/13333105/philadelphia-phillies-trade-jonathan-papelbon-washington-nationals.

3 Tim Rohan, "Mets Trade for Yoenis Cespedes as Yankees Stand Pat," *New York Times*, July 31, 2015.

4 Ibid.

5 Tim Rohan, "Matt Harvey Falters, but the Mets Storm Back for a Victory," *New York Times*, September 8, 2015.

6 Michael Powell, "A Night of Disconsolation and Redemption for the Mets," *New York Times,* September 9, 2015.

7 Tim Rohan, "Mets Latest Comeback Puts Rivals Far Behind," *New York Times*, September 9, 2015.

8 Thomas Boswell, "Fight Between Papelbon, Harper Turns Nationals' Wake Into a Public Viewing," *Washington Post*, September 27, 2015.

9 Tim Rohan, "Matt Harvey Falters, but the Mets Storm Back for a Victory."

10 Thomas Boswell, "After Another Buckle, the Nationals Prove They Need a Stronger Spine," *Washington Post*, September 9, 2015.

METS EDGE THE DODGERS TO ADVANCE TO THE NLCS

OCTOBER 15, 2015: NEW YORK METS 3, LOS ANGELES DODGERS 2, AT DODGER STADIUM
GAME FIVE OF THE 2015 NATIONAL LEAGUE DIVISION SERIES

By Bob Webster

The New York Mets beat the heavily favored Los Angeles Dodgers, 3-2, in the National League Division Series winner-take-all Game Five at Dodger Stadium, before a crowd of 54,602. Daniel Murphy of the Mets, who hit .281 with 14 home runs during the regular season, played the role of hero in the game by going 3-for-4 with a double and a homer and scoring after a heads-up play on the basepaths in the fourth inning.

The teams had split the first two games in LA and did the same at New York's Citi Field. Now, with Clayton Kershaw having picked up the win in Game Four and the Dodgers handing the ball to Zack Greinke for Game Five, the Dodgers figured they were in a pretty good position to win the series.

Jacob deGrom took the mound for the Mets. In a Game One win, the 2014 NL Rookie of the Year,[1] pitched seven shutout innings, giving up five hits while striking out 13 Dodgers. During the regular season, deGrom went 14-8 with a 2.54 ERA and 205 strikeouts in 191 innings pitched.

The Dodgers starter was Zack Greinke, the regular-season ERA leader, who picked up the win in Game Two of the series. Greinke was 19-3 with a league-leading ERA of 1.66 in 32 starts during the regular season, striking out 200 in 202⅔ innings pitched.

DeGrom had a 3.66 ERA in three career regular-season starts against LA. Greinke, who had held the Mets to two runs in Game Two, had limited his opponents to three or fewer runs in all but two of his regular-season starts.[2]

The Dodgers finished first in the NL West with a 92-70 record; the Mets at 90-72 were the champions of the NL East.

Mets leadoff hitter Curtis Granderson grounded to third baseman Justin Turner, who in the shift was playing between first and second. Granderson was called out at first, but after review, the call was overturned and he was safe. After David Wright struck out swinging, Murphy doubled into the left-field gap and advanced to third when Enrique Hernandez bobbled the ball, scoring Granderson. Greinke buckled down and struck out Yoenis Cespedes and Lucas Duda to get out of the inning.

Howie Kendrick led off against deGrom and lined his third pitch to first baseman Duda. Corey Seager lined a base hit to left field. Adrian

The latest in a line of great Mets pitchers, Jacob deGrom won the NL Rookie of the Year in 2014 and made the All-Star team in 2015.

Gonzalez followed with a single to right, sending Seager to third. Justin Turner followed with a single to right, driving in Seager and advancing Gonzalez to third. Andre Ethier singled on a soft pop fly to left, scoring Gonzalez, with Turner taking second. Dan Warthen, the Mets pitching coach, came out to calm down deGrom. It must have worked; deGrom struck out Yasmani Grandal and Enrique Hernandez to end the inning with the Dodgers leading, 2-1. The three runs scored on five singles and a double, with five of the six outs recorded as strikeouts.

Greinke retired the Mets in order in the top of the second while striking out Travis d'Arnaud and Wilmer Flores. With one out, Michael Conforto drove the ball to the warning track down the right-field line, but a diving Andre Ethier tracked it down.

The Dodgers threatened again in their half of the second. Joc Pederson walked and advanced to second on Greinke's bunt. Howie Kendrick reached on an error by shortstop Flores, whose high throw pulled Duda off the bag. Peterson held at second. But deGrom struck out Seager and Gonzalez to get out of the jam.

The Mets were retired 1-2-3 in the top of the third. Justin Turner, playing with a banged-up knee, led off the bottom of the third inning by doubling into the left field corner. Andre Ethier lined out to Conforto in left. With a 2-and-0 count on Grandal, Turner stole third. Grandal reached first on a walk, bringing out Mets manager Terry Collins. DeGrom got Hernandez to ground into a 1-6-3 double play to end the inning.

Daniel Murphy singled to left to lead off the Mets fourth. After Cespedes flied out to center, Duda walked. In a heads-up play, as Murphy jogged to second on the walk he noticed no one was covering third because the shift was on, so as soon as he reached second, he broke for third. The Dodgers had three infielders to the right of second base and Seager was very close to second base when Murphy arrived there. Murphy, who stole only two bases during the regular season, took off for third hoping that nobody had called time out. "Just trying to casually walk to second and hoping that nobody called time because I look like an idiot if somebody calls time and I run to third," Murphy said. "I'm not sure who was supposed to cover, but there was nobody there. I'm not the fleetest of foot, but just fast enough for that one."[3] Murphy's alertness paid off: When Travis d'Arnaud hit a foul fly to Ethier in right, Murphy tagged up and scored, tying the game at 2-2. Conforto grounded out to end the inning.

With one out in the top of the sixth, Murphy again came through, hitting a home run to right to give the Mets a 3-2 lead and silencing the crowd at Chavez Ravine. Greinke had allowed only five baserunners in six innings, but Murphy was a triple short of a cycle.[4]

Neither starting pitcher made it out of the seventh inning. With two down in the Mets' half, Flores singled to center. Kelly Johnson, pinch-hitting for deGrom, singled to second baseman Howie Kendrick, bringing Dodgers manager Don Mattingly out of the dugout to take the ball from Greinke. Luis Avilan replaced Greinke and retired Granderson on a fly ball to Hernandez in left.

Noah Syndergaard came in to pitch the bottom of the seventh and allowed only a two-out walk to Gonzalez. It was the rookie's first big-league relief appearance.

Chris Hatcher replaced Avilan in the top of the eighth and retired the side in order. Jeurys Familia came in to replace Syndergaard in the bottom of the eighth, and did the same.

The Dodgers' Kenley Jansen came in to pitch in the top of the ninth to try to hold the Mets at bay. He got Duda to pop out to short and d'Arnaud to pop out to first baseman Gonzalez in foul territory. Juan Lagares doubled down the left-field line and Jansen intentionally walked Flores with Familia coming up to bat. Familia, in his first plate appearance of 2015 (he had only four in his major-league career),[5] struck out swinging, giving the Dodgers one last chance to keep their season alive.

Chase Utley, making his first appearance since serving a two-game suspension for his take-out slide in Game Two of the series that broke the leg of Mets shortstop Ruben Tejada, lined out to Granderson in right field.[6] Familia then struck out A.J. Ellis and Howie Kendrick to pick up the save, his second of the series and send the Mets to the NL Championship Series against the Chicago Cubs.

Murphy had three hits off Greinke. Murphy batted .333 in the series and homered three times, twice off Greinke and once off Kershaw. He was voted the series' MVP.

"Daniel was a tough out all series," Dodgers manager Mattingly said. "He's always to me been a guy that's been a tough out. Pretty much hits everybody's fastball."[7]

Sporting flowing locks and a triple-digit heater, Noah Syndergaard struck out 218 batters in 2016.

DeGrom won two games in the series, both on the road. Fifty-eight of his 105 pitches were with runners in scoring position.

Sources

In addition to the sources cited in the Notes, the author also accessed MLB.com, MLB.TV, and Retrosheet.org.

Notes

1 Associated Press, "Mets Eliminate $307-Million Dodgers," *San Francisco Examiner,* October 15, 2015. sfexaminer.com/mets-eliminate-307-million-dodgers/.

2 Anthony DiComo and Ken Gurnick, "Daniel Boon: Murphy Lifts Mets Unto NLCS!" MLB.com, October 16, 2015. mlb.com/news/mets-defeat-dodgers-in-game-5-advance-to-nlcs/c-154600686.

3 "Mets Eliminate $307-Million Dodgers."

4 "Mets 3, Dodgers 2: NLDS Game 5 Recap," October 15, 2015. nytimes.com/live/new-york-mets-los-angeles-dodgers-nlds-game-5/.

5 Ibid.

6 Scott Polacek, "Mets vs. Dodgers: Game 5 Score and Twitter Reaction From 2015 MLB Playoffs," bleacherreport.com, October 15, 2015. bleacherreport.com/articles/2579659-mets-vs-dodgers-game-5-score-and-twitter-reaction-from-2015-mlb-playoffs

7 "Mets Eliminate $307-Million Dodgers."

SIXTH STRAIGHT FOR MURPHY KEYS NEW YORK SWEEP OF CHICAGO

OCTOBER 21, 2015: NEW YORK METS 8, CHICAGO CUBS 3, AT WRIGLEY FIELD
GAME FOUR OF THE 2015 NATIONAL LEAGUE CHAMPIONSHIP SERIES

By David Rickard

A single major-league baseball season spans … well, *seasons* … and for that reason alone both good stretches and bad can often seem never-ending. Just as players are prone to streaks and slumps, so too are teams as a whole or any component thereof. For the 2015 New York Mets, pitching and hitting were on vastly different trajectories for much of the spring and summer, until a single player acquisition at the trade deadline invigorated the club and set it on the path that led eventually to fall baseball and Game Four of the National League Championship Series.

Yoenis Cespedes, who came to the Mets via trade with Detroit as the final minutes ticked down before the trade deadline on July 31, did not singlehandedly resuscitate the New York offense. But his arrival, coinciding dramatically with a crucial three-game series against Washington, provided a much-needed spark to a struggling batting order and had a galvanizing effect on his teammates. However, the Cuban outfielder's contribution, though critical to the pennant drive, was only the prelude to a record-setting postseason display from a hitherto unexpected source.

The Mets bolted from the gate in 2015, and were in first place in the National League East with a 16-8 mark on May Day. Then came injuries to David Wright and Travis d'Arnaud, and what had been a tepid offense became one of eye-averting futility. Through July New York was last in the league in runs scored; on one inglorious day the players batting fourth and fifth had batting averages of .170 and .179, respectively, only the second time in the live-ball era that a team sported such woeful numbers in the heart of the order.[1] Through it all, the starting rotation featuring Matt Harvey, Jacob deGrom, Noah Syndergaard, Steven Matz, and Bartolo Colon kept the Mets in contention, despite the dearth of run support. "The Mets," wrote Mike Pesca of the imbalance between offense and defense, "were like restaurant owners with a team of brilliant young chefs turning out four-star dishes, only to have a bumbling wait staff trip and spill Consomme in customers' laps."[2]

Despite its struggles, the team had a sub-.500 record only once after the season's fifth game, at 36-37 on June 24, and that lasted only a day. Then came the Cespedes deal. He didn't suit up for the first Washington game, a 12-inning 2-1 win that ended on a walk-off home run from Wilmer Flores. He was in the lineup for the subsequent 3-2 and 5-2 victories, after which the teams were tied for the NL East lead. One day later the Mets had sole possession of first place, and there they stayed. New York went 38-22 after the trade, with five of the losses following the September 26 division clincher over Cincinnati.

The Chicago Cubs came into the NLCS with a groundswell of national support. After 100 years without a pennant, a new ownership team took over in 2009, and two years later Theo Epstein and Jed Hoyer came aboard. The new administration assured fans the transformation of the Cubs wouldn't happen overnight, and it didn't – the Cubs remained losers during the first three years after Epstein took over as president of baseball operations, finishing last in the Central Division twice. They won a few more games each season, however, and in 2015 broke loose, posting a 97-65 mark and finishing third behind St. Louis and Pittsburgh. A wild-card win over the Pirates preceded a four-game dispatch of the Cardinals, setting up their meeting with New York.

But storylines change as events dictate. While the Chicago team's narrative had an obvious hook, it was in the Dodgers-Mets Division Series that the most compelling individual achievement of the postseason got underway. Leading off the fourth inning of a scoreless affair at Dodger Stadium, second baseman Daniel Murphy deposited a Clayton Kershaw fastball deep into the Mets bullpen. New York went on to win the game, 3-1, and at the time the story was that Kershaw had lost rather than that Murphy had gone deep. But the Mets went on to take the series in five, and Murphy homered in Games Four and Five – off Kershaw again, and Zack Greinke.

And then he just kept on slugging. The Mets, behind Harvey, won Game One of the NLCS, 4-2, a task made easier by Murphy's first-inning homer. He duplicated the feat, a two-run shot this time, in a 4-1 victory the following night. In Chicago for Game Three, Murphy drew the Mets even in the third stanza with still another long ball, then singled and scored a run in the seventh as New York pushed the Cubs to the brink of elimination. Going into Game Four, Murphy had homered in five straight postseason games, tying him for the record set in 2004 by Carlos Beltran.

In contrast to the regular season, which had an obvious turning point, Game Four of the NLCS had no such pivotal moment; before starter Matz had so much as toed the Wrigley Field rubber for the first time, his teammates had given him all the runs the Mets would need in the game. Curtis Granderson opened matters with a single, but Wright struck out and Murphy fouled out. Chicago's relief at retiring Murphy was almost palpable, but Cespedes drew a walk.

Then Lucas Duda – who, commentator Ron Darling informed the national television audience, had "put on a display, home run after home run," during batting practice[3] – silenced the crowd as surely as if he'd cut a wire, drilling a Jason Hammel fastball into the center-field seats. The Mets, having won five of six to that point in the postseason when striking first, jumped in front, 3-0. Two pitches later the lead was four, courtesy of an opposite-field clout by d'Arnaud. A hit batsman, a misplayed fly ball, a stolen base, and a tricky drive into the right-field corner followed, and though they didn't add to New York's advantage, they did suggest a relentlessness that didn't bode well for the home team.

Travis Wood took over for Hammel in the second with one out and one on, surrendered a single to Murphy, and struck out Cespedes. This brought Duda to the plate again, who once more worked the count to 3-and-2 before slapping a double into the right-center-field gap. Wright and Murphy scored, giving Duda five runs batted in and the Mets a 6-0 lead. The big first baseman, who entered the game with three hits in 24 postseason at-bats, hit it so sharply that Chicago shortstop Javier Baez was unable to do more than pivot and watch as the ball caromed off the grass 20 feet past him.

Matz failed to earn the win, leaving one out shy of the required five innings after Dexter Fowler and Jorge Soler hit back-to-back two-out singles. Colon, pitching out of the bullpen, ended the threat by striking out Kris Bryant and then tossed a scoreless sixth to get credit for the win.

The middle innings didn't see an expansion of New York's lead – the Cubs, in fact, cut into it with a run in the fourth – but the impression deepened of a team on the cusp of committing additional mayhem. The Mets threatened in the sixth, but a leadoff triple by Wilmer Flores was wasted. In the seventh they loaded the bases with one out, starting with a double to the center-field wall by the lethal Murphy, but again were unable to score.

Then came the eighth, and Murphy's ascent into the record book. Facing Fernando Rodney with two outs and a man on, he squared up a 1-and-1 fastball and lifted it into the netting atop the fence in right-center field. In addition to capturing the consecutive games home-run record, Murphy's seven total homers against Los Angeles and Chicago tied him for fourth on the all-time list with Troy Glaus, Melvin Upton, and Jayson Werth, trailing only Beltran, Barry Bonds, and Nelson Cruz with eight each.[4]

With an 8-1 lead and only six outs separating the Mets from a sweep, the two-run homer by Kris Bryant in the bottom of the inning was more a harbinger of the next season than a serious threat to extend the current one. The fans cheered, but 30 minutes later most were on their way home, and the Mets were on their way to Kansas City and a World Series meeting with the Royals. Though Murphy's historic spree came to a halt and the Mets fell to the Royals in five games, Game Four of the 2015 NLCS remains a high point in franchise history.

Sources

In addition to the sources cited in the Notes, the author also accessed Baseball-Reference.com and the Ultimate Mets Database.

Notes

1 Patrick Dubuque, Sam Miller, and Jason Wojciechowski, *Baseball Prospectus 2016: The Essential Guide to the 2016 Season* (Nashville: Turner Publishing Company, 2016), 319.
2 Ibid.
3 Major League Baseball on TBS: youtube.com/watch?v=8gaf3hb92Ww.
4 Victor Mather, "Daniel Murphy Breaks a Record With Another Postseason Homer," *New York Times*, October 22, 2015.

METS STAGE THREE COMEBACKS AND DEFEAT PHILLIES WITH CABRERA EXTRA-INNING WALK-OFF

SEPTEMBER 22, 2016: NEW YORK METS 9, PHILADELPHIA PHILLIES 8, AT CITI FIELD

by Michael Huber

You know the old cliché: Some fans claim they've seen it all. Yet only a crowd of 35,759 at Citi Field can state that they have witnessed in person perhaps one of the greatest comebacks in the history of New York Mets baseball. In a "win that defied all logic,"[1] Asdrubal Cabrera led the New Yorkers with a walk-off, game-winning, three-run home run in the bottom of the 11th.

With only 10 games left in the 2016 regular season, New York was nine games out of first place in the National League's East Division. The Mets had just been swept by the Atlanta Braves in a three-game series. It was crucial that they win this four-game series against the Phillies. Their manager, Terry Collins, said, "We talked before the game and said, 'It's a 10-game season.' Best team gets in."[2] Philadelphia, on the other hand, was 20 games behind the division-leading Washington Nationals, even after winning four of five coming to New York.

Constantly affable and generous, Curtis Granderson averaged 26 home runs in his four full seasons as a Met—reaching 30 in 2016.

Rookie righty Seth Lugo (4-2, 2.35 ERA) took to the mound for the Mets, opposed by Phillies left-hander Adam Morgan (2-10, 5.57 ERA). It was Lugo's first appearance against the Phillies. Morgan had pitched against Philly on August 26, earning a loss after yielding six runs in five innings. In this game, both pitchers were sharp in the first inning, retiring batters in order. Lugo struck out two Phillies, while Morgan struck out the side. After the Phillies went again with three-up, three-down, thanks to a double play, New York's T.J. Rivera singled to start the bottom of the second. Curtis Granderson was in the hole with an 0-and-2 count when he launched a ball deep down the right-field line for a two-run homer. Morgan retired the next three Mets batters, but New York had an early lead.

In the top of the fourth, the Phillies batters were seeing Lugo for the second time. Cesar Hernandez tripled to right to start a Philadelphia rally. Roman Quinn drove him in with a groundout to second, but Lugo quickly got Odubel Herrera and Maikel Franco to fly out. In the fourth, Lugo was not so lucky. Ryan Howard and Cameron Rupp hit back-to-back home runs, on the first pitches thrown by Lugo to each, and Philadelphia had taken the lead. Lugo seemed a bit rattled. He survived the inning, but he walked Aaron Altherr and Hernandez before getting the third out.

In the bottom of the fifth, the Mets hitters were getting their third time through the order. After Alejandro De Aza struck out, Ty Kelly pinch-hit for Lugo and drew a walk. Reyes flied out to deep center, and Cabrera reached on an infield single. With Yoenis Cespedes batting, Morgan uncorked a wild pitch and Kelly scampered to third. Cespedes then singled into right field, and the score was tied, 3-3. Two innings later, Reyes walked with two outs. Cabrera singled, and Cespedes doubled to left with Reyes scoring. Comeback number one.

Each starter pitched five innings. Luis Garcia replaced Morgan to open the bottom of the sixth. Then the managers inserted pitchers in a matchup mode. Collins wore out a path from the dugout to the mound, and none of his nine relievers pitched more than one inning. For the Phils, eight calls were made to the bullpen. Jeurys Familia pitched 1⅔ innings to lead the workload.

With New York ahead 4-3 entering the eighth inning, Philadelphia managed a rally. Hernandez singled to lead off. Quinn sacrificed Hernandez to second. Herrera hit a tough grounder to second and made a head-first dive into first base, and umpire Kerwin Danley called him safe on the bang-bang play. The Mets challenged the decision, but after replay review, the call was confirmed: safe. Herrera had held up at third. Franco then crushed a fastball by Addison Reed (the fourth Mets reliever) into the Phillies bullpen, and suddenly, the Mets were down by two tallies. Franco's dramatic three-run homer had "stabbed the Mets."[3] It was Franco's first round-tripper since mid-August.

True fans stayed at Citi Field to watch their Mets come to the plate in the bottom of the ninth. Pinch-hitter Brandon Nimmo stroked a line-drive single to right. Jay Bruce struck out swinging, and then Reyes "destroyed a hanging change-up over the 370-foot mark in right field"[4] for comeback number two. In an instant, the ballgame was tied. To extra innings they went.

Both teams were three-up and three-down in the 10th, but in the 11th, Phillies shortstop Freddy Galvis drove a liner to deep left-center for a leadoff double. Familia, who had come on to pitch the 10th, struck out Altherr. Tommy Joseph followed with a groundout to second, but Galvis moved to third on the out. Collins ordered Familia to intentionally walk Hernandez. With a 1-and-1 count, A.J. Ellis singled into short right field, and Galvis scored the go-ahead run with Hernandez going to third. Jerry Blevins came on to relieve Familia, but he hit Herrera with a 3-and-2 pitch, loading the bases. Jim Henderson was summoned from the bullpen, and after he threw nine pitches to Franco, who kept fouling them off, Franco took ball four, and Hernandez scored the Phillies' eighth run. Peter Bourjos grounded out to third baseman Reyes, who stepped on the bag for the third and final out.

Down by two runs but not out, New York did not give up. Edubray Ramos came in to pitch for Philadelphia in place of Severino Gonzalez. Nimmo grounded out to short. Then Michael Conforto pinch-hit for pitcher Henderson and drew a four-pitch walk. Reyes singled to left, and the fans were on their feet. Ramos's first offering to Cabrera was a ball, but the next pitch was a "slider up and out over the plate, and Cabrera hit it far enough that no Phillies outfielder had any chance to catch it,"[5] for comeback number three. Cabrera's smash, his 22nd of the 2016 campaign, meant a 9-8 win for the home team, and he boasted, "As soon as I hit it, I knew it would be out."[6] Not even out of the batter's box, he tossed his bat into the air and threw his arms skyward to punctuate the victory.

The top of the Mets order provided the bulk of the damage against the Phillies. Reyes was 2-for-5 with a walk, a homer, three runs scored, and two RBIs. Cabrera was 3-for-6 with the three-run blast. Cespedes went 3-for-4 with a walk and two RBIs. Granderson, batting fifth, added a home run and drove in the other two New York runs.

The two teams combined to get 49 players (19 pitchers) into the game. Phillies skipper Pete Mackanin labeled this "probably the toughest loss of the season."[7] He added, "The offense did a heck of a good job coming back twice, going ahead, and we just let them right back in."[8] Gomez, who picked up his sixth blown save of the season, told the sportswriters, "Today was another bad day, probably one of the worst days I've had."[9] In the New York clubhouse, Reyes said, "We had to win this game, to set the tone after the series we had with the Braves."[10] Collins added, "Tonight's game personifies exactly what the season is like. Up and down, up and down. You've just got to keep playing."[11]

The Mets' comeback victory allowed them to hold onto one of the National League's wild-card spots. They took three of four in this series from the Phillies, and the Mets won seven of their last 10 to clinch the wild-card berth and a second straight trip into the postseason.[12]

Sources

In addition to the sources mentioned in the Notes, the author consulted Baseball-Reference.com, mlb.com, and Retrosheet.org.

A recap of the leap-frogging comebacks from mlb.tv can be seen at youtube.com/watch?v=omeXDvZq8sA.

Built adjacent to Shea Stadium, Citi Field's first official major league game occurred on April 13, 2009 against San Diego.

Notes

1 Matt Gelb, "Gomez Blows Save, Phils Lose Heartbreaker," *Philadelphia Inquirer*, September 23, 2016: C01.
2 Danny Knobler and Todd Zolecki, "Mets Win Thriller on Cabrera's Walk-Off homer," m/mlb.com/news/article/202801934/mets-win-on-asdrubel-cabreras-walk-off-homer/?game_pk=449153, posted September 23, 2016.
3 Gelb.
4 Ibid.
5 Knobler and Zolecki.
6 Ibid.
7 Gelb.
8 Knobler and Zolecki.
9 Gelb.
10 Knobler and Zolecki.
11 Maria Guardado, "Resilient Mets rally twice to beat Phillies in wildest win of the season," nj.com/mets/index.ssf/2016/09/mets_win_emotional_tug_of_war_vs_phillies.html, posted September 23, 2016.
12 The Mets hosted the San Francisco Giants in a one-game wild-card game but lost, 3-0. However, for the second time in franchise history, the Mets had made the postseason in consecutive years (previously in 1999-2000).

CONTRIBUTORS

THOMAS J. BROWN JR. is a lifelong Mets fan who became a Durham Bulls fan after moving to North Carolina in the early 1980s. He was a national board certified high school science teacher for 34 years before retiring in 2016. Tom still volunteers with the ELL students at his former high school, serving as a mentor to those students and the teachers who now work with them. He also provides support and guidance for his former ELL students when they embark on different career paths after graduation. Tom has been a member of SABR since 1995 when he learned about the organization during a visit to Cooperstown on his honeymoon. He has become active in the organization since his retirement. Tom has written numerous biographies and game stories, mostly about the NY Mets. He also enjoys traveling as much as possible with his wife and has visited major-league and minor-league baseball parks across the country on his many trips. He also loves to cook and makes all the meals for at his house while writing about those meals on his blog, Cooking and My Family.

FREDERICK C. (RICK) BUSH, his wife Michelle, and their three sons Michael, Andrew, and Daniel live in the greater Houston area, and he teaches English at Wharton County Junior College in Sugar Land. An avid Astros fan, he was overjoyed about the team's first World Series championship but nevertheless fears it may be a sign of an impending apocalypse. Bill Nowlin and Rick co-edited *Bittersweet Goodbye: The Black Barons, the Grays, and the 1948 Negro League World Series* and are currently co-editing a book about the 1946 Newark Eagles, a team that featured four Hall of Fame players in addition to the only woman enshrined in the HOF, co-owner Effa Manley.

ALAN COHEN has been a SABR member since 2011, serves as Vice President-Treasurer of the Connecticut Smoky Joe Wood Chapter, and is the datacaster (stringer) for the Hartford Yard Goats, the Double-A affiliate of the Colorado Rockies. His first visit to Shea Stadium was for the Mets-Giants doubleheader on May 31, 1964 – Baseball's Longest Day. He has written more than 40 biographies for SABR's BioProject, more than 30 games for SABR's Games Project, and has contributed stories to *The National Pastime* and *Baseball Research Journal*. He has expanded his *BRJ* article on the Hearst Sandlot Classic (1946-1965), an annual youth All-Star game which launched the careers of 88 major-league players. He has four children and six grandchildren and resides in West Hartford, Connecticut with his wife Frances, one cat (Morty) and two dogs (Sam and Sheba).

RORY COSTELLO, a lifelong Mets fan, watched plenty of the games covered in this book on TV and had the good fortune to attend some of them in person, too. He lives in Brooklyn, New York, with his wife Noriko and son Kai.

TOM CUGGINO is a native of Bronxville, New York but currently lives in Wheaton, Illinois where he works as a financial controller for Cisco Systems and enjoys an active family life with his wife and three daughters. He is interested in all things Yankees and Cubs, rivalries, ballparks and their influence on cities, rituals and traditions, the Pacific Coast League, and Latin America's influence on baseball.

RICHARD CUICCHI joined SABR in 1983 and is an active member of the Schott-Pelican Chapter. Since his retirement as an information technology executive, Richard authored *Family Ties: A Comprehensive Collection of Facts and Trivia about Baseball's Relatives*. He has contributed to numerous SABR BioProject and Games publications. He does freelance writing and blogging about a variety of baseball topics on his website TheTenthInning.com. Richard lives in New Orleans with his wife, Mary.

BRIAN FRANK is passionate about documenting the history of major and minor league baseball. He is the creator of the website The Herd Chronicles (www.herdchronicles.com), which is dedicated to preserving the history of the Buffalo Bisons. His articles can also be read on the official website of the Bisons. He is a frequent contributor to SABR publications. Brian and his wife Jenny enjoy traveling around the country in their camper to major and minor league ballparks and taking an annual trip to Europe. Brian was a history major at Canisius College where he earned a Bachelor of Arts. He also received a Juris Doctor from the University at Buffalo School of Law.

IRV GOLDFARB has been a member of SABR since 1999 and has written numerous articles, bios, and book reviews for various SABR publications. He and his wife Mercedes live in Union City, New Jersey, with their dog and two cats. All are admitted Met fans.

PAUL HOFMANN, a SABR member since 2002, is the Associate Vice President for International Programs at Sacramento State University. He is a native of Detroit, Michigan and lifelong Detroit Tigers fan. Paul currently resides in Folsom, California.

SABR member **MICHAEL HUBER** is Professor of Mathematics at Muhlenberg College in Allentown, Pennsylvania, where he teaches an undergraduate course titled "Reasoning With Sabermetrics." He has published his sabermetrics research in several books and journals, including *The Baseball Research Journal, Chance,* and *Base Ball,* and he genuinely enjoys contributing to SABR's Baseball Games Project.

TARA KRIEGER has been an active member of SABR since 2005. Although her current day job is as an attorney with the City of New York, she has previously been on staff as a sports writer at *Newsday* and as an editorial producer for MLB Advanced Media. With SABR, she is an editor and contributor to BioProject and has participated in the publication of several SABR books, including *No-Hitters, Van Lingle Mungo, The Miracle Has Landed, Bridging Two Dynasties, Go-Go to Glory,* and *Minnesotans in Baseball*. She also presented original research, "Andy Coakley vs. the Cubs: Baseball's Forgotten Labor Struggle," at the 2015 SABR national convention in Chicago.

KEVIN LARKIN retired after being a police officer for 24 years. He has always been a baseball fan and has been going to minor-league and major-league games for most of his life. He has authored three books on baseball. *Baseball in the Bay State* (a history of baseball in Massachusetts) and *Gehrig: Game by Game* (an account of all of the professional ball games played by Gehrig, Larkin's favorite player of all time.) He also co-authored *Baseball in the Berkshires* with three others, Tom Daly, Jim Overmyer, and Larry Moore, with this book detailing the history of baseball in the area where he grew up. He has authored articles for SABR and recently for the online site Legends On Deck he completed a list of who he thought were the 100 Greatest black baseball/Negro League players of all-time. He also does fact checking and hyperlinking for SABR.

LEN LEVIN, a retired newspaper editor, has been the copyeditor for many SABR books. It's a carryover from his earlier career, when he was the copy desk chief at the *Providence Journal*. He also keeps busy editing the decisions of the Rhode Island Supreme Court.

Seth Moland-Kovash is a lifelong passionate baseball fan and amateur historian. He grew up in Minnesota and his love of the game and the Twins has carried through many years, many moves, and many Twins eras. During the day, Seth is a Lutheran pastor in suburban Chicago where he lives with his wife Jennifer and their son Carl. Carl has also inherited the love of baseball and plays whenever the fields are not covered by snow. Seth's favorite teams are the Twins and whatever team Carl is on.

BILL NOWLIN has nothing against the Mets – even if they did beat the Red Sox in the 1986 World Series. A former political science professor, and co-founder of Rounder Records in 1970, when he met Ted Williams and joined SABR it helped open up whole new worlds. He now spends most of his time in Cambridge, Massachusetts writing bios and collaborating on books. His latest full book is *Tom Yawkey: Patriarch of the Boston Red Sox*.

ALAN RAYLESBERG is an attorney in New York City. He is a lifelong baseball fan who enjoys baseball history and roots for the Yankees and the Mets. Alan also has a strong interest in baseball analytics and is a devotee of baseball simulation games, participating both in draft leagues and historical replays.

Met-rospectives

DAVID RICKARD was born in Los Angeles, California, and raised in Fresno. The former explains his lifelong affinity for the Dodgers, while the latter explains why the 2008 College World Series might just be his greatest baseball memory ever. He graduated from San Jose State with a degree in Journalism in 1987, then promptly moved to Portland, Oregon, where he has lived ever since. Today he works with autistic students at a local middle school. He is married to Peggy, and they have one son, Denis.

CARL RIECHERS retired from United Parcel Service in 2012 after 35 years of service. With more free time, he became a SABR member that same year. Born and raised in the suburbs of St. Louis, he became a big fan of the Cardinals. He and his wife Janet have three children and is the proud grandpa of two.

JOEL RIPPEL, a Minnesota native and graduate of the University of Minnesota, is the author or co-author of nine books on Minnesota sports history and has contributed as an editor or writer to several books published by SABR.

JOE SCHUSTER is the author of *The Might Have Been*, which was a finalist for the CASEY Award for the best baseball book of 2012, as well as *One Season in the Sun,* a short book about ballplayers whose major league careers lasted a few weeks or less and which he wrote for Gemma Open Door's series for adult literacy programs. Recently retired as a professor after 32 years as a member of the faculty at Webster University in St. Louis, he is a frequent contributor to the St. Louis Cardinals *Gameday* magazine, the team's official publication. He is married and the father of five rabid Redbird fans.

MATTHEW SILVERMAN is the author of more than a dozen books, including the forthcoming *Shea Stadium Remembered* along with *One-Year Dynasty, Swinging '73*, and *100 Things Mets Fans Should Know and Do Before They Die*. He co-wrote *Shea Goodbye* (with Keith Hernandez), *Mets by the Numbers* (with Jon Springer), *Red Sox by the Numbers* (with Bill Nowlin), and *Cubs by the Numbers* (with Al Yellon and Kasey Ignarski). With Ken Samelson, he co-edited the SABR collaboration *The Miracle Has Landed: The Amazin' Story of How the 1969 Mets Shocked the World*. He was managing editor for *Total Baseball, Total Football*, and *The ESPN Football Encyclopedia*. He served as associate editor for five editions of *The ESPN Baseball Encyclopedia*. He resides with his family in High Falls, New York.

BRUCE SLUTSKY holds a master's degree in chemistry from the University of Rhode Island and a master's degree in library science from Pratt Institute. He recently retired as a science/engineering librarian at the New Jersey Institute of Technology after 40 years of service to his profession. Bruce joined SABR in 2014 and has been active in the Games Project. He has been an avid Met fan since the inception of the team in 1962 and lives within walking distance of Citi Field.

MARK S. STERNMAN rooted for the Mets when Felix Millan, his favorite player, manned the keystone sack in Queens. New York's release of Millan made Sternman a fan of the Yankees, a team for whom he has faithfully rooted for the past 40 years. A SABR member since 1990, he has enjoyed writing for various SABR outlets, mostly but not exclusively about players who toiled for Boston's National League entry and games involving the Yanks. Sternman dedicates these recaps to his father and brother, who have the misfortune of loyally following the Mets.

TONY VALLEY is a retired public school administrator. He worked in rural schools in Alaska and Oregon for 32 years. After earning a Doctorate in Education Administration in 2003, he became an adjunct instructor for several universities, and is still teaching. A lifelong baseball fan, he has contributed 11 stories to the SABR Games Project. He lives in Silverton, Oregon, with his wife Pam and two demanding cats.

COSME VIVANCO is a Chicago-based writer who received his Master of Fine Arts in Creative Writing from Columbia College in 2010. As a small child, he developed an incredible passion for baseball history. His other areas of interest are politics and music. He has participated in the Chicago Marathon on four different occasions and hopes to do it again in 2019. His biography on Steve Carlton was included in SABR's *20-Game Losers*.

JOSEPH WANCHO lives in Westlake, Ohio, and is a lifelong Cleveland Indians fan. He has been a SABR member since 2005 and serves as the chair of SABR's Minor Leagues Research Committee. He was the editor of the book *Pitching to the Pennant: The 1954 Cleveland Indians* (University of Nebraska Press, 2014) and authored *So You Think You're a Cleveland Indians Fan?* (Sports Publishing, 2018)

BOB WEBSTER grew up in Northwest Indiana and has been a Cubs fan since 1963. Earned a BS in Accounting from Linfield College and an MBA from Marylhurst University. Now living in Portland, Oregon and retired from Intel, Bob is currently working on the History of the Northwest League as well as writing SABR biographies and game stories. Has been a stats stringer for MLB Gameday at the Hillsboro Hops (Short-Season Single-A) games since 2016. He is a member of the Northwest Chapter of SABR, on the Board of Directors of the Old-Timers Baseball Association of Portland, and a manager in the Great American Fantasy League.

STEVEN C. WEINER, a SABR member since 2015, is a retired chemical engineer and a lifelong baseball fan starting with the Brooklyn Dodgers of the 1950s. During his undergraduate years at Rutgers University, Steven authored newspaper articles and helped prepare media guides for the sports information office. On WRSU radio, he enjoyed doing baseball and basketball play-by-play in addition to evening sports news and interviews. Steven obtained his doctoral degree in engineering and applied science from Yale University. He has contributed hydrogen and fuel cell safety knowledge to the *International Conference on Hydrogen Safety* and technical literature to the *International Journal of Hydrogen Energy*. Steven currently contributes essays to the SABR Games Project, volunteers as an in-classroom tutor at a local middle school, and serves as a fundraising volunteer for the Washington Nationals Dream Foundation. You can often find him at Nationals Park for a ballgame.

A lifelong Pirates fan, **GREGORY H. WOLF** was born in Pittsburgh, but now resides in the Chicagoland area with his wife, Margaret, and daughter, Gabriela. A professor of German studies and holder of the Dennis and Jean Bauman Endowed Chair in the Humanities at North Central College in Naperville, Illinois, he has edited eight books for SABR. He is currently working on projects about Wrigley Field and Comiskey Park in Chicago, and the 1982 Milwaukee Brewers. As of January 2017, he serves as co-director of SABR's BioProject, which you can follow on Facebook and Twitter.

BRIAN WRIGHT is the author of *Mets in 10s: Best and Worst of an Amazin' History*, which was released by Arcadia Publishing and The History Press in April 2018. Brian has been featured in *Bleacher Report*, the *Washington Examiner*, and on NESN.com, SB Nation, and The Cauldron. For three years, he was the lead MLB writer for *The Sports Daily*. From 2014 through 2017, he hosted his own sports history podcast, "Profiles in Sports" – featuring in-depth interviews with such notables as Mario Andretti, Jack Ham, Ken Burns, and Tony Perez. He has also contributed to SABR books on the greatest games at Wrigley Field, Comiskey Park and in the history of the San Diego Padres. He currently resides in Washington D.C., or approximately 355 miles from Citi Field.

MIKE WUEST has been a SABR member since 2016. He is a longtime fan of the Red Sox and whatever team Ichiro happens to be playing for. Originally from Pensacola, Florida, he lives in Cayce, South Carolina with his wife and their dog and cat. This is his first time writing for SABR.

JACK ZERBY, a retired attorney and trusts/estates administrator, was fascinated by the Mets when they entered the National League as an expansion team. With the departure of Casey Stengel and his troupe of loveable losers, though, Jack returned to his home-area Pirates and later, living in the South, became an Atlanta Braves fan who now sees the Mets as just another National League East rival. A member of SABR since 1994, Jack writes, edits, and does fact checks for the Games Project and the BioProject, which he joined at inception in 2002. He lives in Brevard, in the Blue Ridge Mountains of North Carolina, with his wife Diana, a professional violinist. While living in southwest Florida, he co-founded the SABR Seymour-Mills regional chapter there with colleague Mel Poplock.